Colorado Ghost Towns and Mining Camps

University of Oklahoma Press
NORMAN

COLORADO GHOST TOWNS AND MINING CAMPS

BY SANDRA DALLAS

PHOTOGRAPHS BY KENDAL ATCHISON

Other books by Sandra Dallas

Gaslights & Gingerbread (Denver, 1965; reprint, Athens, Ohio, 1984)
No More than Five in a Bed (Norman, 1967)
Cherry Creek Gothic (Norman, 1971)
Sacred Paint (Kansas City, 1979)

Library of Congress Cataloging in Publication Data

Dallas, Sandra.
    Colorado ghost towns and mining camps.

Bibliography: p. 243
    Includes index.
    1. Cities and towns, Ruined, extinct, etc.—Colorado—History.   2. Colorado—History, Local.   3. Mines and
mineral resources—Colorado—History.   I. Title.
F778.D35   1984   978.8   84-17377
ISBN 978-0-8061-2084-3 (paper)

The paper in this book meets the guidelines for permanence and durability of the Committee on Production Guide-lines for Book Longevity of the Council on Library Resources, Inc. ⊗

12   13   14

For Michael, who shared his mountains with us

Contents

Maps

viii

Acknowledgments

Writing a ghost town book today is like mining an ore dump. The proverbial old-timers, mined by early ghost town writers, are gone; therefore, I am indebted to those who came before me for preserving the history of these communities. Muriel Sibell Wolle's *Stampede to Timberline,* Perry Eberhart's *Guide to the Colorado Ghost Towns and Mining Camps,* and Robert L. Brown's ghost town guides for jeepers were invaluable in helping me identify and locate ghost towns.

Because local firsthand knowledge today seems to come from guidebooks and chamber of commerce literature, I was dependent on the real repositories of western history, the Denver Public Library Western History Department and the Colorado Historical Society Library. Special thanks are in order to Eleanor Gehres at DPL and her fine staff, Augie Mastrogiuseppe and Pam Patrick, as well as to Fred Yonce, Don Dilley, George DeLuca, Bonnie Hardwick, Susan Myers, Lynn Taylor, and Susan Kotarba; and to Maxine Benson and the staff of the historical society, Catherine Engel, Glee Georgia, Diane Rabson, Rachel Homer, Vicki Diker, and Alice Sharp. I'm grateful to Edward A. Shaw at the University of Oklahoma Press for suggesting this book, to John N. Drayton for seeing it through, and to Joaquin S. Rogers and Jeanne Crabtree for their enthusiasm and sensitive handling of the manuscript.

Colorado Ghost Towns and Mining Camps was a journey into my past, but it also was a way of passing on Colorado's heritage to my daughter, Kendal Atchison, whose exceptional photography illustrates *Colorado Ghost Towns and Mining Camps.* A mother-daughter book on Colorado history has to be unique, and the experience of working with Kendal was exhilarating. Not only did she contribute photographs but her enthusiasm, her artist's eye for detail that I missed, and her objective opinions—she suggested I tell readers one particular ghost town was not worth the effort to get there—added immeasurably to the text.

Finally, my thanks to Robert T. Atchison, cartographer and chauffeur, and to my brother, Michael Dallas, who started us out on this journey with four volumes of Frank Hall's *History of the State of Colorado* and a 1919 Continental Oil Company road map.

Sandra Dallas

Denver, Colorado

ix

Colorado Ghost Towns and Mining Camps

Kendal Atchison

Introduction

Poking through the debris of a moldering cabin on the Swan River near Breckenridge a decade ago, I spotted the remains of an ancient packing box. As I picked it up, the rusted nails fell out and the fragile carton broke apart, revealing an address written in a strong hand on rough board:

Tom Earley
Middle Swan, Colo

There is no Middle Swan, Colorado, and I can find no evidence there ever was one. In all its glory, Middle Swan may have been only this single desolate cabin.

And Tom Earley? There is no record of him, either. Perhaps he was just another lonely, faceless miner who came west from Ohio or Mississippi, who found blossom rock—the outcropping of a vein—and mined it for enough money to go home with a silk hat and a gold watch. Maybe he died during the long winter, or went mad; some of them did. Most likely, he just moved on.

In truth, Colorado had a thousand Middle Swans (and many times that number of Tom Earleys), camps birthed by men with cries of gold or silver, settled with a rush of hope and greed, and deserted when the dreams, like the ore, played out. One in ten, or one in a hundred, of these towns lived to be important—Central City, for example, and Aspen. Some, like Swandyke and Crystal, were prosperous for a time and then were deserted, leaving picturesque, ghostly ruins. Most, like Middle Swan, have been crushed into the earth by a hundred brutal winters.

Colorado Ghost Towns and Mining Camps is the story of 147 of these towns, culled from a list of more than a thousand, from Leadville, the wickedest town in the West, to Magnolia, which outlawed saloons. (Leadville was the more prosperous, the result, most likely, of better ore, though good liquor undoubtedly helped.)

The towns flourished during a forty-year period, beginning in early 1859, when eager prospectors pushed out from embryonic Denver searching the hills to the west for gold and founding Mountain City and Idaho Springs. By the time the last of the towns—which include Apex and Bowerman—reached their zeniths, many early camps had become abandoned ruins.

Many of the towns never got beyond the stage of log cabins on rutted streets where every second structure housed a saloon or gambling hall or whorehouse. But those that endured turned into proper Victorian cities where fancy gambling halls, glittering opera houses, and pretentious homes proclaimed success and permanence. In time, the steeples of fine white churches were pushed into the mountain skies, and the doors of trim school buildings were opened to welcome the children of the community.

Historians have loved and written about these charming towns for years, but most Colorado ghost-town books are twenty years old or more, and the research is even older. Muriel Sibell Wolle began collecting information for *Stampede to Timberline* in the 1920s, when most towns were about fifty years old. Since then another fifty years have passed, and these towns today are as different from Muriel Wolle's era as her towns were from their prime. It is time to take another look at Colorado's ghost towns.

"Ghost town" is a misnomer, of course, for a third of the towns in this book are inhabited year-round. Breckenridge and Aspen are no more ghosts than Denver, but they are included because they have their origins in gold and silver strikes and because, despite thriving economies today, they still retain their nineteenth-century flavor. Towns were selected for their historical importance, their picturesqueness, and their accessibility by conventional car. In the early 1980s all could be reached by standard automobile—though some required a brisk walk the last mile or so. Mountain roads decay, however, and anyone visiting deserted towns should check locally before proceeding. Moreover, use of United States Geological Survey maps is suggested for explicit directions in reaching remote locations.

It might be wise to determine whether the town is there at all before starting out. Colorado's ghost towns are fragile; they were put together with hope as much as with nails and boards. The emotion the miners felt is evident in the names they scattered with abandon — Wide Awake, Pass-me-by, Small Hopes, What Cheer, Last Dollar, and Oh-Be-Joyful.

Some towns have been restored and a few stabilized, but each year one or two do not make it through the winter. Others fall victim to vandalism or destruction by squatters. Since that day I visited Tom Earley's cabin at Middle Swan, the logs have rotted into the mountainside. *Colorado Ghost Towns and Mining Camps* well may be the last look at some of Colorado's ghost towns.

4|

To the Reader

The special format of Colorado Ghost Towns and Mining Camps *was designed for convenient reference. The towns appear in alphabetical order, from Alice to Yankee, and along with the page number is printed the alphabetical letter of the towns on that page.*

Directly under the name of each town is listed the county in which it is located, the direction and distance in miles from the nearest present-day town, the number of the map upon which the town is located, and the date when the first post office was established and when it was discontinued.

Alice

COUNTY: *Clear Creek*
LOCATION: *10 mi. northwest of Idaho Springs*
MAP 1
P.O. est. Aug. 20, 1898; discont. January, 1939

Alice began in the 1860s as Yorktown, "a bois- terous mining camp inhabited by an estimated 300 males," according to one account. The name was changed with the discovery of the Alice Mine in 1868. The mine, the richest in the area, was worked first as a placer, producing some $100,000 in fine gold from a ten-acre site. Then hydraulic equipment uncovered a major ore body, and a twenty-five-stamp mill was erected. After only six months, however, the owners found they were recovering only 25 percent of the gold in the ore, and Alice declined.

In 1897 the mine was sold for $250,000 to a New Yorker, who traveled to Denver in a private railroad car to spend four days inspecting the property. He pronounced it a fine prospect and sank some $150,000 more into its development, but the venture lasted only a few years. Later, a group of Denver investors, who described the Alice as a "veritable mountain or quarry of ore," put together an offering to raise $300,000 for a 300-ton mill. In 1936 control of the Alice passed to American Smelting and Refining Company.

The Alice glory hole, a hundred feet wide and fifty feet deep, lies silent above the town of Alice. Several cabins remain, including the house oc- cupied by the schoolteacher near the well-kept white schoolhouse. Built in 1915, it operated until 1936. Mindful of the weather—Alice is lo- cated adjacent to Saint Mary's Glacier—the school administration installed a pipe across the ceiling of the school so that swings could be hung inside during the winter.

The Alice school was built in 1915. *Kendal Atchison*

Next to Christmas, the Fourth of July was the biggest holiday in mining towns. Alma is decked out with bunting and pine boughs in this 1887 photograph. *Courtesy Denver Public Library Western History Department.*

Alma

COUNTY: *Park*
LOCATION: *5 mi. northwest of Fairplay*
MAP 4
P. O. est. March 7, 1873

Established in 1872, Alma was named for Alma James, wife of the town's first merchant and homeowner, according to Frank Hall's *History of the State of Colorado.* Another story claims it was named for the first girl born in the town. Whatever the origin of its name, Alma flourished with the mining activity on nearby Mount Bross. The discovery of silver at Leadville sent prospectors scurrying across Mosquito Pass from Leadville to prospect on Mount Bross and Mount Lincoln, discovering the Dolly Varden, the Hiawatha, the Moose, the Eagle, the True Blue, and the Gertrude mines.

Alma grew steadily, and in the 1880s had a population of between five hundred and a thousand citizens, a weekly newspaper, and several hotels.

The town's main street was nearly destroyed in 1937 when a fire that started in a beer parlor was fanned by fifty-mile-per-hour winds and spread to adjacent buildings. The blaze destroyed a pool hall, a barber shop, a grocery, a restaurant, several shops, and, most disastrous of all, the Gatley Motor Company, a garage where most of the town's cars were parked.

This house on Alma's main street is surrounded by the detritus of more than a century, from mine wastes to cast-off camper shells. *Kendal Atchison*

Alta, 1981. *Kendal Atchison*

Alta

COUNTY: *San Miguel*
LOCATION: *14 mi. south of Telluride*
MAP 10
No P.O.

Perched high above Ophir, Alta sprang up as a company town for the Gold King Mine, which was discovered in 1878 and operated through the 1940s. Ore was transported in aerial tram cars from the Gold King and other Alta mines to the Ophir Loop two miles down the mountain.

Because the cost of hauling coal to the Gold King was exorbitant, the mine experimented with electrical generators, and the Gold King was one of the first mines in the country to use electricity.

In later years Alta's mines were purchased by the Silver Mountain Mining Company, but it has been a generation since the area was mined.

Alta is a collection of fine old buildings, including a boardinghouse, a manager's house with a bay window and fireplace, and several bungalows with traces of their original green and white paint.

Because Alta was not shut down until the 1940s, many of its buildings are standing, though they will not last long. *Kendal Atchison*

Altman at the top of the world, about the time the town was hit by Cripple Creek labor violence. *Courtesy Denver Public Library Western History Department.*

Altman

COUNTY: *Teller*
LOCATION: *3 mi. north of Victor*
MAP 14
P.O. est. Jan. 28, 1894; discont. May 20, 1911

At the height of the labor strife that gripped the Cripple Creek mining district in 1894, the miners of Altman, located at the top of Bull Hill in the center of the district, set up barricades, armed themselves with a catapult that propelled dynamite-loaded beer bottles and a phony cannon made from stovepipe, and announced they had seceded from the country.

Even after the labor war was settled and Altman rejoined the nation, it remained a hotbed of union sympathy. A favorite child's game was called "miners and deputies."

Altman was a miners' town, a colony of shacks and simple pleasures with two restaurants, four boardinghouses, and nine saloons, which suggested the priorities of Altman miners. Altman was garish and "beastly prosperous," *Leslie's Weekly, Illustrated* reported shortly after the labor confrontation. It was garish because of the red building paper used on many buildings,

and it was prosperous because "every man willing to work earns four dollars a day, working only eight hours," *Leslie's* said.

Altman, in terms of its elevation once the highest incorporated town in the nation, had little to boast of architecturally. "But that is not surprising when you remember that it was built in six weeks," reported *Leslie's,* also noting that the population, which peaked in 1899 at twelve hundred, included a sizable number of saloon-keepers, "'tin horn' gamblers and faded soiled doves." But the magazine praised the generosity of the residents, every one of whom turned out for a benefit for a wounded miner. "The good company had been lavish of perfume and pomade," the reporter wrote. "Then, too, everybody was chewing gum."

Even without strikes, Altman was volatile. In 1903 a fire, probably set to collect insurance, destroyed a major portion of the town, leaving 350 of the town's 500 population homeless. The perpetrators had cut a water main and covered their trail with pepper to thwart bloodhounds.

The next year a second bloody strike led to the town's demise. Even the discovery that Altman's streets were paved with gold ore that assayed out at $20 a ton failed to stop the decline.

American City

COUNTY: *Gilpin*
LOCATION: *9 mi. northwest of Black Hawk*
MAP 2
No P.O.

For a few brief years in the 1890s, American City thrived. A combination of gold discoveries and eastern capital sent dozens of miners to the Continental Divide town of American City, a site so windswept that branches grow on only one side of the pine trees.

A few houses, a school, a mill, and a hotel with the prepossessing name of Hotel Del Monte were built to accommodate a hundred or so residents, most of whom worked for the Boston-Occidental Mining Company or the American Mining Company. But the town, which was revived briefly as a filming location during the fledgling days of motion pictures, never amounted to anything.

American City "isn't much of a place so far as size is concerned," noted the *Kansas City Star* in 1906. American City, now privately owned, isn't much of a place now, either.

American City today is privately owned. *Kendal Atchison*

Anaconda

COUNTY: *Teller*
LOCATION: *2 mi. south of Cripple Creek*
MAP 14
P.O. est. March 1, 1892 as Barry; discont. Nov. 15, 1917

"The wild hurrah of the average mining camp is noticeably absent" in Anaconda, reported an 1896 publication touting the Cripple Creek mining district. The statement was obvious hyperbole, since Anaconda had its share of saloons and dance halls.

It also boasted a sizable business district and a number of churches. One of the organists was a pretty young girl, Mary Louise Cecilia Guinan, who left the district for New York. There, as Texas Guinan, she became a celebrated speakeasy operator who greeted her customers with "Hello, Sucker."

Anaconda grew up around the Anaconda Mine, which, like the Mary McKinney, the Blue Bell, and the Republic, was located within the town limits. Another dozen mines were within a five-minute walk.

A fire that started in a meat market destroyed most of the town in 1904, and Anaconda never was rebuilt.

Animas Forks's location high in the mountains meant severe winter storms and bitterly cold weather. *Courtesy Denver Public Library Western History Department.*

Animas Forks

COUNTY: *San Juan*
LOCATION: *12 mi. northeast of Silverton*
MAP 9
P.O. est. Feb. 8, 1875; discont. Nov. 30, 1915

Animas Forks "is in the midst of a wild and rugged country, where nothing but rich mines would induce a human being to live longer than absolutely necessary," wrote George A. Crofutt in his *Crofutt's Grip-Sack Guide of Colorado.*

But rich mines were attraction enough for the hardy miners who braved winters at the 11,584-feet elevation of Animas Forks, at the time the highest incorporated town in Colorado. In the mid-1880s the population reached four hundred in the summer but dropped to a dozen men, three women, and twenty dogs in the winter of 1884. A storm that lasted twenty-three days dumped twenty-five feet of snow on the main street of Animas Forks, and after each storm the trapped miners cut a notch on the telephone pole in front of Frank Thaler's saloon. Despite the constant danger of avalanches, which buried several cabins, the miners holed up for the winter in the saloon and kept the economy going by beating each other at poker.

One immense slide that dumped a mountainside of snow half a mile wide and 250 feet deep was packed so solid that a wagon team could be driven across it. In the spring, when the snow at the bottom melted out, creating a hollow, the stage drove up the creek through the long snow tunnel.

Animas Forks was settled in the 1870s with the discovery of rich timberline lodes. Within a year it had two groceries, a drugstore, and four hotels, one of which advertised "especial attention paid to the comfort of ladies." After a brief, intense boom, the town declined in the late 1880s and was all but deserted by the early 1900s.

Animas Forks is a crumbling ghost town of a dozen houses, a mill, and a small square jail built to thwart breakouts; its walls are constructed of boards laid flat. The town's most elegant house, which is being stabilized today by Silverton residents, sports a gaping bay window, its glass panes long gone. Legend says Thomas Walsh, who discovered the Camp Bird Mine near Ouray, once lived there, but not a scrap of historical evidence exists to back up the claim.

An Animas Forks house, long deserted. *Kendal Atchison*

The Animas Forks jail was constructed of boards laid flat. *Kendal Atchison*

Apex in 1899, at the height of the boom. *Courtesy Denver Public Library Western History Department.*

Apex

COUNTY: *Gilpin*
LOCATION: *7 mi. northwest of Black Hawk*
MAP 2
P.O. est. Nov. 12, 1894; discont. April 30, 1932

Apex was founded in the mid-1890s when discoveries of rich float and promising ore bodies attracted some eight hundred miners, merchants, and assorted hangers-on to the Pine Creek mining district. Within a year or two Apex had more than a hundred buildings, several operating mines and a colorful newspaper called the *Pine Cone*.

Among the more promising strikes were the Schultz Wonder, the Annie H. Mascot, the Huberknocker, and the Yellow Medicine. Apex boasted certain amenities the earlier mining camps lacked, such as a telephone system, but in other ways it was as dangerous and as primitive as its counterparts elsewhere. In 1898 the *Denver Times* noted that a "stage loaded with passengers and mail capsized" on its way to Apex.

"This district is not one of the number of so-called mining boom camps, as it stands upon its merits," the Central City *Register-Call* proclaimed in 1897 with misplaced enthusiasm. Today Apex's merits include a number of cabins located at the end of a good road.

Argentine

COUNTY: *Summit*
LOCATION: *12 mi. east of Keystone*
MAP 4
P.O. est. July 8, 1880 as Conger; discont. Feb. 28, 1907

Argentine had three booms and changed its name for each one. The town was founded in the 1860s by "Commodore" Stephen Decatur, a mine promoter and charlatan of sorts. His real name was Stephen Decatur Bross, and he had skipped out on his wife and family in Illinois and come west. Even when his brother, the

All that remains of Decatur-Rathbone-Argentine is the wreck of the Pennsylvania Mine. *Kendal Atchison*

lieutenant governor of Illinois, tracked him down in 1868, he denied the relationship.

Because it was located near the crest of the 13,000-foot Argentine Pass, Decatur, as it first was called, was so high the miners had difficulty working. One reporter claimed that because of the altitude miners ate more and worked less and could not take the harsh winters, making the mines unprofitable.

But the *Colorado Miner* scoffed at that conclusion: "No matter how great the altitude of a rich silver mine, the ingenuity of man will devise means to work them in winter as well as in summer."

Whether it was the altitude, the poor transportation facilities, or the low-grade ore, Decatur declined. It was revived in the 1890s as Rathbone, but an avalanche in 1899 snuffed out most of the town, which was rebuilt once more on a modest scale a few years later as Argentine, the name by which it is known today.

The town's fortunes through all three booms were based on the Pennsylvania Mine, whose gaunt workings are all that remain of Argentine.

In the early 1900s burros were used to carry equipment for the Shoshone-to-Denver transmission line near Argentine. *Courtesy Public Service Company of Colorado.*

Present-day Ashcroft. At one time it was larger than Aspen. *Kendal Atchison*

Ashcroft

COUNTY: *Pitkin*
LOCATION: *12 mi. south of Aspen*
MAP 6
P.O. est. Aug. 12, 1880; discont. Nov. 30, 1912

Two prospectors, C. B. Culver and W. F. Coxhead, headed up Castle Creek in May, 1880 on their way to Gunnison. They found indications of minerals and decided to try their luck. Coxhead backtracked to Leadville for supplies while his partner prospected—and touted the area to every miner who passed by. Dubbed "Crazy Culver" for this enthusiasm, the prospector was, nonetheless, so persuasive that when Coxhead returned, he found twenty-three men camped in what shortly afterward was named Ashcroft.

Culver was right. The area was promising. In late May two prospectors discovered the first important mine. The next month, the North American was staked, followed by discovery of the Tam O'Shanter and the Montezuma. Crazy Culver was less successful. He started a boardinghouse and later sold out.

By 1883 or so Ashcroft, with its population varying between twenty-five hundred and five thousand, was larger than Aspen. It had six hotels, seventeen saloons, and a female faro player. The town's major producer was the Tam O'Shanter-Montezuma Mine, 50 percent owned by silver king H. A. W. Tabor, who lived for a time with his wife, Baby Doe, in a log cabin overlooking the town.

The Tam O'Shanter-Montezuma ore was not extensive, however. The mine closed in 1884, and Ashcroft's residents hauled their houses to Aspen. By 1892, just before the silver crash doomed silver mining in Ashcroft and elsewhere, the town had only fifty residents. After the last resident, a 77-year-old poet and self-styled mayor, left in 1935, Ashcroft became a ghost town. The skiing Tenth Mountain Division of the army used Ashcroft for training during World War II, and in the 1950s segments of "Sergeant Preston of the Yukon," a television serial, were filmed in Ashcroft.

In 1974 the United States Forest Service and the Aspen Historical Society began restoration of the town, which today is a national historic site.

Ashcroft's buildings have been repaired and stabilized. *Kendal Atchison*

Aspen

COUNTY: *Pitkin*
LOCATION: *41 mi. southeast of Glenwood Springs*
MAP 6
P.O. est. June 7, 1880

Of all Colorado's mining towns, at the present time Aspen is the least ghost-like. While its resident population today is only about half the nineteenth-century high of twelve thousand, Aspen nonetheless is the most densely populated of Colorado's old boomtowns. The town came so close to dying in the 1920s and 1930s, with only a few hundred residents, that it almost became one of Colorado's fabled ghost towns.

Aspen's rich silver mines—the Durant, the Aspen, the Mollie Gibson, and dozens more—were discovered in the frenzy of silver prospecting that followed Leadville's silver boom. In 1879 several prospectors left Leadville to explore the mountains on the west side of Independence Pass. They hit pay dirt almost at once, and one prospector sold his half interest in the Smuggler for $50 and a mule that died a short time later. The Smuggler produced millions.

A handful of prospectors spent the winter in the little settlement they called Ute City at the feet of Aspen, Smuggler, and Red mountains, biding their time until spring. In early 1880 they were joined by B. Clark Wheeler, a promoter and speculator, and a company of men who made the cold trek over Independence Pass to look at the claims.

Wheeler promptly claimed the townsite, renamed it Aspen, and returned to Leadville where his enthusiasm set off a rush of silver prospectors. One determined group built boat-like sleds, which they filled with provisions, and dragged them over the snow to the new settlement.

By summer there were a hundred shacks and tents housing nearly a thousand gold seekers. By the time winter set in, though, the fear of Indians and the winter snows reduced the population to thirty-five, including thirteen women. Among them were H. P. Cowenhoven, a merchant, his wife, his daughter Kate, and his clerk, David R. C. Brown.

Cowenhoven set up shop and became known as the H. A. W. Tabor of Aspen because he was an easy grubstake for any luckless prospector. "The boys had to eat," he explained when asked why he carried so many worthless accounts on his books. One customer who had run up a bill

Early Aspen was a grimy town of false-front buildings and dusty streets. *Courtesy Denver Public Library Western History Department.*

Aspen's "row" lay between the depot and downtown. *Courtesy Denver Public Library Western History Department.*

The building occupied by the Red Onion once housed a brothel. *Sandra Dallas*

An Aspen tennis player at the Lincoln School. *Courtesy Denver Public Library Western History Department.*

Some Aspen high society takes a spin. The Wheeler Opera House is in the background. *Courtesy Denver Public Library Western History Department.*

In the 1920s and 1930s the Hotel Jerome housed drummers and stray tourists. *Courtesy Glenn L. Gebhardt.*

of $400 settled it by palming off on Cowenhoven part interest in the Aspen Mine. It later made fortunes for both Cowenhoven and Kate's husband, the clerk D. R. C. Brown.

Aspen grew slowly and unspectacularly for the next few years. "We believe that mineral, like money, talks better than brag, and we propose to leave the brag to the camps that want it," noted the *Aspen Times* in its first issue in 1881. But mineral did not talk very fast, and Aspen's growth was hampered by both poor transportation and lack of capital.

It took money to develop Aspen's ores. Noted *Harper's Weekly* in 1889:

If an operator can afford to spend from $5000 to $25,000 without interfering with the comfort of his family, he can engage in mining with a fair outlook for success. . . . In the case of a man with only a few hundred dollars to begin work with, the chances are not worth considering.

The economic picture changed in 1883 when Jerome B. Wheeler (no relation to B. Clark Wheeler), a New York merchant vacationing in Colorado, visited Aspen and was so impressed with its prospects that he invested heavily in the camp, encouraging other speculators to put their money on Aspen, too. Along with his investments in mining, Jerome B. Wheeler built the Wheeler Opera House and the Hotel Jerome.

Wheeler brought prosperity to Aspen. By 1885, the *Aspen Times* reported, the town had fifty-five hundred people, ten laundries, sixteen hotels, ten cigar stores, five brick houses, three fruit stands, three water wagons, thirty-one lawyers, one temperance society, 150 eastern "have beens," and fifteen hundred men "hankering for wives." Those lonely men could find some solace in other statistics—one dance hall, fifteen sporting houses, and forty saloons.

In the fall of 1887 the first railroad, the narrow gauge Denver & Rio Grande, reached Aspen to the tumultuous cheers of Aspen residents. Children were dismissed early from school; men placed bets on the time the last rail would be laid; and fireworks and bonfires were set off at the sound of the first whistle—prematurely, it turned out, because the first screech was from a yard whistle, not a locomotive. The Colorado Midland Railway arrived the following year.

By then Aspen was booming. The mines were working three shifts, pouring out millions in silver every year. In fact, the largest silver nugget ever discovered, a 2,060 pound, 93 percent silver nugget (trimmed to 1,840 pounds to get it through the shaft) was hauled out of the Smuggler Mine

In 1936, Aspen had yet to discover there was gold in snow. *Courtesy Denver Public Library Western History Department.*

"THE STORY OF GREECE is written in its monuments; that of America in its hotels," wrote Gene Fowler, once a Denver newspaperman. Nowhere was the story of the West more evident than in the mining camp hostelries. Barely had a boomtown begun shipping ore when plans were made to build the fanciest, most elegant hotel good money and bad taste could create.

The Hotel Jerome, built by Jerome B. Wheeler in 1889 at a cost of $125,000, was one of the best—a marvel of glittering crystal and polished wood, gleaming brass and shining marble. A water-powered elevator whisked guests to dozens of bedrooms on the second and third floors. There were fifteen bathrooms and a greenhouse that provided exotic flowers and vegetables in the middle of winter.

The Jerome was only one of dozens of Colorado hostelries that pandered to the pretensions of Colorado's newly rich. Each had its quirks and foibles, but each was undeniably elegant and styled itself as "the finest west of the Mississippi," or some such superlative.

The Tabor Grand in Leadville, the Jerome's closest rival, had silver dollars inlaid in its floor. The Beaumont in Ouray was built with a stairway that divided at the landing like a wishbone. The Strater in Durango offered pianos in its bedrooms and a harp in the barbershop.

The Jerome followed Aspen's fortunes. It held court for a few splashy years, then crashed with the rest of Aspen in 1893. The hotel fell into the possession of a onetime pencil vendor, spending its ignoble middle years providing accommodations for drummers and tourists.

When Aspen revived, the Jerome did too; particularly its bar, which provided libations for retired prospectors, skiers, musicians, and celebrities such as Gary Cooper and Jill St. John.

If, as Fowler wrote, America's history is in its hotels, then Aspen's story is written well in the Jerome.

in 1894. Aspen's silver production was so extraordinary that one mine owner ordered a set of silverware made from his ore to give to his wife for a silver anniversary present, and Mollie Gibson owners sent a silver and gold statue called the "Silver Queen" to the Chicago World's Fair in 1893.

At its height Aspen boasted three daily newspapers, a substantial business district of handsome brick buildings, and an elegant residential section filled with Victorian mansions and charming cottages. The town's socialites attended musicales, plays, boxing matches, and even a duel at the Wheeler Opera House. They skated and bicycled, and attended masquerade balls, literary gatherings, and horse races. They dined on caviar, lobster, and oyster loaf at John O'Riley's,

Brick malls have replaced many downtown Aspen streets. *Kendal Atchison*

Aspen winter morning, 1967. *Sandra Dallas*

Charlie Helmer's, Adolph Veasey's, the Delmonico, or the La Veta.

Along with the rest of Aspen, they celebrated the Fourth of July by watching the members of Aspen's hose cart companies, dressed in red, white, and blue tight-fitting uniforms, show off their skills. "Noise made all day," headlined the *Aspen Times* after an 1887 Fourth of July celebration, adding: "Many of the ladies" reflected "the radient [*sic*] beauty of health and spirits."

The ladies were not the only ones who re-flected spirits. Hundreds of miners with twinkling lanterns walked down Aspen Mountain each night into a myriad of saloons and gambling halls. Despite the profusion of bars, the closing of even one was cause for grief. In 1885, when the Bank Saloon closed, a *Times* reporter lamented: "Like the chambers of a haunted house, everything round about was dark and still. . . . Those days are gone and with them pleasant reminiscences."

Unlike its neighbor Leadville, Aspen was a

relatively crime-free town. "Even in the earlier days of its career, Aspen never had much of this law-breaking element. The slowness with which the mines were developed, and the comparative nearness of Leadville as a center of criminal disturbance, prevented a dangerous assembling of objectionable characters in the valley of the Roaring Fork," explained *Harper's Weekly* in 1889.

Aspen had strict laws regulating morality. One ordinance stated: "No bawdy house, house of ill-fame, house of assignation, or place for the practice of fornication, or common, ill-governed or disorderly house, shall be kept or maintained within the limits of the city." But, of course, there were plenty of bawdy houses, houses of ill-fame, and houses of assignation. They were located on two out-of-the-way blocks of Durant Avenue. Because of its discreet location, Aspen's red-light district could be ignored, at least until the Colorado Midland located its depot on Durant Avenue and travelers were forced to pass Aspen's immoral row to get into town.

The crash of 1893 knocked the silver pinnings from under Aspen. The silver mines closed, Aspen's population plummeted, and silver kings such as the two Wheelers faced ruin. Despite an attempt in 1909 to reopen Smuggler Mountain by hiring deep-sea divers to dewater a tunnel, silver mining was virtually dead and so, for a time, was Aspen.

Its renaissance came after World War II, and Aspen became the first and most successful of Colorado's ghost towns to be resurrected. Members of the army's skiing Tenth Mountain Division, who trained near Aspen during the war, were enamored of the small mountain town and returned in the late 1940s to convert it into one of the world's top ski areas. At the same time, Chicago industrialist Walter P. Paepcke, intrigued with the idea of reviving Aspen as a cultural mecca, started the Aspen Institute for Humanistic Studies.

The resulting melee has meant a boom far beyond anything the silver miners ever dreamed of. Aspen booms today as it did a hundred years ago. Many of its houses and commercial buildings have been restored, and in an attempt to control the chaos in the heart of the business district, Aspen has converted several streets into brick malls.

Contemporary Aspen offers some intriguing contrasts with the old silver town. While old Aspen was relative crime free, today's Aspen has a nationally publicized and highly lucrative illegal drug trade. The silver miners were tireless boomers, but Aspenites are embroiled today in no-growth battles. And though few Orientals and blacks were welcomed a hundred years ago, Aspen today is an ethnically and racially diverse town. One thing is unchanged—money. Noted *Harper's* in an 1889 article that is as true today: "Aspen is not a poor man's camp."

Baldwin

COUNTY: *Gunnison*
LOCATION: *17 mi. northwest of Gunnison*
MAP 8
P.O. est. Sept. 17, 1883; discont. June, 1949

Coal from the Baldwin Mine, reported Frank Hall in his *History of the State of Colorado*, was known for "burning with a bright flame and emitting intense heat." So was the town of Baldwin—two adjacent towns, actually, the first started in 1881, its successor in 1897. Both suffered from union strife, with a score of men killed in Baldwin mines over the years.

As early as 1886 a nonunion miner was killed by a pro-union "Molly Maguire," and by 1900 the mines had been hit by a dozen strikes. In 1899, "the miners have not worked very much since January, and are in destitute circumstances. Many of them are leaving the camp," reported the *Denver Times*.

The next year strikers blew up a bridge, and in 1913 the Rocky Mountain Fuel Company began a twenty-year shutdown of one mine where violence was prevalent. On Christmas Eve, 1927, a superintendent was killed by a miner, over a labor disagreement. Labor troubles stopped in the 1940s. So did mining.

Baldwin was shut down in the 1940s, but some of its houses were inhabited over the next twenty-five years and still contain old stoves and broken crockery. *Kendal Atchison*

Baltimore

COUNTY: *Gilpin*
LOCATION: *5 mi. west of Rollinsville*
MAP 2
P.O. est. Aug. 28, 1896; discont. Oct. 26, 1904

Not much is known about Baltimore, a small town located in a meadow near South Boulder Creek. The town apparently was supported by paying mines because not only was there a saloon with a billiard table, but there was also a two-story opera house with a fancy canvas backdrop.

Despite its obscurity, Baltimore today is a well-preserved ghost town of log cabins that now do duty as summer homes, and a badly listing two-story log building marked "Town Hall, 1865."

Baltimore survived as a summer encampment. *Courtesy Denver Public Library Western History Department.*

Town hall, built in 1865. *Kendal Atchison*

Basalt has been spruced up, but the one-eyed building in the center would make preservationists blanch. *Kendal Atchison*

Basalt

COUNTY: *Pitkin*
LOCATION: *18 mi. northwest of Aspen*
MAP 6
P.O. est. Feb. 13, 1890 as Aspen Junction

In 1882, Gabriel Lucksinger built a boarding-house at the confluence of the Roaring Fork and the Fryingpan rivers and named the settlement Frying Pan. A few years later, when the Colorado Midland Railway reached the valley, railroad officials encouraged residents to take apart their houses and move them a short distance to a settlement they called Aspen Junction. Then in 1894, because the town was confused so often with both Aspen and Grand Junction, the name was changed to Basalt. That name stuck.

By whatever name, Basalt was and is a sturdy if unspectacular supply and transportation town, overshadowed by both Aspen and Glenwood Springs. President Theodore Roosevelt considered it so inconsequential that he failed to show himself to a crowd of early morning patriots who had decorated the station with bunting and gathered to cheer the touring dignitary passing through in 1903.

Aspen Junction-Basalt boasted half a dozen newspapers over its lifetime, one of which had to be printed on wrapping paper when a railroad shutdown kept newsprint from reaching the town.

Basalt was plagued continuously by fires. In 1892 the Colorado Midland's depot was completely destroyed in a blaze. Part of the town was lost to a fire in 1898 when a kerosene lamp in a boardinghouse exploded and a strong wind flung burning debris over a two-mile-wide area. Then in 1900, there was another kerosene lamp explosion, this one in Nellie Smith's restaurant. It caused a $9,000 loss when the fire burned several buildings, including the Lupton Brothers Saloon. One woman broke both arms when she jumped from a second-story window to avoid the blaze.

Black Hawk boasted thirteen saloons, a brewery, and a cracker factory *(fourth from right). Courtesy Denver Public Library Western History Department.*

Black Hawk

COUNTY: *Gilpin*
LOCATION: *1 mi. east of Central City*
MAP 2
P.O. est. Dec. 6, 1862 as Black Hawk Point; discont. July, 1950.

Black Hawk was born in the frenetic activity that sent men searching the hillsides and streams of Gregory Gulch in the wake of John Gregory's 1859 gold discovery. Thousands of men poured into the area that extended from Black Hawk through Mountain City to Central City and spilled over into Nevadaville. By the mid-1860s Black Hawk had a school and a church high above the town, a newspaper, six groceries and butcher shops, thirteen saloons, a brewery, a cracker factory, and a 10-year-old billiard player who could beat the professionals.

Black Hawk also claimed a young beauty

Clean-up after the July 30, 1895, flood. *Courtesy Denver Public Library Western History Department.*

The Lace House *(above)* has been restored, but many Coloradoans prefer the ghostly look it still had in 1964. *Sandra Dallas.*

Despite the deserted appearance, this building probably was occupied in 1950, since the shades are properly aligned. *Courtesy Robert T. Atchison.*

Black Hawk school. *Kendal Atchison.*

named Elizabeth McCourt Doe, called "Baby Doe" by the miners. Her husband, William Harvey Doe, Jr., was a would-be mining man who lacked the discipline and mining savvy to pursue his career. Before Baby Doe deserted him for Leadville and legend, the couple lived over a Black Hawk store.

Black Hawk, named for a milling company that in turn was named for an Indian chief, developed into the district's milling town, with a population of three thousand at one time. In 1880 writer Frank Fossett listed fifteen stamp mills with 666 stamps operating at Black Hawk, their dull thumps reverberating day and night.

Despite its blue-collar image, Black Hawk claimed the finest house in the district, the fancifully carved Lace House, dripping with jigsaw trim. Built in 1863 for a mining man, the Lace House deteriorated after the turn of the century into a weathered ghost, a boarded-up relic of lost elegance. It was rescued by the town in the 1970s and restored. The Lace House, today a splendid Victorian re-creation, is Black Hawk's major tourist attraction.

Bonanza

COUNTY: *Saquache*
LOCATION: *14 mi. northwest of Villa Grove*
MAP 13
P.O. est. Aug. 12, 1880; discont. June, 1938

When a lucky Kerber Creek prospector yelled out, "Boy, she's a bonanza," the town of Bonanza was born and aptly named. Mining lasted in Bonanza for more than fifty years, from 1880, when the town was established, to the 1930s, and one mine alone, the Rawley, accounted for $6 million in mineral production.

When Anne Ellis, who later wrote *The Life of an Ordinary Woman,* arrived in 1882 with her mother—who barely had time to unload the wagon and do a hurried load of wash before giving birth—Bonanza was a rowdy camp peopled with drunken miners, prostitutes who spent their afternoons riding fast horses, a clutch of get-rich-quick schemers, and an assortment of other colorful characters.

One was Nellie Smeltzer, an elegant, refined young wife who shocked a town accustomed to feedsack dresses with her fashionable clothes.

Times turned bad for Nellie Smeltzer, however. She became a dressmaker and eventually a washerwoman to support herself, but she retained her haughty ways. When an ardent young miner came to call, she opened the door sweetly and threw red pepper in his face. She dumped a bucket of water over another suitor. Mrs. Smeltzer wore her fine clothes to tatters, then added gunny sacks to keep out the cold. She powdered her none-too-clean face daily with flour. But when a group of well-meaning citizens left a sack of groceries on her doorstep, she disdainfully scattered them about the yard.

By the time the Ellises arrived, Bonanza was a booming town with fine restaurants and pool halls, drugstores, and a livery stable with saddle horses and stylish turnouts. "Busted Joe" Wathen was busy putting up a 21-room hotel, though other construction in town had stopped for lack of lumber. There was a reported population of five thousand, though Ellis noted, "in speaking of population, you didn't count people, anyway, you counted saloons and dance-halls. There were thirty-six saloons and seven dance-halls."

There were more than dance-hall girls and whiskey-drinking miners in Bonanza, however. There were women who made homes, who nailed canvas on log walls for warmth, who picked wild gooseberries for pies, and who fed lonely prospectors. They took care of the miners who were down on their luck and turned away by saloon girls; they delivered each other's babies; and they sat with the dying. "Nowhere on earth are neighbors so good as in mining camps," Ellis wrote.

Bonanza's mines were studied closely by prominent investors, including Cripple Creek millionaire Winfield Scott Stratton and former President Ulysses S. Grant, who camped for a week or two just outside Bonanza. Grant, who had his meals sent in from Salida sixty miles away, tried to buy the Bonanza Mine for $40,000 and the Exchequer for $160,000, but he was turned down on both deals.

Like most mining camps, Bonanza boomed intermittently. In 1889 the *San Francisco Chronicle* noted: "Everything boomed except the mines." Population had dropped to about a hundred persons, and the *Denver Times* reported: "From a rustling, prosperous camp, Bonanza sank to a deserted village. . . . Even the chipmunks left it."

Bonanza had thirty-six saloons, seven dance halls, and a population of five thousand. *Courtesy Denver Public Library Western History Department.*

Both vice and population have been reduced considerably. *Kendal Atchison*

When Ellis returned to Bonanza in the 1920s, nearly fifty years after she first saw it as a child, the buildings were "so stooped and gray with age that they lean on each other for support; the windows are all broken like blind eyes; and the sidewalks so torn and warped that they look like twisted hands." That description fit Bonanza fifty years later when the population was only eight. In 1980, Bonanza ranked second only to Keota, in eastern Colorado, as the smallest town in the state.

Boreas

COUNTY: *Summit*
LOCATION: *11 mi. southeast of Breckenridge*
MAP 4
P.O. est. Jan. 2, 1896; discont. Jan. 31, 1905

Like the north wind it was named for, Boreas was a cold and blustery place. During the record-long winter of 1899, when snow kept trains from crossing Bald Mountain between Como and Breckenridge, stir-crazy young men in Breckenridge skied out over Boreas Pass, stopping to warm themselves at the combined telegraph office and section house of the narrow-gauge Denver, South Park & Pacific Railroad Company that stood on the Boreas crest.

Thomas Painsett, "in order to get away from bacon rinds and frozen potatoes," and with "hope for the flesh pots of Denver," made the trip in February, 1899, reported the *Denver Times,* climbing the nine miles to Boreas from Breckenridge in about four hours. He ate lunch with station hands who appreciated the bottle of whiskey he had brought along for emergencies. Here, he declared, was an emergency.

Painsett arrived safely at the fleshpots of Denver, but others were not so lucky. When the station agent himself fled from Boreas, he told a reporter: "They have been coming by my place all winter, and I am sure that some I talked with saw in me the last person they ever saw alive."

Even in the best of weather, Boreas could be treacherous. In 1901 a runaway train derailed

The Boreas station (shown about 1970) provides little protection today against winter storms. *Sandra Dallas*

with thirteen cars of ore, smashing the engine and killing a brakeman.

There were brief moments of respite, however. In summer the train stopped to allow passengers to pick wildflowers, and when P. T. Barnum's circus train failed to make it up the grade, the animal trainer unloaded the elephants to push the train to the Boreas crest. A baby girl born at Boreas in 1882 was dubbed "the highest born lady in Colorado."

Fires over the years destroyed much of Boreas, including an iron turntable and the depot. All that is left of the once sizable village, founded in 1882, are the tarpapered remains of a two-story structure.

Bowerman

Snow was the greatest challenge for both men and machines operating on Boreas Pass. *Author's collection.*

COUNTY: *Gunnison*
LOCATION: *35 mi. east of Gunnison*
MAP 8
P.O. est. Oct. 28, 1903; discont. May 27, 1910

J. C. Bowerman, whose wife supported his prospecting addiction by taking in laundry, staked

This cabin crumbling into the sage and another hidden in the trees are all that is left of Bowerman. *Kendal Atchison*

the Independent Mine between Waunita Hot Springs and Pitkin in 1903, causing a gold rush among prospectors who claimed Bowerman, or Nugget City as it first was called, was another Cripple Creek.

Bowerman and his partner, a Denver & Rio Grande Railway dispatcher who had agreed to pay the prospector a $50-per-month grubstake, claimed their ore assayed at extraordinarily high rates, but they refused to show their mine to anyone. That failed to stop the miners, however. Within weeks several hundred claims had been staked by the five hundred residents, and a dozen saloons, gambling dens, and dance halls were running full blast. A prospector could buy a loaf of bread for only a dime, but he paid 25 cents to get his shirt laundered.

Despite the rich gold nuggets Bowerman and his partner showed to tantalize the prospectors, the two failed to ship ore, claiming they were in deep negotiations with eastern capitalists over the future of the mine. Along with rumors of an impending sale, however, were those that said the mine was made up of only a few pockets of ore.

Bowerman quickly declined, and before the decade was out it was all but deserted.

Breckenridge

COUNTY: *Summit*
LOCATION: *81 mi. west of Denver*
MAP 4
P.O. est. Jan. 18, 1860

The rock piles begin across from Peak One of the Tenmile Range. They spill out of the gulches and move on to Breckenridge, ugly and harsh as the dredges that left them in their wake. The dredges were demons of destruction, huge barges that churned up the mountain streams, sending their buckets down to bedrock in search of gold. When they had passed on, the mountain streams were gone, choked by piles of stone higher than a town. Two generations later the rock piles remain, unyielding. Only a few clumps of grass and a few sturdy aspens grow on them.

The rock piles are in the detritus of Breckenridge's third and longest boom—dredging. The first began in 1859 when gold seekers swarmed over the Front Range to placer mine the streams of the Tenmile. They settled a dozen towns, but Breckenridge became the most important of them when its residents stole county records from Parkville and established Breckenridge as county seat.

Gold was discovered on the Blue River August 10, 1859, when a party of prospectors picked Ruben J. Spalding, an experienced California

Patriotic celebrations generally brought out the whole town. In a less festive time, the infamous Pug Ryan robbed the Denver Hotel. Buildings on the far left and far right are the only ones still standing. *Author's collection.*

Skiing, now Breckenridge's economic mainstay, has been popular as both a sport and a mode of transportation since before the turn of the century. *Author's collection.*

miner, to work the first pan of dirt. He recovered 13 cents' worth of gold. The second pan yielded 27 cents. "Our little party now felt jubilant . . . and began to realize that here lay the fulfillment of their most ardent hopes," Spalding told historian Frank Hall. Spalding traded his mule for two sacks of stale flour and 175 feet of lumber to build long toms. Wrapping his feet in pieces of saddle blanket, Spalding worked in ankle-deep water. The first day netted $10 and a bad cold.

Even luckier was William H. Iliff, just across the river from Spalding, who scratched out $7,000 in gold from a patch 40 feet square. When Iliff told of his good fortune in Denver, some two thousand men stampeded into the area.

In early 1860 prospectors organized the town of Breckinridge, naming it for United States Vice-President John C. Breckinridge. The chances of getting a post office designation were greater if the town was named for a political official; there are nine Breckenridges or Breckinridges in the United States. After Abraham

Lincoln was elected president and John Breckinridge defected to the South, Union supporters changed the spelling to "Breckenridge."

The placer mines lasted about three years. By 1868 when Samuel Bowles visited Breckenridge, it was a settlement of only twenty or thirty cabins, "scarcely habitable in winter," Bowles wrote. He also noted that Breckenridge had a good hotel with a "broad buxom matron and black-eyed beauties of daughters"—probably the family of Judge Marshall Silverthorne, who was so sickly when he crossed the Missouri River for Colorado in 1859 that one party refused to allow him to join them. Only after Silverthorne challenged the biggest man in camp to a fight did they agree to allow the plucky invalid to go with them. Nevertheless, they slipped a few boards into the bottom of a wagon for a coffin.

Another early settler was Edwin Carter, who went to the mountains in search of gold but stayed to become the state's most prominent naturalist. Carter killed and mounted hundreds of animals and displayed them in his Breckenridge museum. Forty years of breathing the arsenic then used in taxidermy contributed to Carter's death in 1900, and his collection was acquired by the city of Denver as the foundation of the city's Museum of Natural History.

The discovery of gold in fissures and veins in the early 1880s caused a second rush to Breckenridge. Dozens of mines were established in the gulches and on the mountainsides around Breckenridge, on Farncomb Hill, where wire gold was discovered, on Shock and Nigger hills, and along Georgia Gulch and the Swan River.

By 1885 there were two thousand residents in Breckenridge, and the townspeople had begun to replace the log cabins with false-fronted stores, gingerbread-trimmed houses, and commercial buildings dripping with carved wooden icing.

The most elaborate were the hotels—the Hotel Arlington with its scalloped false front and the double-gabled Denver Hotel. Managed by Robert Foote, the Denver Hotel was a haven for traveling men, gamblers, local merchants, and occasional blackguards. One summer evening in 1898 a tough named Pug Ryan and a gang of henchmen robbed the patrons of the Denver Hotel. Intent on plundering the hotel safe and robbing a local merchant who spent his evenings dozing

Two types of Breckenridge mining. Placer mining. *Author's collection.* Gold dredging near Breckenridge in 1926. *Courtesy Glenn L. Gebhardt.*

Main Street, Breckenridge, 1982. *Kendal Atchison*

Breckenridge from the ski-hill road. *Kendal Atchison*

Billiard saloon operators Peter and George Engle kept customers' valuables in their vault until they discovered banking was more lucrative than billiards and opened the Engle Brothers Exchange Bank. *Author's collection.*

in the lobby, the robbers changed their plans when a gun discharged accidentally. They quickly took the cash from the barroom till and relieved the customers of their money and jewelry.

The robbers were tracked to a cabin near Kokomo, between Breckenridge and Leadville, and in a bloody shoot-out, two members of the gang and two lawmen were killed. Ryan escaped and was not captured until four years later in Seattle when the tattoo "PUG" on his arm gave him away. He was jailed but escaped; he was recaptured and eventually sent to prison, where he died in 1931.

Ten years after the robbery, schoolchildren on a picnic found part of the loot from the robbery, including a watch belonging to Foote, that Ryan had stashed in a log near the Kokomo cabin. When Foote heard of the discovery, he took the train to Kokomo and scratched in the dirt until he found his stolen diamond stickpin.

Dredging, Breckenridge's third gold boom, began on the Swan River in 1898 when Ben Stanley Revett, a mining engineer, launched the first dredge boat, a 100-foot barge with a clamoring bucket line. It flew a silk flag designed by Revett himself. Revett, a mountain of a man, directed dredging operations from his home on the Swan River, called Swan's Nest. The house was built with outsize doorways so he did not have to turn sideways to get from room to room.

The dredges began operations in the gulches and slowly moved down the rivers to Breckenridge, making such a persistent din that residents woke up in the middle of the night if the bucket lines stopped. Dredges were tolerated because they provided jobs at a time when mines all over Colorado were closing down. But Breckenridge residents had a love-hate relationship with the barges that extended even to the children. The daughter of a dredge master recalled

Helen Rich. *Courtesy Summit Historical Society.*

Belle Turnbull. *Courtesy Summit Historical Society.*

FAR DOWN THE VALLEY a tiny black car jumped and jerked across the corduroy of the Goose Pasture, skittish as a snow skiff on the Ten-mile Range. The lady writers from Colorado Springs were making their way through the valley, impatient to reach Breckenridge. Helen Rich, a reporter, was born in Sauk Centre where her sister's high-school beau was Sinclair Lewis. She was handsome and tenacious as a timberline pine. Beside her was Belle Turnbull, a schoolteacher; she was as pale as an alpine columbine and as delicate as its mauve-tinted petals that darted and bobbed under the lodgepole pines.

After spending several summers in Breckenridge, the two moved there permanently in 1938, later purchasing a log cabin on French Street once owned by a gambler. They had a passion for the high mountains and the mountain folk, a love that shone through in their writing as they rejected the romantic and the glamorous and wrote about the harsh reality of living too near the sky. They were among the best of the twentieth-century writers who wrote about the mountain towns. In Rich's novels, *The Willow-Bender* and *The Spring Begins,* and in Turnbull's books of poetry, *The Tenmile Range* and *Goldboat,* they told of the mountains' hold on the people, of prospectors whose search for gold was a sickness, of women who went crazy from the long winters and the loneliness.

From that house, the "ladies of French Street," as they came to be known, served what they called "drinkin' whiskey" in crystal glasses to old miners, aging madams, and visiting literati. They chopped their own wood and burned it in a Franklin stove, and they baked their bread in a cookstove.

Like the people they wrote about, Rich and Turnbull could not leave Breckenridge for long; their blood was too thin, and they developed a terrible longing for the mountains. Turnbull died in 1970. Rich moved to a Denver nursing home with a view of the mountains but fought to go home to French Street. "I like my mountains close up, and harsh," she said. She died on French Street in 1971.

forty years later that her playmates loved to taunt her when the dredge broke down, chanting: "Your dad's bucket line is in the pond."

Like the mine owners elsewhere, the dredge officials were the elite of Breckenridge society. In the early 1900s George H. Evans, manager of the Gold Pan Company, built a hall onto his house where he showed motion pictures and his wife gave violin concerts. Evans, an Englishman, drove a white Stanley Steamer and hired a governess for his children. When he asked an associate, Robert Gore, to buy a pair of gloves at Gano Downs, an elegant department store in Denver, he contemptuously refused to accept the purchase because Gore had paid a niggardly $12.50 for the gloves.

Despite such pretensions, Breckenridge was wide open. One evening when Mrs. Gore was entertaining a church group, her daughter answered a knock at the door to find a drunk who lunged at her, crying: "I'll take you, Katy." The drunk, new in town, had asked directions to the whorehouse but had been pointed instead to the Gore house.

Most of the whorehouses were "over the Blue," across the river to the west of town, and they included the Blue Goose, the Pines, and the Columbine Rest. The prostitutes kept to themselves, mixing only during town celebrations or when there was trouble. The last of the madams, May Nicholson, who lived until the 1960s, bragged that she led the Fourth of July parade carrying the American flag. Another madam agreed to sell a house she owned to a family with seven or eight children, but before the deal was closed, the husband died of flu. After the funeral, the madam quietly presented the deed to the house to the widow.

When the financially precarious dredging operations finally shut down during World War II, the brothels were closed and the prostitutes moved on or became part of the town fabric. Some of the girls who stayed on lived with former customers, and if the relationship looked as though it might last, the women began to be called by the men's names. Then Breckenridge people said the woman had "risen from over the Blue."

After the dredges stopped and the young men went off to war, the town was in limbo. Then, in 1962, a ski area was opened on Peak Eight

to the west of Breckenridge, and skiers swarmed into town, remodeling the houses into Victorian chalets. Successive waves of vacationers have built towering condominiums on the mountainsides and Victorianesque houses in town. They have turned Main Street into a boutique mining camp. But the rock piles remain.

Buckskin Joe

COUNTY: *Park*
LOCATION: *2 mi. west of Alma*
MAP 4
P.O. est. June 1, 1861; discont. Jan. 24, 1873

A single arastra, the last of a dozen that once operated in Buckskin Gulch, is all that is left of Buckskin Joe, one of Colorado's earliest and wildest mining camps. It was settled in 1859 by a group of prospectors and named "Buckskin Joe's Diggings" for their leader, Joseph Higganbottom. Called "Buckskin Joe" for his deerskin dress, Higganbottom a year later traded his interest in the camp for a horse, a gun, and settlement of a bar bill and disappeared.

The miners who stayed behind prospered, and $1.6 million in gold was taken out of the diggings in the first few years, much of it crushed in the arastras. An arastra was a basin cut in rock to hold the ore that was then crushed by a heavy boulder rotated by mule power; the crushed ore was panned to remove the gold.

Buckskin Joe's arastra. *Kendal Atchison*

Early Buckskin Joe was as elegant as Denver. One visitor reported that to his astonishment there was a carpet in his room at the Pacific House. The town had its share of "gentry," as one visitor called them, who attended brilliant balls and did not care in the least that these glittering evenings ended with supper in a saloon. Minstrel shows and theatrical performances were held in Laurette Hall. A performance by Mlle. Julia Cotton drew such rave reviews from the editor of the *Western Mountaineer* that a correspondent for the *Rocky Mountain News* accused him of hoping to "'cotton up' to a histrionic Senorita of like charm and style and maturer years."

Buckskin Joe had its rawer side. A *News* reporter noted that half the town's population "are sitting in their houses or tents, watching the weather and as a 'general business' playing 'high low jack' or 'seven-up' for the whiskey." Buckskin Joe was rife with saloons, gambling hells, and dance halls, whose denizens included the legendary "Silver Heels," a beautiful dance-hall girl named for her fancy slippers. When smallpox hit the camp, Silver Heels stayed to nurse the miners. She caught the disease, which left her disfigured, and she fled. From time to time in later years, a heavily veiled woman was seen laying wildflowers on the graves of smallpox victims. Legend says it was Silver Heels.

As Buckskin Joe matured, its residents voted to rename it a more refined Lauret or Laurette, but the name never really took. In 1866 the postmaster at Buckskin officially notified the United States Post Office Department that the name of the town had been changed back to Buckskin. The postmaster was an obscure grocer named H. A. W. Tabor.

Camp Bird

COUNTY: *Ouray*
LOCATION: *5 mi. southwest of Ouray*
MAP 9
P.O. est. April 28, 1898 as Campbird; discont. March 15, 1918

Camp Bird was the company town that grew up around the Camp Bird Mine, the fabulously rich gold producer that made its owner, Thomas Walsh, a companion of kings and his daughter, Evalyn, a confidante of presidents.

Walsh discovered rich gold ore in Imogene Basin above Ouray in 1896 and began acquiring claims—more than a hundred—that he consolidated under the name of Camp Bird. Within a few years his mine was making $95,000 a month.

With profits from the Camp Bird, Walsh bought a mansion in Washington, D.C., and launched his wife and daughter in international society. Evalyn married Edward B. McLean, whose family owned the *Washington Post,* and each family gave the couple $100,000 pin money as a wedding gift. They spent it before the honeymoon was over. Evalyn Walsh McLean later purchased the Hope Diamond, which she had set in a necklace and flaunted in the faces of society matrons and shop girls alike.

The hundreds of employees at the Camp Bird lived well. The men slept in enameled iron beds and ate from china plates. Walsh provided them with the latest magazines and newspapers, which they read by electric lights. The piano in the miners' recreation hall was purchased by mining magnate Harry Payne Whitney, who lost a poker game in which the players agreed the stakes were a piano for the miners.

In 1902, Walsh, who had taken several million dollars worth of gold out of the mine, sold the Camp Bird to an English syndicate for a total of $5.2 million—$3.1 million in cash, $100,000 in stock, and another $2 million in royalties. He rewarded employees with checks of up to $5,000.

Under its new ownership, the Camp Bird continued to be profitable, and by 1916, when the first shutdown occurred, the Camp Bird had produced $27 million, with a profit of nearly $18 million.

Capitol City

COUNTY: *Hinsdale*
LOCATION: *10 mi. west of Lake City*
MAP 8
P.O. est. May 18, 1877; discont. Oct. 30, 1920

Only a few crumbling bricks mark the site of the red brick house George S. Lee built for use as Colorado's governor's mansion. So certain was he that Colorado would move its capitol to the San Juans that he changed the name of his town from Galena City to Capitol City.

Capitol City sprang up in 1877 with the discovery of silver deposits. Early-day journalists rushed to describe the scene: "Capitol is said to be two weeks old. This may be a day or two out of the way . . . but it looks very fresh indeed," wrote a *Rocky Mountain News* journalist, who counted more than twenty-five completed houses and a hundred foundations for more.

A week later a *News* reporter noted that Capitol City was two and half weeks old and said: "My hotel was a frame of new boards about fourteen feet square. The kitchen a slab lean-to about eight feet square at the rear. The landlord said he had been in business about a week, but it was clear that his house was already full to overflowing with boarders."

Despite the activity, the population never reached more than about four hundred in 1881, when Capitol City had a general store, two saloons, a hotel, two mining companies, and, of course, a red brick governor's mansion.

"The handsome brick residence of George S. Lee and lady, distinguished for their hospitality, is a landmark . . . ," wrote Frank Fossett in his book on Colorado mines. At that time, Capitol City, located in a valley at the end of a narrow, winding canyon that runs all the way from Lake City, was a booming smelter town treating ores from the silver mines that sur-

rounded it. George S. Lee and lady gave brilliant parties. Lady Lee even gave long-distance concerts, singing over the telephone with a friend in Lake City while her neighbors listened in.

The 1893 silver crash doomed Capitol City and George S. Lee's dreams. The governor's mansion is gone, and only two cabins and a beehive-shaped brick oven mark the site of Capitol City.

Caribou

COUNTY: *Boulder*
LOCATION: *5 mi. west of Nederland*
MAP 3
P.O. est. Jan. 31, 1871; discont. March 31, 1917

Prospector Sam Conger discovered the rich silver ore at Caribou in 1860 when he stopped to finger a piece of rock while hunting elk. At the time he failed to recognize that the ore contained silver. Nine years later, after seeing similar ore in Wyoming, Conger returned with a party of five other prospectors, and in a single day they discovered the Caribou Mine—so called because one of the party had worked in the Cariboo district of British Columbia—and the Poorman. Mines on Caribou Hill produced $20 million in silver, with the Caribou Mine itself

The masonry remains of Caribou. *Kendal Atchison*

giving up $8 million. Silver from the Caribou was made into silver bricks that were placed in the sidewalk in front of the Teller House in Central City for Ulysses S. Grant's visit.

The discovery party spent the winter of 1869-1870 in Caribou. By spring, when word leaked out about their discovery, a hundred miners were camped on Caribou Hill. By mid-1871, Caribou—the spelling of the name was determined by the United States Post Office—had two billiard rooms, four saloons, five grocery stores, three bakeries, several hotels, a millinery shop, and a photograph gallery.

Located in a high mountain meadow, Caribou was a bleak, wind-swept place in winter. A visitor who came in 1874 had to drive his horses and sleigh through 25-foot drifts on the steep road from Nederland, and on arriving he found only the stovepipes of houses sticking through the snow to tell him where the town was. One man who fell into a drift yelled for a ladder.

Miners crawled to work on hands and knees, and hotel guests climbed through second-story windows to get to their rooms. The snowbank outside one hotel was dubbed the Sherman House elevator.

Production peaked in 1875 when Caribou's population reached three thousand. Then the town declined, and after an 1879 fire, it was only partially rebuilt. Another fire in 1899 destroyed much of what was left. Today only the stone skeletons of an old hotel and the assay office remain.

Central City

COUNTY: *Gilpin*
LOCATION: *34 mi. west of Denver*
MAP 2
P.O. est. Jan. 17, 1860 as Mountain City

The gold seekers who poured into Denver in

Central City during its heyday in the 1880s. *Courtesy Denver Public Library Western History Department.*

1858 soon realized that the flakes of gold they washed out of Cherry Creek came from the high mountains to the west. Most of them waited out the winter in Denver saloons, drinking Taos Lightning and playing cards. A few were too impatient to let the snows melt in the mountain gulches, though. Among them was John Gregory, a wiry, red-haired Georgia cracker, who followed a stream out of Golden and hiked through the snow up the twisted canyon until, early in 1859, he found gold.

When news of his discovery leaked out, prospectors swarmed up the canyon, muddying the waters of the creek with their gold pans and long toms, cutting the pines to make cabins or to fuel their fires. They named the place Gregory Gulch, but it became famous as Central City, dubbed "the richest square mile on earth," and for a time it was. But not for John Gregory. He made a modest sum selling his claim and apparently spent it; before he dropped out of sight, he told a Golden journalist: "I believe that I am the only living being who has not benefited by this discovery."

A few months after Gregory's strike there were five thousand people in Gregory Gulch, and hundreds more poured in daily. The hills were pockmarked with prospect holes and denuded of trees; there was a stench of garbage and offal and unwashed men. Meat sold for 50 cents a pound, and the few women in the camp washed shirts for $3 a dozen. When Horace Greeley arrived to inspect the diggings, he gave a speech cautioning the miners about drinking and gambling. His importunings had no noticeable effect, but the articles he wrote about Gregory gold served to attract even more prospectors.

For about five years Central City was the most important town in Colorado Territory, eclipsing even Denver. It was in Central City, says his-

Top: The Wells, Fargo building, foreground, was one of the few left standing after the disastrous fire of 1874. *Courtesy Denver Public Library Western History Department. Middle:* A parade down Main Street. Most of the buildings still stand. *Courtesy Denver Public Library Western History Department. Bottom:* Business at the First National Bank had begun to cool by 1899. The Teller House is next door. *Courtesy Denver Public Library Western History Department.*

Artist Herndon Davis painted "The Face on the Barroom Floor" during a Teller House restoration in the 1930s. The inspiration was a melodramatic Victorian poem called "The Face Upon the Floor," but the model was the artist's wife. *Courtesy Denver Public Library Western History Department.*

torian Frank Hall, who was editor of the Central City *Miners' Register,*

in a bleak and wholly uninviting region, where is not to be found a space sufficiently level to serve as a site for even a small circus tent, or an eligible cemetery, not a tree, shrub, flower, or grass plot to relieve the tiresome monotony of brown rocks and verdureless soil . . . we find the birthplace and cradle of American civilization in the great central region. . . .

It was not civilization, however, but the American dream of instant wealth, of striking it rich, that brought thousands of gold seekers into the godforsaken gulch. Many of them did indeed strike it rich. Pat Casey, an illiterate, hard-drinking Irishman, discovered the Casey Mine and spent the proceeds on his barfly companions, whom he called his "night hands." Casey carried a huge gold watch, though he could not tell time, and inspired a dozen tales of his stupidity and gullibility.

"How many of youse are down there?" he supposedly yelled to his workers in the Casey Mine one day.

"Five," came the reply.

Casey scratched his head for a minute then called: "Well, half of youse come up for a drink."

Casey went through his fortune, but other gold seekers who got rich from Gregory Gulch gold were more prudent, including Nathaniel Hill, a Brown University professor who developed a method for treating gold ore, and Henry Teller, a lawyer and railroad builder. Both men were elected to the United States Senate, as was a onetime Central City resident, William A. Clark, who later made a fortune in copper in Butte, Montana.

Central City offered something for those who could not hope to strike it rich but who were seeking a better way of life. Some Cornishmen immigrated to the American West searching for new homes or hoping to build a nest egg to make life easier when they returned to Cornwall, and they were welcomed by the West's new mining entrepreneurs for their ability at timbering and stonemasonry; examples of their superb workmanship are easy to find today.

They were clannish, these Cornishmen. Whenever there was a job opening, a Cornish worker quickly said he had a Cousin Jack who could fill the job, and the Cornish miners soon were called "Cousin Jacks" and their wives "Cousin Jennies."

A day at the opera. *Courtesy Denver Public Library Western History Department.*

With their sweet voices and their sense of humor, the Cornish people added to the rich ethnic and cultural mix in the gulch that included Chinese, Irish, and blacks. The miners carried Cornish pasties—leftovers baked in a crust—and pungent saffron buns thick with currents in their dinner pails. At Christmas they marched up the gulch at night carrying pine branches twisted into circles with candles set in them.

Central City, the largest of the towns strung out along Gregory Gulch, was thronged with saloons and gambling dens, variety theaters and dance halls. The sidewalks were so crowded on Saturday nights that anyone in a hurry had to walk down the center of the street.

Jack Langrishe and Mike Dougherty (who was to die shortly from alcoholism) performed before packed crowds when they played at the candle-lit Montana Theater in the early 1860s. Dougherty's popular act, "Pat Casey's Night Hands," a spoof of Central City's champagne-swilling buffoon, had drawn raves in Denver, and it was only natural for Dougherty to take it to Gregory Gulch. Casey, however, was outraged at the public spoofing. He gathered his "night hands," armed them with eggs and stones, and prepared to pelt Dougherty if he sang a particularly objectionable song. Dougherty, in turn, called out the Elbert Guards, whose presence quelled the night hands and allowed the show to go on.

Central City's most popular performer was "Mlle." Rose Haydee, who played at the Montana with her two less talented sisters. The miners were smitten with the virginal Mlle. Haydee, and confused by the "Mlle." They called her "Millie." When she eloped they were so outraged they threatened to lynch her husband.

The variety theaters and dance halls and saloons continued to attract crowds of miners, but as the mines went deeper, requiring huge sums of money for development, the prospectors sold out and were replaced by college-educated mining men, often accompanied by wives and children. These newcomers demanded schools and churches and culture.

Father Joseph P. Machebeuf, tired of tending his Central City Catholic flock first in a theater, then in a billiard room, and finally in a store, locked the door one day and refused to allow his parishioners to leave until they had pledged enough money to build a church. Using less drastic methods, the Methodists built Saint James. Until it was built, they met in private homes, including one belonging to Aunt Clara Brown, a former slave who had bought her own freedom and then, working as a Central City washerwoman, saved enough to bring other blacks west.

In 1872 the Teller House opened and was described variously as the finest hotel in the West (outside Denver) and as a building that looked more like a factory than a hotel. It was good enough for Central City, however. When Ulysses S. Grant visited the Teller House, he walked across a sidewalk laid with $12,000 worth of silver bricks.

Bayard Taylor, who visited the gulch in 1866, called it "the most outrageously expensive place in Colorado. You pay more and get less for the money than in any other part of the world," he wrote. Taylor noted the houses were dry as tinder and jammed together. "A fire starting at the top of the town . . . would wipe out the place in half an hour," he predicted.

Actually, it took several hours. In May, 1874, a fire that started in the house of a Chinese resident who was burning incense destroyed 150 buildings, leaving only the Teller House and a few other structures standing. Fire fighters came from as far away as Golden, where a special

CENTRAL CITY PLAY FESTIVAL
July 16-30, 1938

"RUY BLAS"
A Melodrama of Old Spain

By VICTOR HUGO

English Version by Brian Hooker

Designed and Produced by........................ ROBERT EDMOND JONES

Music Arranged and Conducted by........................ WALDO WILLIAMSON

Associate Producer........................ Richard Aldrich

Central City program, 1938. *Author's collection.*

train hauled a hand pump to the gulch, but the lack of water made it useless. The town was rebuild of brick and stone and iron, and Central City became a high Victorian town of whimsical buildings with cast-iron fronts, fluted columns, lacy stone trim, and wide expanses of plate glass. The finest building of all was the Opera House, a stone structure designed by Denver architect Robert S. Roeschlaub. It had two fanciful staircases that spiraled upward from either side of the lobby to the balcony. The ornate theater not only attracted Central City's growing "upper crust," but it brought in renowned performers such as Lotta Crabtree and Edwin Booth.

The theater's heyday lasted only a few years. By 1880 the richest ore in Central City's mines was depleted, and the capitalists and merchants and miners moved on to Denver or to Leadville. Central City began a fifty-year decline. By the 1930s Central City was merely another quaint mining town at the end of a dusty road. A back room of the Teller House was a chicken roost, and pigeons and pack rats inhabited the Opera House.

Nevertheless, the town's musty charm and its close location to Denver made it a tourist attraction. Many of Denver's elite felt a fondness for the town that had provided their family fortunes. Thus there was considerable public support in 1932 for the novel idea of reopening the Opera House for summer performances. Restoration of the building was funded in part by $100 donations from individuals who wanted family names carved on the backs of theater chairs.

The murals in the Teller House were repainted, including those of the one-breasted goddess and the goddess with two left feet. One night artist Herndon Davis, well into his cups, painted his wife's portrait on the Teller House floor. Promoters quickly suggested that the face had inspired the maudlin barroom poem, "The Face Upon the Floor." No matter that the poem was written in the nineteenth century.

When the Opera House reopened in 1932 with Lillian Gish as Camille, Denver society women pinched themselves into wasp-waisted Victorian gowns and flocked to Central City for what became one of the West's most glittering social events. In the years to come, social luminaries such as Evalyn Walsh McLean and Lucius Beebe motored up the winding road to Central City to attend the opera.

Eureka Street with the Teller House on the right. *Kendal Atchison*

The descendants of the Cornish miners and the Irish saloonkeepers rediscovered Central City, too. While their social betters mingled at the Teller House or the Opera House at the top of Eureka Street, the tourists in family coupes and on motorcycles brought a revival of Main Street. Less interested in culture than in good times, they patronized souvenir stands and popcorn concessions, beer parlors and honky-tonks. This dichotomous revival has kept Central City going another fifty years. With its mix of cultural elite and low-class rowdies, Central City today is a twentieth-century continuation of its nineteenth-century heritage.

Columbine, 1982. *Kendal Atchison*

Columbine

COUNTY: *Routt*
LOCATION: *5 mi. north of Hahns Peak*
MAP 12
P.O. est. Jan. 5, 1896; discont. 1967

Columbine was founded in the flush of the Hahns Peak gold discoveries when prospectors spread out across the country around Hahns Peak in search of gold. Mining was moderately successful, with the discovery of several mines that were incorporated into the Royal Flush.

While the area was settled in the 1870s, Columbine was not officially laid out until 1897, and never was more than a collection of log cabins (today rented by fishermen) and several commercial buildings, including, of course, a saloon. Legend has it that one night a sheepman, Joe Belardi, gambling in the Columbine saloon, lost not only his wages but those of his two herders. Rather than admit his folly to his employees, he went back to camp, killed the herders, and roasted their bodies over a campfire.

Como

COUNTY: *Park*
LOCATION: *10 mi. northeast of Fairplay*
MAP 4
P.O. est. Jan. 23, 1879; discont. Aug. 31, 1963

The discovery of coal and the arrival of the Denver, South Park & Pacific Railroad turned Como, a tiny settlement known as Stubbs Ranch, into a bustling community. Established in 1879 as a tent city with rutted streets, Como quickly grew into an established community with six thousand residents who had access to two Chinese laundries, three hotels, a red-light district,

The ghost of Como's roundhouse. *Kendal Atchison*

A deserted butcher shop. *Kendal Atchison*

and innumerable saloons—as many as eight in one block.

A mining and railroad town—the stone roundhouse is Como's most distinctive building—Como was a rough, violent place. A mine explosion in 1893 killed more than twenty men, and many others were maimed or killed in saloon fights and racial brawls. "A church service has not been heard of by the citizens," the *Rocky Mountain News* noted in 1880. Racial fights between the Chinese and the Italians or between the Cornish and the Italians were so common that the *Denver Republican* reported in 1881: "Nearly every street corner and bar-room had a fistic encounter or a shooting affray."

Como's violence was a legacy from its early days when some outlaws known as the Reynolds Gang robbed a stagecoach of its gold box in 1864 near the site of Como. Six of the bandits were killed by a posse, and the remaining six were shot before they came to trial, supposedly for not telling where they hid the gold. It was never found.

As late as 1902, when Como was on the decline, a professional pool player known as "Billy the Kid" was shot by a local man when the pool player refused to give up his seat at a minstrel show to a lady.

In 1909 a fire destroyed much of the railroad's Como operations, which were not rebuilt. The

One writer noted that Creede, shown in the early 1890s, looked like "a city of fresh cardboard." *Courtesy Denver Public Library Western History Department.*

roundhouse itself caught fire in 1935, but by then Como's railroad days were almost over. The line was abandoned in 1937.

Creede

COUNTY: *Mineral*
LOCATION: *37 mi. northwest of Del Norte*
MAP 11
P.O. est. May 12, 1891 as Willow

While exploring the mountains above Wagon Wheel Gap in 1889, Nicholas C. Creede, a down-on-his-luck prospector, picked aimlessly at an outcropping near where he had stopped for lunch. He examined the ore and gulped, "Holy Moses!" He gave the epithet to the mine and his name to the town that spilled down the narrow canyon nearby.

Creede actually was two settlements threaded between hulking cliffs. Today's Creede originally was called Gintown and later Jimtown before taking the name Creede. North Creede, today just a few cabins farther up the canyon, originally was named Creede.

Nicholas Creede's discovery caused a flurry of interest that turned into a silver rush when capitalist David Moffat paid $65,000 for an interest in the Holy Moses. Creede himself discovered a second mine, the Ethel, and when two prospectors showed him promising ore they had discovered on Bachelor Mountain—ore that became the Last Chance Mine—Creede promptly filed on an adjacent claim and discovered his third mine, the Amethyst.

By 1892, Denver was agog with talk of the town of Creede, and photographs of it adorned shop windows. Maps of Creede and specimens from the Holy Moses were offered for sale. Trains leaving Denver were jammed with prospectors, self-important mine owners, and eastern college graduates self-consciously dressed in fur coats and laced boots, all on their way to Creede to make a fortune.

The town itself was less than impressive. It looked like "a city of fresh card-board," noted popular writer Richard Harding Davis in 1892. "There is not a brick, a painted front, nor an awning. . . ." He likened the town to a circus tent and implied that the residents were the clowns and the freaks.

With as many as two hundred men arriving

every day, Creede was thronged with gold seekers who spent their days in the hills and their nights in the smoky, dimly lit saloons, dance halls, and keno parlors, some built on logs laid across the creek because such sites were cheaper than town lots. Culture of a sort touched Creede in 1892 when the Theatre Comique opened to a crowded house that applauded wildly for a rope-skipping exhibition by Miss May De Rose. Other forms of entertainment were more profitable, however, and the theater soon removed the benches and became a dance hall. "Beer is still sold there at an exorbitant price," the *Creede Candle* noted.

Before long, as many as three of every four arrivals came to prey on the miners. Poker Alice Tubbs dealt cards, and swindler Soapy Smith sold bars of soap ostensibly wrapped in $5 bills. Soapy was the prince of the bunco artists, but he himself was a soft touch. When Parson Tom Uzzell, who preached hellfire in most of the mining camps, was robbed of his pants containing the money he had made by passing the hat, Soapy bought him a new pair of pants and replaced the collection.

Tempers were short in Creede, and the usual way to settle differences of opinion was with guns. When a drunk slapped the notorious Bat Masterson, the saloon crowd stopped drinking to watch the famed gunman take revenge. Masterson, however, merely laughed and told the drunk to try again when he was sober.

Bob Ford, who had shot Jesse James in the back, ran a Creede saloon until he too was

Life could be dreary for the families of miners *(above)*. Men generally had a more exciting time *(below)*. Courtesy *Denver Public Library Western History Department.*

The immutable rock cliffs look the same, but Creede had changed considerably by the 1920s. *Courtesy Denver Public Library Western History Department.*

The town had changed even more by 1981.
Kendal Atchison

gunned down. At Ford's funeral, the preacher, hard-pressed for something good to say, intoned: "Charity covereth a multitude of sins."

Prostitute Rose Vastine, called "Timberline," wearied of life and attempted to commit suicide, but was saved. Lulu Slain, one of her frail sisters, was more successful when she and her cabin mate, the Mormon Queen, turned to morphine. "Lulu is dead; the Queen lives," reported the *Candle.*

Life was difficult for everyone. A six-year-old Creede boy watched his overworked mother, who ran a boardinghouse, moan from the heavy work, and he vowed to buy her a mansion with servants one day. As a successful prizefighter, Jack Dempsey made good on his promise.

Creede never shut down. "Creede was one of the liveliest communities in the state," wrote Frank Hall in his Colorado history. "It never was and never will be a pleasant place to live in. . . ." The gambling and drinking and fighting went on day and night, inspiring Cy Warman, a Creede newspaper editor, to write his famous poem, "Creede":

Here's a land where all are equal—
        Of high or lowly birth
A land where men make millions,
        Dug from the dreary earth.
Here the meek and mild-eyed burro
        On mineral mountains feed—
It's day all day, in the day-time,
        And there is no night in Creede.

Not until 1906, long after Creede peaked, was there a successful attempt to close down the gambling halls. A group of women descended on a meeting of aldermen and demanded that all gambling apparatus be removed from the saloons and that all drinking establishments be closed on Sundays. The new law did not last long, however. The *Candle* expressed ambivalence about it. "As to public gambling it does no one no good," the paper editorialized. But it took exception to Sunday saloon closings, arguing such a law inflicted hardship on miners, who "do not have comfortable quarters during winter in which to spend the evenings. Their rooms have no stoves and they have no place where they can mingle with their associates other than on the cold streets or in a cold dismal room and the results generally are that they decamp for other climes." Moved by sheer compassion, the aldermen reopened the saloons.

Creede, crammed into a narrow river canyon and built with unpainted wood shacks jammed together, was a prime candidate for flood and fire, both of which hit with depressing regularity. In 1892 a flood wiped out part of Creede's business district. The same year a fire consumed a million dollars worth of buildings and goods and left hundreds of people homeless. Three years later the town was ignited again when a hotel proprietor set fire to his own building to collect the insurance.

Creede's heyday was intense but brief. The 1893 drop in silver prices led to an immediate decline in mining, though Creede continued to produce silver and still does. But with the 1893 silver depression, the gamblers and bunco artists, dance-hall girls and prostitutes deserted Creede for Cripple Creek and other more prosperous camps. Before he, too, abandoned Creede, Cy Warman wrote "The Rise and Fall of Creede":

The winter winds blow bleak and chill,
        The quaking, quivering aspen waves
About the summit of the hill—
        Above the unrecorded graves
Where halt, abandoned burros feed
        And coyotes call—and this is Creede.

Crested Butte

County: *Gunnison*
Location: *29 mi. north of Gunnison*
Map 8
P.O. est. May 26, 1879

While early gold discoveries attracted miners

Crested Butte's Elk Avenue. Note the makeshift ramps from street to board sidewalks. *Courtesy Denver Public Library Western History Department.*

The Cunningham Hose Team #1 takes off in a July 4 contest. *Courtesy Denver Public Library Western History Department.*

Elk Avenue, 1982. *Kendal Atchison*

Crested Butte's carpenter Gothic buildings. *Kendal Atchison*

to Crested Butte, the town gained prominence first as a supply center and a way station for travelers between Gunnison and Aspen, and then as a coal town.

The first major coal mine was the Jokerville, but it was closed after an underground explosion killed fifty-eight miners. Like other mines in the area—the Horace, the Bulkley, and the Big Mine—it was owned by the Colorado Fuel and Iron Company, eventually part of CF & I Steel Corporation, which operated coal mines in the Crested Butte area into the 1950s.

As a coal-mining town, Crested Butte suffered the excesses of the coal companies. Miners were paid in script even after such payment was outlawed. Wage confrontations and strikes brought conflict; young boys barely into their teens did men's work in the mines; and cave-ins and underground death were a way of life.

Many of the residents of Crested Butte were Slavs and Italians, who brought with them their rich traditions, old-country dress, and pungent foods. For the most part, though, they embraced

Colorado mining camp architecture. In fact, Crested Butte is such a sparkling example of middle-class Victorian architecture that the town is listed on the National Register of Historic Places. Crested Butte added one unique touch to American architectural design—the two-story outhouse. The lower story was used in summer, the upper in winter when deep snow made the first floor inaccessible.

A decade after the last coal mine closed, Crested Butte reemerged as a ski town when a group of entrepreneurs purchased a ranch outside the town and developed it as a winter resort. In the 1970s, Crested Butte appeared destined to become a mining town once again when Amax Incorporated planned to turn Mount Emmons, west of Crested Butte, into a major molybdenum mine. Low molybdenum prices forced Amax to shelve the project, however, to the glee of skiers and preservationists, who feared Crested Butte would suffer irreparable damage by becoming a boomtown.

Crestone

COUNTY: *Saguache*
LOCATION: *13 mi. west of Moffat*
MAP 13
P.O. est. Nov. 16, 1880

Nestled at the foot of the jagged Crestone Needle of the Sangre de Cristos Mountains, Crestone, with its mountain stream and giant willow trees, appears more like a rural community than a mining camp. Despite boomtown tensions and a legal decision that forced many miners from their homes, Crestone was an orderly town. The most heinous crime committed was the destruction of a saloon by town matrons protesting a policy of hiring bar girls.

Ore was discovered near Crestone, a farm town, in 1875. A second flurry of activity came in the 1880s when several promising ore bodies were found. Most promising of all was a cave discovered by two prospectors caught in a storm. When they lit a candle, they discovered three bars of gold and three human skulls. The two stumbled back to Crestone with the gold and the story but could not find the cave again.

Crestone's boom was cut short when the owners of the vast Baca Grant, which traces its origin to a grant awarded Don Luis Maria Cabeza de Vaca by the Spanish crown in 1822, evicted

Never completely a ghost town, Crestone has undergone a recent revival *(below)*. Crestone gateway. *Kendal Atchison*

57
C

hapless miners. The court upheld the rights of the owners of the grant over those of gold seekers who had settled on the land believing it was open to mining.

In 1900, with building sites selling for as much as $600, Crestone boasted five general stores, four saloons, a millinery shop, an undertaker, a sign painter, "and several hundred good citizens," according to the *Crestone Miner.* At the peak of the boom, in February, 1901, the *Denver Times* touted Crestone as having "quicker return for the money invested than any other new camp."

The *Times,* of course, was wrong. Less than six months later it reported: "A slump of the most decided character has occurred. People are leaving the camp by dozens and business is terribly overdone." The Independent Mine shut its mill, ostensibly for modernization, and though the Independent did reopen, the Crestone boom was over. Within a few years most of the miners were gone. Business was so bad that the small house on the hill that served as Crestone's red-light district was hauled into town and became a home.

Cripple Creek

COUNTY: *Teller*
LOCATION: *45 mi. west of Colorado Springs*
MAP 14
P.O. est. July 29, 1891 as Fremont

For ten years Robert Womack, a cowboy and a prospector, had been telling saloon bums in the dives of Colorado City that there was a fortune to be made in gold at Cripple Creek, the yard-wide stream that ran through his cow pasture. For a time, when news of a gold find sent scores of prospectors to the area, it appeared Womack might be right. But the claim turned out to be a salted mine; thus whenever mining men were tempted to listen to Womack, they recalled the Mount Pisgah Hoax, as it was known, and put their money instead into the newly discovered silver mines at Creede. When Womack did at last find gold ore, he failed to interest investors, and eventually he sold the claim for $300. Later $5 million in gold was taken from the mine.

Despite the initial lack of interest, Cripple Creek was too rich to go undiscovered for long.

Two fires within a week devastated Cripple Creek, which was rebuilt with brick. *Courtesy Denver Public Library Western History Department.*

Despite the glum looks on the faces of patrons and bar girls, drinking was Cripple Creek's favorite form of recreation. *Courtesy Denver Public Library Western History Department.*

The dapper gentleman *fifth from left* in this group of swells is Spencer Penrose, who made fortunes in both Cripple Creek gold and Utah copper. *Courtesy Denver Public Library Western History Department.*

Gold mining began its decline at the turn of the century, but Cripple Creek had a sizable population into the depression years. *Author's collection.*

Inveterate prospectors like Womack, Colorado Springs carpenter Winfield Scott Stratton, and tenderfoots such as James Burns and James Doyle, two Irishmen from Portland, Maine, began digging holes in the hills. Before long, the mountains around Cripple Creek were so pock-marked with prospect holes "that a map of one of the mountains looks as if some one had loaded a cannon with claims and shot them up against a piece of card board," noted Cy Warman, the Creede editor, who went to Cripple Creek to look around.

The break for Cripple Creek came in 1893 when the silver crash decimated the silver camps and threw Colorado into a depression. The gold mines at Cripple Creek, just then proving out, pulled in millions of dollars in investment money and revived Colorado's economy.

Cripple Creek was the last of the West's great gold camps and the greatest. Before it was over, the district, which included twelve towns, produced hundreds of millions of dollars in gold and created some twenty-five millionaires.

Gold was everywhere. "Free gold sticks out of the rock like raisins out of a fruit cake," noted a reporter. Miners following the vein of the Cresson struck a "vug," a room of almost pure gold worth more than a million dollars. A young suitor grubstaked his girlfriend's father and found himself both married and a mine owner. And a drugstore clerk threw his hat into

the air and dug where it landed, discovering the Pharmacist Mine.

Many of the district's mine owners were ordinary prospectors, like Stratton, the district's first millionaire, who sold his Independence Mine for $11 million; he would wish later he had sold out earlier at $155,000. Wealth did not wear well for many, and Stratton became deeply morose. Others, observed a reporter, acted as though they had "fallen into a fortune as a benighted ranchman falls into an irrigation ditch. . . . He has been the hired man all his life and ought not to have been promoted."

A number of the successful mine operators were eastern-educated bluebloods who understood investment and risk taking as well as speculation and stock manipulation. Cripple Creek, developed late in western mining, was part of a sophisticated era when discoveries required enormous amounts of capital just to fight off lawsuits. "Cripple Creek ought to be a lawyers' paradise," Warman noted. And indeed it was, with ninety-one lawyers by 1900.

With many of Colorado's mining camps doomed, prospectors and miners swarmed into the Cripple Creek district, and right on their heels were gamblers and prostitutes, swindlers, and footpads. It cost four bits to sleep in a chair in a hotel lobby. Miners formed long lines outside restaurants at mealtimes. When one family moved out of a tent, another moved in before

Left: Mr. and Mrs. John Crooks in their fashionably cluttered Cripple Creek home, 1911. *Courtesy Hazel Mavity.*

Below: The third building from the right housed the elegant Turf Club. To the left of it is the Tutt Building, named for one of Penrose's partners. *Kendal Atchison*

the ashes in the cookstove were cold. As late as 1900, prices still were twice as high as in nearby Colorado Springs. "Two stage lines, two telegraph lines, two dance halls, two hotels, time locks on the dinin' rum do's, waite's on rolah-skates an' head waite's on hossback—I reckon we'er purt nigh in it," a stage driver told a journalist in 1895. Actually, he was low on the number of dance halls.

Despite boomtown conditions, Cripple Creek offered comforts unique among budding mining camps. The train from Colorado Springs stopped

The Old Homestead appears as lonely as a streetwalker, all that is left of once glittering Myers Avenue. *Kendal Atchison*

only eighteen miles away. The climate was mild and the terrain was tame. It was possible to rent a rig and prospect from a buggy.

Cripple Creek, named when both a cow and a rancher were lamed near the stream, gave its name to the little settlement that grew up around Bob Womack's 1890 discovery. It was a flim-flam town of saloons, dance halls, and whore-houses—Johnnie Nolan's Saloon, Crapper Jack's, the Topic Dance Hall, the Bucket of Blood, the Turf Club, the Mikado, and the Old Homestead, laid out along Bennett and Myers avenues.

Horace Bennett and Julius Myers, Denver real estate men, had purchased the Cripple Creek area for $5,000 down and a $20,000 note in 1885 because Myers liked the fishing. When word came that gold seekers were throwing up shacks on the partners' ranch, the two promptly platted the town and sold lots. They named the two main streets for themselves. Bennett Avenue became the town's business boulevard, with banks, hotels, and brokerage houses. Myers Avenue was known worldwide as the fanciest red-light district in the West.

Fire hit Cripple Creek in 1896 when a bar-tender from the Topic and his girlfriend got into an argument and knocked over a stove. In three hours the fire destroyed the Central Dance Hall, the Topic, and a good stretch of Myers Avenue buildings, along with several blocks of more sedate Cripple Creek. Some fifteen hun-dred persons were left homeless. Four days later, a second fire, started when a pot of grease ig-nited at the Portland Hotel, consumed most of what was left, ironically leaving Poverty Gulch untouched. Thousands of people were left home-less, with dozens financially ruined, but Cripple Creek emerged a more substantial community.

Before the last fire was extinguished, the peo-ple of Colorado Springs had begun filling relief trains with food, blankets, and tents. Stratton told the stores to send the bills to him. Colo-rado Springs financiers also advanced the capi-tal necessary to rebuild Cripple Creek, not just as a boom camp but as a brick and stone city with an air of prosperity and permanence. Ben-nett Avenue was crowded with handsome brick buildings, proudly bearing the names of their builders or owners. Stone rosettes, stained-glass insets, and cast-iron pillars decorated the stores and business blocks. The most elegant building of all was the National Hotel, built to rival the Brown Palace in Denver. Stratton leased a suite for fifty years in the National but probably never stayed there. Later he bought the Brown Palace.

The elegant new Cripple Creek was more to the liking of the town's rich young bloods, who divided their time between their investments and the Old Homestead or the gambling clubs. They called themselves the Socialites and were the most elegant and most eligible men in town. Albert Carlton, who turned down an offer to

SHE was a splendid whore. Whenever Pearl DeVere went driving, dressed in a French gown, an ostrich plume in her dyed red hair, men sighed, women stared, and little girls swooned in envy. She served the finest wines at the Old Homestead, which was the most elegant bagnio in Cripple Creek, and she threw spectacular parties. In 1897, while some of the town swells and millionaires swilled champagne in a parlor bedecked with hothouse flowers, Pearl DeVere went upstairs and took an overdose of morphine. An anonymous gentleman paid the funeral costs, and the Elks band marched in her funeral parade, playing "Good-bye, Little Girl, Good-bye."

From the glittering brothels of Cripple Creek's Myers Avenue to the cribs of Leadville's Stillborn Alley, named for the dead infants—the detritus of prostitution—found in its garbage heaps, prostitution was part of the mining town economy. Few prostitutes lived as regally as Pearl DeVere, but most died like her, from drugs or disease, too destitute to pay for their funerals.

Glamorized by historians—most of them male—prostitution was in truth the noxious underside of western life, attracting women who had no other way of earning a living. Hundreds of women found their way into prostitution in Colorado's mining camps. A few even found their way out. Red Stockings, a popular Leadville nymph, supposedly saved $100,000 from her ill-gotten earnings, threw a farewell party, and became a born-again woman of virtue. Most, however, stayed in the nether world of the gaslights, changing their names to such colorful appellations as Sallie Purple, Timberline, the Mormon Queen, Liverlip, Dirty Neck Nell, and the Victor Pig.

While a handful of prostitutes operated out of elegant brothels like the Old Homestead, which had stoves in each room, crystal chandeliers, and Oriental carpets, and where only gentlemen known to the madam were welcome, the majority of Cripple Creek's three hundred prostitutes lived in shacks along Myers Avenue and Poverty Gulch, accepting all comers.

Cripple Creek's row was so infamous that when Julian Street, a writer for *Collier's* and author of *Abroad at Home*, visited the district, he spent all his time ogling Myers Avenue's habitués. Street called Cripple Creek "the most awful little city in the world" and described in detail a visit with a blowzy, outsize prostitute named Leo the Lion. Cripple Creek fathers returned the insult. They renamed Myers Avenue "Julian Street."

buy into the Independence for $500 because he had come west to die, controlled Cripple Creek's freight business and later controlled the district's mines as well. After he decided he would live after all, he married one of the town's young beauties, Ethel Frizzell, who lived so regally her servant sold her cast-off dresses to Cripple Creek's prostitutes for $100 each.

The most intriguing member of the Socialites was Spencer Penrose, a handsome Philadelphian who bought into the C.O.D. Mine. Penrose wired his older brother Boies, an eastern backroom politician, for investment money, but Boies wired back $150 so he could buy a ticket home. Penrose promptly sank the money into the C.O.D. and later sent Boies a $10,000 check as a return on the $150 investment.

Penrose's real fortune came when he backed a scheme advanced by a young Cripple Creek engineer who claimed he could extract copper from low-grade ore in Utah. Penrose became a founder of Utah Copper Company and one of the West's great nabobs; he was builder of the Broadmoor in Colorado Springs and a civic benefactor.

As the major town of the Cripple Creek district—a town of 50,000 in 1900—Cripple Creek was hurt by the volatile labor strife of 1903. When the violence as over, Cripple Creek, along with the rest of the district, never fully recovered though mining lasted another half century. In 1941, Ethel Carlton, whose husband had lived until 1931, built the Carlton Tunnel to drain water from the district's major mines, and later added a $2 million cyanide mill. But those steps failed to combat the combination of low gold prices, high mining costs, and declining ore grades, and late in the 1950s the district's last mines shut down.

The town of Cripple Creek did not, however. By the time the mining stopped, Cripple Creek had made a name for itself as a summer theater center. Melodrama at the Imperial Hotel (never as grand as the National but still standing, which is more than can be said for the National) attracts hundreds of tourists each summer, many of whom have turned Cripple Creek's Victorian cottages into summer homes. Another attraction is the Old Homestead, now a museum; the nominal fee charged is a bargain compared to what the madams charged for entrance eighty years ago.

Crisman's general store. *Courtesy Denver Public Library Western History Department.*

Crisman

COUNTY: *Boulder*
LOCATION: *7 mi. west of Boulder*
MAP 3
P.O. est. July 20, 1876; discont. May 31, 1918

Obed Crisman, who built the first concentration mill in the area, stamped his name on the town, which he founded in the mid-1880s. The Yellow Pine Mine, which gave up some $500,000 before the 1893 silver crash, and the Great Logan, which once produced "the richest specimens of any mine in the country," according to the *Denver Times,* were the town's major mines. The major citizen was mine owner Pierre Ardourel, a Frenchman who built a fine house containing a spacious wine cellar. In 1894 an inauspicious rerouting of the narrow-gauge rail track near the house blocked the wine cellar, and legend says the bottles are still aging nicely.

Crystal

COUNTY: *Gunnison*
LOCATION: *5 mi. east of Marble*
MAP 6
P.O. est. July 28, 1882; discont. Oct. 31, 1909

A group of prospectors discovered crystal-like quartz along Rock Creek (later the Crystal River) in 1880 and named their settlement Crystal City. By 1883, when a good road was built to the town, allowing wagons to replace jack trains for ore hauling, Crystal blossomed into a metropolis of several hundred residents, most working in the Black Queen, the Lead King, and the Sheep Mountain Tunnel along with lesser mines, the Whopper, the Cinnamon Pride, the Daisy, and the Laura.

By the mid-1880s Crystal was booming with a newspaper, the *Crystal River Current,* two general stores, dozens of houses, a handful of sa-

The remains of the Crystal Mill are among Colorado's most famous ghost town sights. *Kendal Atchison*

The Crystal Club was an all-male domain. *Kendal Atchison*

loons, and the Crystal Club (which still stands), catering to an all-male clientele with a variety of games and libations.

About that time Crystal dropped the "city" from its name, a portent of things to come. Transportation was a persistent problem for the remote town, and despite talk of a railroad from Carbondale, the mines were forced to rely on wagons to transport their ore. The 1893 silver crash doomed Crystal as a silver town, though at the turn of the century activity picked up when mining companies began extracting the lead and copper from ores that had been thrown out on the dumps. Mining in some form lasted in Crystal until World War I.

Crystal is well known today for more than its magnificent setting on the Crystal River and its orderly collection of cabins. The picturesque remains of the Crystal Mill on the Crystal River, once used to provide power for the Sheep Mountain Tunnel, is one of the most photographed relics of Colorado's mining days.

Dorchester's most substantial building, the general store and post office, shown in 1909, still stands. *Courtesy Colorado Historical Society.*

Dorchester

COUNTY: *Gunnison*
LOCATION: *22 mi. north of Tin Cup*
MAP 8
P.O. est. Aug. 2, 1900; discont. July 31, 1912

Founded in the mid-1890s, Dorchester blossomed after the turn of the century when the Star and the Enterprise mines were shipping

ore. The town never amounted to more than a few commercial establishments and some log cabins.

The Star was run by a French widow who had persuaded her friends to invest in the mine. Despite her personal supervision, the Star was not profitable, and the widow cashed in her shares and left. So did the rest of Dorchester.

Dumont

COUNTY: *Clear Creek*
LOCATION: *5 mi. northwest of Idaho Springs*
MAP 1
P.O. est. July 5, 1861, as Mill City

The miners of Clear Creek had great hopes for the log cabin settlement they built in 1860 and named Mill City after the arastras they used to crush ore. "It has a large belt of lodes which give external appearance of great value, but thus far have been almost invariably disappointing," wrote Frank Hall in his *History of the State of Colorado.*

Twenty years later, the camp was renamed Dumont for John M. Dumont, a part owner of the Freeland, the Whale, and the Lone Tree

mines, who attempted to resurrect the community. The *Rocky Mountain News* reported Dumont "is a right busy camp," but that activity also did not last long.

In 1900, Dumont attempted another revival, this time as a gambling resort. "The camp of Dumont . . . was started up last night as a wide open camp. A number of gamblers came up from Denver and with other sports carried on gambling throughout the night," the *Denver Times* reported. Gambling died out even faster than mining had.

Dunton

COUNTY: *Dolores*
LOCATION: *36 mi. northeast of Dolores*
MAP 10
P.O. est. Aug. 9, 1892; discont. date unknown

Dunton is a splendid ghost town of eighteen buildings, most of them log cabins and all of them in excellent condition. Old bottles, pieces of machinery, and other mining camp memorabilia decorate the exteriors.

The town is in a pristine setting along a road lined with wild iris and aspen, and the town

Dumont no longer is a "right busy camp." *Kendal Atchison*

Dunton today attracts cross-country skiers and hunters. *Kendal Atchison*

Mining camp memorabilia, Dunton. *Kendal Atchison*

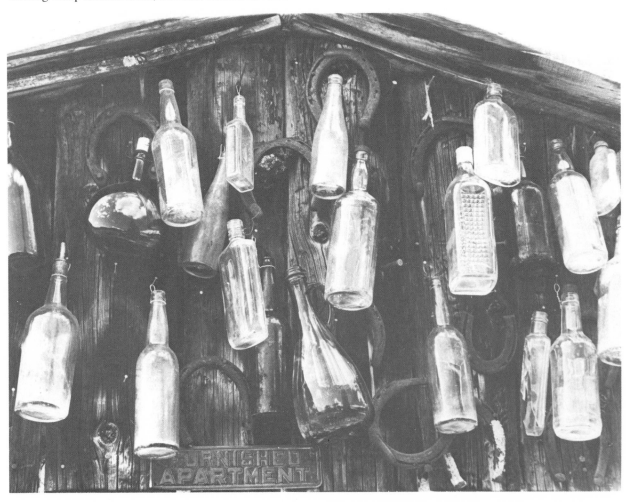

today, a haven for hunters and cross-country skiers, is a far cry from the raucous town where legend says Butch Cassidy holed up after robbing a Telluride bank.

Dunton was founded in the 1880s when the Emma Mine, just south of town, was discovered. The town reached its peak at the turn of the century, when the Emma complex employed 125 men, the Mount Goram group was booming, and there was feverish activity on Democrat Mountain.

Mining did not last long after that. By 1917, when a hot spring in the town was turned into a tourist attraction, Dunton was better known as a resort than as a mining camp.

Dyersville

COUNTY: *Summit*
LOCATION: *11 mi. southeast of Breckenridge*
MAP 4
No P.O.

Preacher John L. Dyer, the fire-and-brimstone Methodist circuit rider, was as much in demand for his ability as a locator of mines as he was for his rousing sermons, and locating paid better. He employed a method called dowsing that, like witching for water, involved the use of a forked stick. Dyer was so proficient at dowsing that prospectors often sat through his lengthy ser-

The remains of Dyersville, 1981. *Kendal Atchison*

Dyersville is located in a mountain valley a half-mile walk from the Boreas Pass road. *Kendal Atchison*

mons just for the opportunity of talking with him afterward about mining.

Since preaching paid almost nothing, and the collection was usually skimpy, Dyer used his mining skill to supplement his income. His most successful investment was the Warrior's Mark Mine ten miles above Breckenridge, where he made $2,000. On January 1, 1881, in part to watch his investment, Dyer began construction of a log cabin with a loft not far from his mine. On February 19, Dyer moved his wife into the house, a respectable cabin that was seventeen by seventeen feet square, with a shingle roof.

Before long the town of Dyersville grew up around the preacher's home, in order to provide housing for Warrior's Mark employees. Dyer, familiarly known as "Father Dyer" throughout the mining country, did not like the management of the mine and disapproved of high overhead costs. Moreover, according to his autobiography, *The Snow-Shoe Itinerant,* he scorned "the whiskey, cards, and fancy women," and the nearby saloon, inappropriately named Angels Rest. Late in 1882, Dyer sold his interest in the mine and moved away.

Methodist preacher John L. Dyer, known to the miners as "Father Dyer," was more successful at preaching than at prospecting. *Author's collection.*

Once considered a young rival to Cripple Creek, Eldora never reached the famed gold camp's prominence. *Kendal Atchison*

Eldora

COUNTY: *Boulder*
LOCATION: *4 mi. west of Nederland*
MAP 3
P.O. est. Feb. 13, 1897; discont. May 19, 1967

The *Rocky Mountain News* in 1898 called Eldora "the youngest rival of Cripple Creek," and the *Denver Republican* said the frenzy at Eldora was like the beginning of the rush into Leadville. There was a decided difference between Eldora and those sinful gold camps of Colorado's earlier years, however. "There is not a dance house in the town, nor will there be. . . . The pioneers of the camp . . . are all experienced miners and know the limitation of morality in a new and prosperous camp," the *Republican* noted. The town employed only one police officer, and six months into the boom "there has not been a single instance of an affray of any character," the paper continued.

Keeping Eldora moral during its 1898 boom proved to be more than one officer could handle. Miners filled the half-dozen coaches that ran from Boulder to Eldora each day, swelling the population by forty or fifty newcomers daily. By mid-1898 there were fifteen hundred residents in the area and some three hundred new buildings.

Eldora was founded as Happy Valley, but it was rechristened El Dorado when news of the camp's rich sulfide ore leaked out. The United States Post Office changed the name to Eldora because of mail mix-ups with El Dorado, California.

Despite its intensity, Eldora's boom was brief. It peaked about the turn of the century, along with the town's immorality, it might seem. Town gossips whispered that Mrs. Givens, who ran the Gold Miner Hotel, which still stands, was actually the wife of the man who had assassinated President James A. Garfield. And workers at the Baily Mill, incensed at not being paid, went gunning for their employer and shot him.

Elkton

COUNTY: *Teller*
LOCATION: *2 mi. north of Victor*
MAP 14
P.O. est. April 12, 1895; discont. Nov. 15, 1926

A tenderfoot prospector discovered the Elkton Mine just north of Victor in the 1890s, named it for the elk antlers he found nearby, and offered half interest in the mine to settle a grocery bill of $34, or $36.50, depending on the story. The Elkton went on to produce millions and to spawn the town of Elkton, a pleasant community served by three railroads and an electric line. Elkton's decline began with the 1904 Cripple Creek labor war, though the mine itself continued to produce well into the twentieth century.

Emma

COUNTY: *Pitkin*
LOCATION: *2 mi. southwest of Basalt*
MAP 6
P.O. est. date unknown; discont. 1947

Emma appears more like the remains of a midwestern farm town than the ruins of an outpost on the Denver & Rio Grande between the silver town of Aspen and the once elegant resort of Glenwood Springs. Emma was originally a small collection of railroad buildings that later were supplanted by a fine brick store embellished with cast-iron columns and fancy brickwork, a trim schoolhouse, and a brick Victorian mansion and barn that were grand even by Aspen standards. They remain in crumbling splendor, bypassed by the affluence of Aspen and the prosperity of Glenwood Springs.

Tin siding on an Eldora building. *Kendal Atchison*

This Elkton storefront is slowly crumbling into the mountain grasses. *Kendal Atchison*

Deserted storefronts at Emma, 1982. *Kendal Atchison*

Empire

COUNTY: *Clear Creek*
LOCATION: *9 mi. west of Idaho Springs*
MAP 1
P.O. est. June 28, 1861 as Empire City

Empire City is "a title which must have been given more in the spirit of prophecy than from any existing applicability, for the only sign of a city existed in about a dozen mean log-huts and a few brace of frame houses," wrote an 1864 visitor.

The town consisted of a hotel—"a modicum of hay in sacking was given you for a shake-down," the visitor continued, a blacksmith shop, and a store with a post office.

Founded as a mining camp in 1860 and named for New York, the Empire State, Empire quickly grew to become a settlement of several hundred people, but it declined just as rapidly, and by the mid-1860s the population was down to a handful of people. Mining was revived in the 1870s, and Empire settled down to a long if un-spectacular career as a mining town.

Empire's most enduring family was the Pecks. James Peck, a Chicago merchant, arrived about 1862, intent on starting a mining career. His

Empire's main street, 1981. *Kendal Atchison*

The Peck House with the Peck family arrayed on the porch. *Courtesy Colorado Historical Society.*

wife, Mary Grace, reached Empire shortly afterward, bringing a wardrobe of silk ball gowns and fine jewelry. She took one look at Empire, packed up the dresses, and set out to bring hospitality to Empire. She served her guests milk, mush, and popcorn as if they were lobster and champagne, and was such a successful hostess that in 1872 the Pecks turned their home into a hotel. The Peck family sold the hotel, the Peck House, in 1945, but they never really let go. Perceptive guests say today that Mary Grace Peck's granddaughter Gracie, who died of tuberculosis in the house in 1885 when she was fourteen years old, still wanders the halls.

The town of Eureka is gone. Only the foundation of the Sunnyside Mill, stair-stepped up the mountainside, remains. *Courtesy Denver Public Library Western History Department.*

Eureka

COUNTY: *San Juan*
LOCATION: *8 mi. northeast of Silverton*
MAP 9
P.O. est. Aug. 9, 1875; discont. May, 1942

In 1874 a member of F. V. Hayden's survey team came across a collection of log cabins and a "flaring signboard" bearing the name "Eureka." "What had been found here to suggest the name was not immediately apparent," he wrote.

Not apparent to the surveyor, perhaps, but to the miners who lived there was the Sunnyside Mine, which had been located the year before and was destined to become one of the West's great producers. It operated steadily until 1931, when it was worked intermittently. Today the mine is operated by Standard Metals Corpora-

The stagecoach trip from Denver to Fairplay was long, uncomfortable, and often dangerous. *Courtesy Colorado Historical Society.*

tion from the other side of the mountain. All that remains of Eureka is a flat townsite and the skeleton of the enormous Sunnyside Mill, its levels cut into the mountain like giant steps.

If the Hayden surveyor found Eureka unworthy of the name, others did not. Within a few years it boasted a population of three thousand and a booming business section with stores, meat markets, a restaurant, and a post office.

The best building in town was a saloon, however, and Eureka had its own recognized society. The *Silver World* describes an 1877 dance at which the women arrived on burros. The ball began with the "San Juan Polka," "which resembled a Sioux war dance," the paper noted, and so much dust was raised the dancers could hardly see. Still, they danced until morning, stopping only to feast on ground hog and ox meat.

Later entertainments were more genteel. A former Eureka resident recalls in *Timberline Tailings* that she went to dances at the Gold Prince boardinghouse where miners and sheepherders, who outnumbered the women ten to one, danced the waltz and offered their partners ice cream and cake.

Railroad builder Otto Mears routed his Silverton railroad through Eureka, and it operated until the Sunnyside shut down in the 1930s. Toward the end of its operation, the railroad's steam engines were replaced by an ungainly amalgamation of automobile and locomotive parts called "Casey Jones." An ugly duckling cousin of the Galloping Goose, the Casey Jones, which could carry a dozen riders, swooped down the tracks between Silverton and Eureka, making the screeching eight-mile run in a death-defying twenty minutes. To clear snow off the tracks, the Casey Jones carried brooms tied behind the cowcatcher.

In 1976 the state of Colorado decided the town had had no municipal government for the past five years and declared Eureka formally abandoned.

Fairplay

COUNTY: *Park*
LOCATION: *81 mi. southwest of Denver*
MAP 4
P.O. est. Aug. 2, 1862 as Fair Play

Angry with the greed of the early settlers of

A slow day at the mercantile company, perhaps because the boys were up the street at the saloon. *Courtesy Colorado Historical Society.*

Orientals were discriminated against in most mining camps. In Fairplay they were allowed to placer mine only in the areas where white miners had given up. *Courtesy Colorado Historical Society.*

Tarryall, who claimed all the best placer sites for themselves, disgruntled gold seekers dubbed the settlement "Graball" and moved to a spot on the South Platte where they organized a more egalitarian town. They called it Fair Play (now Fairplay), but for all its aspirations the town, founded in 1859, was little more honorable than Tarryall.

One of Fairplay's organizers was Jim Reynolds, a Confederate raider and highwayman, who was killed after a robbery not far from Fairplay. For a time Fairplay was terrorized by the crazed Espinoza brothers, who claimed nearly two dozen victims.

Still, the idea of fair play held. In 1880 when Judge Thomas M. Bowen, who later made a fortune at Summitville, sentenced a murderer to only eight years in prison, a group of enraged citizens hanged the guilty man from a courthouse window.

With all that evil about, it was only natural that Fairplay attracted reformers. Father Dyer, the Methodist itinerant preacher, moved a hotel from Montgomery, a dying town a few miles away, to Fairplay for use as a church and in-

As Park County seat, Fairplay remained an active community during the depression years of the 1930s. *Courtesy Denver Public Library Western History Department.*

stalled W. F. Warren as pastor. Not only did local toughs shave Warren's horse, but someone tried to steal the church. "If hell is any worse than Fairplay," muttered the beleaguered preacher, "I certainly want to be saved from going there." In 1873 the church burned down in a fire that destroyed much of the town.

The Presbyterians, apparently, had an easier time of it. In 1874, Sheldon Jackson built Fairplay's quaint carpenter Gothic church, a splendid architectural whimsy in a drab, windswept town.

Fairplay was settled by placer miners, and when they turned to hydraulic mining, Chinese

Fairplay's South Park City is a collection of mining camp buildings. *Kendal Atchison*

Named for an early Fairplay parson, the Sheldon Jackson Memorial Chapel is one of the state's best examples of ecclesiastical carpenter Gothic. *Sandra Dallas*

Freeland

COUNTY: *Clear Creek*
LOCATION: *5 mi. west of Idaho Springs*
MAP 1
P.O. est. Jan. 16, 1879; discont. Sept. 15, 1908

The rich ores of the Freeland, the Lone Tree, and other mines near the stringtown of Freeland attracted a number of prominent mining investors. One was Cripple Creek millionaire Winfield Scott Stratton. Another was Comstock king John W. Mackay, who headed a group of Californians investing in the Freeland and nearby Stanley properties. Mackay brought in one of

workers came in to work the placers. As mining played out, Fairplay became a supply and transportation center for the mines west of the town. In 1867 it wrested the Park County seat away from Buckskin Joe.

Nearly a hundred years after it was settled, Fairplay emerged as a protypical wild west town when buildings from all over the county were hauled to Fairplay and refurbished. The block-long restoration, called South Park City, includes a Chinese tong house similar to that used by Fairplay's Chinese workers, a morgue, a drug store, a photography gallery, and various other commercial and residential structures that give visitors a glimpse of how a century-old mountain town looked during its heyday.

At Freeland, rock walls built with mud as mortar are still sturdy after more than a century. *Kendal Atchison*

his Comstock lieutenants at a $25,000 a year salary to "show the old-timers something," an Idaho Springs man gleefully reported in the *Denver Times*. What he showed them was how to spend "money like water. They were amazed and bewildered at the lavish way in which the representative of the bonanza king spent money."

So lavish was the manager, who spent most of his time in Denver, that other mine owners closed their operations and went to work for the Mackay venture. Though Mackay took out millions in ore during his short ownership, there were no profits, and his Freeland experience soured him on Colorado mining.

Other owners were more prudent and more profitable, including John M. Dumont, who owned the Freeland before the Mackay group.

The town of Freeland was started in 1877, and within a year seventeen dwellings had been completed and more were under way. Everyone in town was "employed either developing the various mines or building homes for their families," reported the Georgetown *Colorado Miner*, which added that there was a school with twenty-seven students and a church and Sunday school were not far behind.

Despite the hasty construction, the structures of Freeland were durable, in part because Cor-

nish miners were responsible for the stonework, which was so finely executed that mud used as mortar held the rock walls together—some for a century. There are several hewn-log cabins and frame houses still standing in Freeland, but the fancier houses were sawed in half and hauled to Idaho Springs.

Frisco

COUNTY: *Summit*
LOCATION: *9 mi. north of Breckenridge*
MAP 4
P.O. est. Aug. 29, 1879

Indian scout Captain Henry Learned hacked "Frisco" into a log and nailed it above a log cabin at the north end of the Tenmile Range, naming the tiny settlement. He stayed on to become Frisco's business leader and mayor. The first cabin was built in 1873, though Captain Learned did not come along for several years. By 1881, Frisco had two hotels, a grocery, a hardware store, a clothing store, a blacksmith shop, and a saw mill.

The town thrived as a railroad stop and once had two depots to serve the Denver & Rio Grande and the Denver, South Park & Pacific.

A Public Service Company crew rides to work near Frisco. *Courtesy Public Service Company of Colorado.*

Despite modern attempts to disguise it, Frisco buildings occasionally aspired to architectural pretension. *Kendal Atchison*

Cans, bottles, and other mining camp implements collected near Fulford. *Kendal Atchison*

Frisco acted as a supply center for the gold and silver mines along the Tenmile Range. The boom slackened in 1893 with the fall in silver prices and an exodus of merchants. Enterprising local residents turned a nearly completed saloon into a school.

Fulford

COUNTY: *Eagle*
LOCATION: *22 mi. southeast of Eagle*
MAP 6
P.O. est. Feb. 5, 1892; discont. May 15, 1910

Fulford—originally three towns named Fulford, Polar City, and Gee's Addition—was settled in 1889 when rich ores were discovered in the area. The towns were consolidated under the name of Fulford after Arthur H. Fulford, one of the pioneers, was killed in an avalanche. Local residents had a propensity for naming places after the victims of disasters. A nearby creek was

named Nolan Creek for William Nolan, who died when he accidentally shot himself.

Population peaked in the late 1890s at about six hundred, and after the turn of the century only a few families were left. Fulford had a revival in 1913 when the *Denver Republican* counted fifteen men sitting on the porch of the local hotel swapping stories and comparing ore specimens. Today Fulford is two towns. Upper Fulford has two deserted cabins, and Lower Fulford is a thriving summer community of cabins along two rutted streets.

Georgetown

COUNTY: *Clear Creek*
LOCATION: *45 mi. west of Denver*
MAP 1
P.O. est. June 19, 1866

Brothers George and David Griffith, Kentucky gold seekers, arrived in Auraria in 1858 and set out with the throngs of prospectors who poured into the mountain gulches in search of gold. The brothers built a cabin in a pretty valley among towering mountains, then struck pay dirt in a nearby crevice. Their mine was the only gold mine of consequence ever found in the Georgetown area.

As miners crowded in on the brothers' find the Griffiths organized the settlement of Georgetown and an adjacent camp called Elizabethtown, probably named for their sister. In time the two communities were merged into Georgetown, which Isabella Bird, the indomitable English traveler visiting Colorado in 1873, called "the only town I have seen in America to which the epithet picturesque could be applied."

The Georgetown that Isabella Bird saw, already dubbed the "Silver Queen" for the rich silver mines discovered in the vicinity, was an attractive mix of handsome brick business blocks and quaint Victorian cottages trimmed with gingerbread. While founded as a gold camp, Georgetown emerged as a silver town in 1864 when R. W. Steele picked up blossom rock heavy in sil-

ver. Actually, the first gold prospectors had encountered silver, but because they were looking for gold they failed to recognize the precious ore. After Steele discovered the Belmont, Georgetown's first silver mine, the Pelican and the Dives mines (later combined), the Seven-thirty, the Payrock, the Paymaster, the Sunburst, and several dozen other paying mines were developed. "Fortunes were made in a few days or weeks, and nearly as speedily squandered," noted one observer.

Those fortunes sometimes led to violence. In 1875 one of the owners of the Pelican Mine was murdered in daylight on a Georgetown street by an employee of the Dives, climaxing a four-year clash between the two operations.

Despite that bloodshed, Georgetown was relatively tame compared to other silver towns such as Leadville. Still, it had its share of bawdy houses and drinking establishments. "Saloons multiplied on every hand; gamblers plied their pernicious trade, fleecing hundreds of the innocent and unwary," historian Frank Hall reported. Saloons and gambling hall rowdies caused fre-

Winter morning on Argentine Street in Georgetown. Hamill House is to the left of the dark brick mansion. *Courtesy Denver Public Library Western History Department.*

The town's fine homes
required pressed-wood
rocking chairs and
punched-tin pie safes.
*Courtesy Denver Public
Library Western History
Department.*

Interior of the
Georgetown Courier
office. *Courtesy Denver
Public Library Western
History Department.*

The Hotel de Paris was a bit of Normandy in the Colorado Rockies. *Courtesy Colorado Historical Society.*

quent problems. "Only last sabbath we saw two ladies pushed into the gutter on Main street, trembling in fear, trying to shield a child in its carriage from eight young men and boys who were riding at full speed," reported the George-town *Colorado Miner* in 1872, demanding the town pass an ordinance against fast riding. The newspaper also requested a dog ordinance. "It would not only cheapen the price of beef, but it would enable our people to sleep nights." And it occasionally suggested beautification projects: "Wouldn't it be appropriate . . . for all the men to visit Billy Cooper's Bath House . . . and there purify the body as well as streets."

The *Colorado Miner* was, like the independent newspapers of other Colorado mining towns, witty and irreverent, indulging in the sort of personal attack that led to canings and duels. One editor kept a gun lying within easy reach on his desk; when he left his office, he always walked down the center of the street, armed with an arsenal.

The *Miner* was begun in 1867 by Dr. J. E. Wharton and A. W. Barnard. Wharton, a contemporary noted, "loved the pure, unadulterated corn-juice, of which he was a prodigious consumer, and drank early and often." Temperance or the lack of it was a concern of other *Miner* editors. "We have always been earnestly in favor of total abstinence; but if you will drink, fond reader, we know of no better place than Joe Garbarino's," noted one editor, piously coming to terms with temperance and his own livelihood.

While saloonkeeper Garbarino had more than thirty competitors, giving Georgetown a saloon for every 150 residents, the town was among the more refined of Colorado's mining towns. Meeting halls and opera houses attracted harpists, minstrels, circus acts, and lecturers on the Holy Land. Suffragettes were especially popular, eliciting cute comments from the *Miner*. "Who will have and take care of the babies when women go into politics and get all their rights?"

Above: Half a dozen raw oysters in the Hotel de Paris dining room cost 35 cents. *Courtesy Colorado Historical Society. Right:* Other restaurants served an entire meal for 35 cents. *Courtesy Denver Public Library Western History Department.*

the *Miner* asked in 1869, following a women's rights lecture by Redelia Bates. The paper expressed surprise that Miss Bates was a lady. "We have sometimes the good reason for believing that much, very much of the unfriendliness contained in the wide-spread and popular opposition to women's becoming a voter . . . is directly traceable to the seeming bitterness and uncompromising hostility too frequently displayed," the paper noted in a patronizing argument still being used a century later.

Men were better prepared for the dirty world of politics, most Georgetown residents agreed, and none more up to the task than William A.

Hamill. A successful mining investor, Hamill was a power in Republican politics during Colorado's early statehood years and even was considered a senatorial candidate. He dabbled in real estate, operating several agricultural properties and erecting commercial buildings in Georgetown. His long-lasting legacy to Colorado was his own home, the Hamill House, now a fine museum. Originally a modest frame house with pretty Gothic windows, Hamill House became more opulent as Hamill became wealthier. He added bay windows, a solarium with curved glass panels, two stone outbuildings to serve as stable and office, and a six-seat outhouse—three walnut seats for the family, three pine ones for servants. During restoration of the Hamill House, preservationists excavated the long-unused privy to learn about the family china. Maids who broke plates or crystal often dropped the pieces

Below: Alpine Street, 1982. *Right:* Georgetown's school has been deserted for years. *Kendal Atchison*

through a hole in the outhouse to hide the evidence of their carelessness.

Until the silver crash, William and Priscilla Hamill and their children, one an embarrassing reprobate, presided over Georgetown society, attending oyster suppers and masked balls. Georgetown had become an elegant town with pretentious Victorian houses, the most fanciful of which was the Maxwell House, to this day, immaculately kept and considered one of the best examples of Victorian architecture in the country. Like the Hamill House, the Maxwell House was a modest structure that took on airs when its owner, a grocer who grubstaked a successful prospector, became wealthy.

Georgetown's hotels were equally lavish. The Barton House, which burned and was rebuilt in 1871, was the town's finest and was host to Ulysses S. Grant. But the most extraordinary was the Hotel de Paris, built by Louis Dupuy, an army deserter, in 1875. The hotel was built as a French country inn and furnished with heavy walnut pieces, including a matched pair of double beds in the bridal suite. The hotel bottled its own wine and kept small trout in an indoor fountain so that Dupuy could cook fresh fish for his guests. He served elegant dinners of quail and mountain sheep, truffles and anchovies in the splendid dining room, which had a floor of maple and walnut laid in alternating strips.

Dupuy had a reputation as a misogynist, but he placed vases of wildflowers in the rooms of female guests, and when he died in 1900 he left the hotel to his housekeeper. In the 1950s the furnished hotel was acquired by the National Society of Colonial Dames, which operates it as a museum.

Following the silver crash, Georgetown settled in as a sleepy mountain town. Because of its pristine setting and proximity to Denver, it attracted summer residents who maintained the Victorian houses and helped keep the town from decaying. In 1966, Georgetown and neighboring Silver Plume were named a national historic landmark district, and four years later residents formed the Georgetown Society, Incorporated, to acquire the Hamill House, which has been extensively restored. Due in part to the society, which has purchased other properties and fought off development that would destroy the town's charm, Georgetown today is Colorado's best-preserved Victorian town.

Gillett

COUNTY: *Teller*
LOCATION: *7 mi. north of Victor*
MAP 14
P.O. est. Aug. 29, 1894; discont. March 15, 1913

Colorado's only bullfight was held in 1895 in Gillett, a gold camp known as the "Monte Carlo of the West." Gillett contained the Cripple Creek district's race track, which drew hundreds of people, and the town was popular as a site for sporting events. It bragged of fourteen saloons, open twenty-four hours a day, and three dance halls.

The weekend of the bullfight, the town, whose population never reached a thousand, swelled to accommodate the thousands who crowded onto a hastily built midway, gaudy with bunting and complete with bunco artists plying suckers. The promoters, a local casino owner and a wild west show proprietor, brought in five Mexican bullfighters, one of them a woman, all described by the *Rocky Mountain News* as "swarthy foreigners."

The first afternoon of the three-day event the crowd included a hundred women, most of them prostitutes, and a smattering of nervous humane society officials and local law enforcement agents, who fined the promoters $5 for cruelty to animals and then let the show proceed.

The fight was a blaze of showmanship, blood, and torture that sickened many of the spectators. The bulls were poorly chosen and were too frightened to fight. The first was tortured for twenty minutes before it was killed, and the second was shot by a deputy.

The promoters' dreams of an American bullfight fortune ended in a nightmare. While several thousand spectators showed up the first two days, only two hundred came for the third round of bullfights. And when the receipts were totaled, the organizers took in only $2,600 against $7,000 in expenses. The pickpockets, prostitutes, and con men, including Soapy Smith, fared much better.

Thousands of men crowded into Gillett during the Cripple Creek gold rush. *Courtesy Denver Public Library Western History Department.*

Gillett's bullfight was a fiasco, in part because it attracted as many pickpockets and con men as legitimate patrons. *Courtesy Denver Public Library Western History Department.*

There is little about present-day Gillett to suggest its infamous past. *Kendal Atchison*

Gilman's setting is more spectacular than its history. *Kendal Atchison*

Gilman

COUNTY: *Eagle*
LOCATION: *5 mi. north of Redcliff*
MAP 5
P.O. est. Nov. 3, 1886

Perched on Battle Mountain, 1,000 feet above the Eagle River, the town of Gilman was settled by miners who worked the Iron Mask, the Star of the West, and the Belden, and who did not want to walk the three miles from Redcliff, especially in winter.

The two towns competed for years, and in the 1890s, Gilman (originally called Clinton) actually boasted more residents than Redcliff.

About the time of World War I, the New Jersey Zinc Company purchased the mines on Battle Mountain and consolidated them into a massive underground mining operation, turning Gilman into a company town, a status it kept until 1977 when New Jersey Zinc shut down its operations.

Gilpin

COUNTY: *Gilpin*
LOCATION: *6 mi. south of Rollinsville*
MAP 2
P.O. est. April 7, 1897; discont. Sept. 29, 1917

Gilpin was one of hundreds of mining towns founded for mines that never paid off. Named for Colorado's first territorial governor, William Gilpin, the town was established in Gamble Gulch near Rollinsville. At one time it had a number of residences and boardinghouses, a blacksmith shop, a school, and a baseball team. By the turn of the century the population had dwindled to fifty. Today it has been eclipsed by a vacation subdivision, though a few old buildings still stand.

Gladstone

COUNTY: *San Juan*
LOCATION: *7 mi. north of Silverton*
MAP 9
P.O. est. Jan. 24, 1878; discont. Jan. 15, 1912

Settled in the 1870s, Gladstone boomed in the 1890s with the development of the Gold King Mine. It was discovered by a part-time prospector who worked the mine for a few years, then died. His widow sold the property for $15,000, and within three years of the sale it had produced $1 million in gold, silver, and copper.

Not all of Gladstone's mines were successful. The *Denver Times* remarked in 1899 that a pair of prospector brothers "have been plodding along on the old mountain for about a quarter of a century. Nobody knows but them how much of the yellow metal they have lured from the crevices of the rocks up there."

By the turn of the century, Gladstone was a

A pair of shacks mark the site of Gladstone. *Kendal Atchison*

Above: Mine dumps near Goldfield. *Below:* Goldfield's combined town hall and fire station is being restored. *Kendal Atchison*

tidy town of neat miners' cottages occupied by men working the Gold King, the Pride of the West, and the Grand Mogul (whose mill remains are about all that is left of Gladstone today).

The town grew quickly, reported the editor of the *Gladstone Kibosh*: "Last week's census showed 102 inhabitants, and we received 204 votes and our opponent 53." Gladstone apparently granted female suffrage, because the editor noted: "The ladies from Means Dancing parlors voted early and late."

The election he described was spirited. "Miller, the reform candidate, was under the influence of at least a quart of 'demon delight,' working the temperance ward," the *Kibosh* noted. The editor concluded cynically: "The election was quiet and clean."

Goldfield

COUNTY: *Teller*
LOCATION: *1 mi. northeast of Victor*
MAP 14
P.O. est. May 5, 1894; discont. August, 1932

Platted with the symmetry of a prairie town, Goldfield, the third largest town of the Cripple Creek district, was in some ways the most domesticated. Called "the city of homes," it boasted several schools, fine residences, two newspapers, and almost as many churches as saloons. Founded in 1895 by the owners of the fabulously wealthy Portland Mine, Goldfield had become so influential in 1899 that it vied with Cripple Creek for county seat of the newly formed Teller County. Goldfield lost.

As a miners' town, Goldfield was heavily unionized and suffered in the 1904 labor confrontation when strikers, several of them town officials, were forced to leave the district.

Today the elegant carpenter Gothic town hall and firehouse stands guard over the boarded-up homes with their weathered scroll-sawn trim.

Gold Hill

COUNTY: *Boulder*
LOCATION: *11 mi. northwest of Boulder*
MAP 3
P.O. est. Jan. 13, 1863; discont. October, 1952

When gold was discovered in the mountains

Gold Hill, 1964. *Sandra Dallas*

northwest of Boulder near Gold Hill in 1859, thousands of prospectors swarmed into the area to work the placers, which produced handsomely for a year or two. Then came the discovery of gold-bearing quartz at the Horsfal Mine, which produced $300,000 in its first two years.

Not everyone hit pay dirt. One early prospector complained: "The only thing I took out . . . was Peabody." Peabody, he explained, was his partner.

The first Gold Hill was burned in an 1860 fire. The town was rebuilt, and in 1861 the the *Rocky Mountain News* commented on the orderly streets, the number of families, and the fine school that presented an "agreeable contrast to the scenes of '59 when the revolver, cards and infamous mean whiskey, too often held sway." In 1872, when tellurium ore was discovered, a new town of Gold Hill was located a short distance from the original one.

Early miners had voted to keep out saloons, but by the time of Gold Hill's second boom, liquor was plentiful, particularly at the Wentworth House, a thirty-room log hotel with a bridal suite, built by a Central City hotel proprietor.

The Wentworth was a favorite hangout of Denver newspaperman Eugene Field, who favored Gold Hill for his drinking bouts. Later the author of treacly children's poems, Field was a somewhat better poet when he wrote about Gold Hill, which he dubbed "Red Hoss Moun-

An expanding population has reclaimed many of Gold Hill's boarded-up buildings. *Kendal Atchison*

The Wentworth House, the original "Casey's." *Courtesy Denver Public Library Western History Department.*

tain," and the foibles of uneducated miners or the sadness of a mother, Martha, who had lost her child. He titled that poem "Marthy's Younkit."

Field's best-known Colorado work was about the Wentworth—which has been resurrected today as the Gold Hill Inn—in a poem entitled "Casey's Table D'Hote":

*Oh, them days on Red Hoss Mountain, when the
skies was fair 'nd blue;
When the money flowed like likker, 'nd
the folks was brave 'nd true!
When the nights wuz crisp 'nd balmy, 'nd
the camp wuz all astir,
With the joints all throwed wide open 'nd
no sheriff to demur!
Oh, them times on Red Hoss Mountain in the
Rockies fur away—
There's no sich place nor times like them
as I kin find to-day!
What, though the camp hez busted? I seem to
see it still
A-lyin', like it love it, on that big 'nd
warty hill;
And I feel a sort of yearnin' 'nd a chokin'
in my throat
When I think of Red Hoss Mountain 'nd of
Casey's tabble dote!*

Sometime after Field left, Creede newspaperman Cy Warman visited Gold Hill and found it nearly deserted. He wrote a parody of it and Field in "Old Red Hoss Mountain":

*I've been to Red Hoss Mountain, where Field
once dwelt and wrote;
I've seen the Place de Casey, but Casey's
table d'hote
Is gone; and so is Casey. A solitary pine
The fires have spared now shadows the Gosh-all-
Hemlock Mine . . . .*

*The brook that sang so "lonesome-like, an'
loitered on its way"
Is singing just as softly and lonesome-like to-day.
One pine above the hemlock and just one willow
weeps
Down in the ragged canyon where "Martha's younket"
sleeps.*

Gold Park

COUNTY: *Eagle*
LOCATION: *26 mi. northwest of Leadville*
MAP 5
P.O. est. May 31, 1881; discont. Oct. 5, 1883

For a few years, when the ores on French Mountain and along Fancy Creek looked promising, the town of Gold Park was in full swing. It had four hundred residents in 1881, the year after it was founded, a general store, and two hotels, the Homestake and the Gold Park.

The Gold Park Mining and Milling Company, which owned more than thirty mining properties,

Gold Park has been virtually deserted since 1884. *Kendal Atchison*

built a twenty-stamp mill. "Managers and principal stockholders have abundant faith in the mines . . . they expect shortly to reap a rich harvest," reported the *Rocky Mountain News* in 1881. Alas, they never did, and by 1884 Gold Park was all but deserted.

Gothic

COUNTY: *Gunnison*
LOCATION: *8 mi. north of Crested Butte*
MAP 8
P.O. est. Aug. 5, 1879; discont. Jan. 31, 1914

Two prospectors, grubstaked by a Chicago hotelier who had come west to die, discovered the Sylvanite Mine in 1879 and started the stampede to Gothic.

Within a few weeks, merchants were selling flour for $7 per 100-pound bag, nails for a penny each, and whiskey for as much as $10 a gallon to the hundreds of miners who flocked in. Most of the gold seekers returned to Gunnison for the winter. In fact, only twelve men and two women spent the winter in Gothic, but with the first sign of spring, the prospectors once again headed for the gold town. The *Gunnison Review* reported one party spent nine days shoveling its way from Gunnison to Gothic. Noted the paper: "Gothic resembles a Pennsylvania coal camp in appearance, 154 buildings visible and no doubt more hidden in deep snow."

Gothic's busiest years were 1880 and 1881 when its population was estimated at anywhere from four hundred to four thousand. Wages were $3 a day and board for miners; carpenters and mechanics made up to $5. Room and board cost $10 a week, with individual meals priced at fifty cents. The town listed a newspaper, backed by silver king H. A. W. Tabor, four hundred buildings, eight saloons, and a dance hall, where the "ladies" frolicked in near nudity wearing dresses cut up to their knees.

Gothic had a wicked reputation. Racist miners hanged in effigy a Chinese who announced plans to open a laundry. Newspapers across the country picked up the hanging, omitting the fact it was in effigy, further spreading Gothic's reputation as a lawless frontier town. The image was not helped when one of the town founders was arrested for murder and escaped—twice.

Gothic town hall, 1982. *Kendal Atchison*

But lawlessness had its appeal. When Ulysses S. Grant expressed a wish to see a wild mining town, he promptly was taken to Gothic.

Gothic, alas, lacked one necessity of a successful mining town—good ore. Despite some promising wire silver specimens, the cylvanite proved disappointing. The miners left almost as quickly as they had come, except for one. Garwood Hall Judd, a saloonkeeper, stayed on, and on. A curious relic of mining days, Judd was known as the mayor of Gothic, but he much preferred the title of "the man who stayed," and, in fact, he nailed a sign with that title over his door. As the last resident of Gothic, Judd remained until his death in 1930. In his own way, he tarried even longer, because his ashes were scattered over Gothic.

About the time Judd died, the town was sold for $200 in taxes to the Rocky Mountain Biological Laboratory, which conducts ecological research in Gothic every summer.

Granite

COUNTY: *Chaffee*
LOCATION: *17 mi. south of Leadville*
MAP 7
P.O. est. Nov. 30, 1868; discont. March 25, 1966

Granite was as hard and as bleak as its name, the scene of brawls, vengeance, and one of Colorado's infamous murders. In 1875, Judge Elias Dyer, son of Methodist preacher John Dyer, was shot to death in his courtroom. Dyer, who had sided with the wrong faction in a feud, was "in the discharge of his duty as an officer of the law," noted one newspaper. But another reporter claimed: "He was well-known to have been the associate and defender of midnight assassins, incendiaries, and thieves. . . ."

The feud began when a man named Elijah Gibbs was acquitted of killing a neighbor. The dead man's friends quickly formed a vigilante committee to threaten anyone who sided with Gibbs, including Dyer. When the judge issued warrants for the arrest of several of the vigilantes, he apparently signed his own death warrant. Only minutes after the charges against the men were dismissed for lack of evidence, Dyer was shot. No one ever was arrested for the murder.

Placer gold was discovered in the Granite area in 1859, but the diggings quickly played out. In 1867 the discovery of gold lodes caused a second rush to Granite. Within a year, the *Rocky Mountain News* reported: "It's pleasantly situated, and with its stores, hotels, and saloons, bears quite a business, sir."

But Granite's life was erratic. In 1872 the *News* noted: "Granite looks a little rusty, and most of the houses are for let."

Granite boomed again at the time of the Dyer controversy, which was called the Lake County War. Among investors in local mines at that time was H. A. W. Tabor, a former Granite storekeeper, who purchased an interest in Elias Dyer's mine after his murder. In 1880, Granite lost its designation as Chaffee County seat to Buena Vista. The booms stopped in the 1880s, and Granite, supported by a little mining and transportation, slid into obscurity.

Guston

COUNTY: *Ouray*
LOCATION: *11 mi. south of Ouray*
MAP 9
P.O. est. Jan. 26, 1892; discont. Nov. 16, 1898

Guston was named for the Guston Mine, a major silver and lead producer discovered in 1881. A few years later Otto Mears built a railroad

The Guston Mine and its dump. *Kendal Atchison*

Hahns Peak was once the seat of Routt County. *Kendal Atchison*

from Silverton to the three mining towns strung out along Red Mountain Pass—Guston, Ironton, and Red Mountain.

Guston's Congregational church was built in 1892 by the Reverend William Davis, who had failed to convince the wicked at nearby Red Mountain they needed a house of worship. The day the Guston church was dedicated, according to the reverend's daughter in *Timberline Tailings,* a fire broke out at Red Mountain that destroyed its business district. This event caused one Red Mountain resident to compare his town to Sodom and Gomorrah and to note ruefully: "You can't fight God and prosper."

By 1899 the town was on the decline. No trace of Guston remains today, although there are fine ruins of the Guston Mine complex next to a stream that runs red through yellow mill tailings.

Hahns Peak

COUNTY: *Routt*
LOCATION: *27 mi. north of Steamboat Springs*
MAP 12
P.O. est. May 3, 1877; discont. December, 1941

In 1866, Joseph Henne and a group of forty miners made their way from Empire to north-western Colorado where a member of their party claimed he once had found float. The men worked through the summer, but headed back to Empire when winter threatened, leaving Henne and two companions, George Way and William Doyle.

Way left shortly afterward, probably to get supplies, and never returned. The two remaining prospectors lived through the winter at a near-starvation level, finally snowshoeing out when spring arrived. Henne, weak and ill, died on the bank of a stream, and Doyle trudged on, finally arriving in Hot Sulphur Springs snow blind and raving. He told his rescuers he had left Henne dead twenty miles upstream, but when the body eventually was found, it was only a mile away. Miners gave Henne's name to the volcanic cone that marked the site of the party's gold activity—Hahns Peak—and the town that grew up near its base took the same name.

Interest in the Hahns Peak district fell off following Joseph Henne's death, though prospectors continued to explore the area. By the mid-1870s their perseverance paid off, and Hahns Peak began to attract capitalists who consolidated the placer claims. Several hundred men crowded into Hahns Peak, which had a church and a reading room but no saloons. Since Hahns

Peak was sober, carnal pleasures were satisfied at Poverty Flats just above Hahns Peak, while Bugtown, just below, became a bedroom community for mining-company brass.

Hahns Peak was county seat of Routt County from 1879 to 1912, about the time mining shut down. Most of the houses fell apart or were hauled away, leaving only a rambling street of tin-roofed log cabins and summer cottages.

Hancock

COUNTY: *Chaffee*
LOCATION: *5 mi. south of Saint Elmo*
MAP 7
P.O. est. Sept. 10, 1880; discont. Dec. 31, 1904

"It's a rather pretty location, almost at timberline," the *Denver Tribune* described Hancock in August, 1880, when the town was barely a month old. Within six months Hancock had five stores, two sawmills, a variety of saloons and restaurants, and five hundred residents. There

The existence of Hancock today is as precarious as this old mine structure. *Kendal Atchison.*

Hancock, when construction of the Alpine tunnel caused a building boom. *Courtesy Denver Public Library.*

was some mining in the area—the town name comes from the Hancock Placer—but Hancock was better known as a railroad town for workers building the Denver, South Park & Pacific's Alpine tunnel, the first railroad tunnel to pierce the Continental Divide.

Despite its "rather pretty location," Hancock was a treacherous place in the winter. Newly hired tunnel workers who arrived on the morning train often rode out in disgust in the afternoon. In 1899, a winter of awesome snowfall, food was so scarce that a Hancock man, fearful his horses would be killed for food or starve, decided to take the animals to Romley. Eight men trampled the snow between Romley and Hancock, two and a half miles away, then lined the trail with strips of canvas, moving the pieces ahead as the horses slowly made their way along the trail. The trip took three days.

Henson

COUNTY: *Hinsdale*
LOCATION: *5 mi. west of Lake City*
MAP 8
P.O. est. May 17, 1883; discont. Nov. 30, 1913

Midway between Lake City and Capitol City—and never as large or as fine as either—Henson

was named for Henry Henson, one of the discoverers of the Ute and the Ulay veins in 1871. The mines, which were among the most prosperous in the area, were sold to the Crooke brothers of Lake City in 1876, and they built a smelter next to Henson Creek. A concentrator was added several years later. The townsite of Henson was platted in 1880, and as late as 1910 it had a hundred residents.

Hesperus

COUNTY: *La Plata*
LOCATION: *11 mi. west of Durango*
MAP 9
P.O. est. Oct. 10, 1891

Hesperus, founded in 1894, was a coal town that supplied energy for Durango and other nearby towns. Residents complained that high transportation costs, brought about by the Denver & Rio Grande's monopoly, made it unprofitable to ship coal farther.

John Porter, a prominent western slope mining investor, opened the first coal mines in the Hesperus area in the early 1880s, and eventually his Porter Fuel Company, which employed 175 men, had an annual production of 150,000 tons.

Henson, 1982. *Kendal Atchison*

The yellow and orange Catholic church at Hesperus. *Sandra Dallas*

Howardsville

COUNTY: *San Juan*
LOCATION: *4 mi. northeast of Silverton*
MAP 9
P.O. est. Jan. 24, 1874; discont. November, 1939

When George W. Howard built the first permanent cabin in the town he named for himself, he hauled in a stack of logs and a barrel of whiskey and offered a drink to each prospector who passed his building site. As each miner got liquored up, Howard asked him to give him a hand, and before long the cabin was in place.

Other buildings, erected by more conventional methods, followed quickly until in 1874 there were thirty structures, including stores, saloons, and a reduction works.

Howardsville was so prosperous by 1874 that it was named western Colorado's first county seat. La Plata County records were moved to Silverton a few months later, and Howardsville eventually became part of San Juan County.

In 1875 the first stove and earthenware dishes were hauled in on a wagon pulled by four horses and two mules. The next year the town had a sizable livery stable that rented horses to ride to Silverton for $2.50 and to the mines for $4. Since there was no grain for the horses, the stable owner turned them out in the fall and bought new ones in the spring.

Howardsville acted as supply center for the mines of nearby Cunningham Gulch, which included the Pride of the West, the Green Mountain, and the Highland Mary. Discovered in 1875 by two brothers who paid a spiritualist $50,000 to locate an ore body, the Highland Mary cost its discoverers $1 million to develop. It was developed according to instructions written by their occultist consultant, who charted a maze

Howardsville was western Colorado's first county seat. *Courtesy Denver Public Library Western History Department.*

of tunnels and stopes that bore no relationship to any ore body, though quite by accident the workings crossed several good veins. After going bankrupt in 1885 in their search for a lake of gold foretold by the medium, the brothers lost the mine to operators who developed the Highland Mary along conventional lines and turned it into one of the gulch's biggest producers.

Idaho Springs

COUNTY: *Clear Creek*
LOCATION: *34 mi. west of Denver*
MAP 1
P.O. est. March 22, 1862 as Idaho

Smoke rising from behind a hill made prospector George Jackson cautious. He had left his companions near Denver and ventured out on his own to look for gold in the mountains to the west. Since he had encountered no other white men, he believed the smoke meant Indians. He crept forward stealthily and peered over the ridge to discover that instead of smoke

from Indian campfires, he had seen steam rising from hot springs. More impressive for Jackson, however, were the traces of gold in the nearby stream.

The town that grew up around Jackson's find was called Jackson's Diggings, Sacramento City, Idahoe City, Idaho, and finally Idaho Springs. The first cabin was built in July, 1859, an event celebrated by a horse race, a foot race, two fights, and, shortly afterward, two more cabins.

"There is not much of it yet, but it takes but a few days to make a town if located in the right spot," the *Rocky Mountain Herald* noted in an article about the settlement.

And, indeed, within a few months, Idaho Springs had ten saloons, a hundred and fifty dwellings, half a dozen stores, and a first-class hotel. The town forbade the practice of law and for a time allowed women to frequent billiard saloons.

A few years later when Bayard Taylor visited Idaho Springs, he called the town "a straggling village of log-huts . . . [a] queer, almost aborigi-

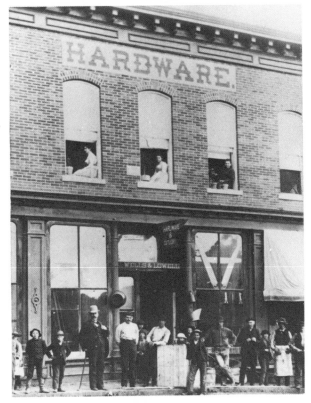

Above: Miner Street, Idaho Springs. *Below:* The men posed in front of Wells & Lowell's hardware store are probably employees and customers. The occupation of the women upstairs is not known. *Courtesy Denver Public Library Western History Department.*

nal village." But he noted it had the best hotel in Colorado, the Beebe House, a truly splendid establishment that in its prime was replete with thick carpets, shiny horse-hair-stuffed sofas, and elaborate mirrors. The Beebe House dining room seated 125, or fifty fashionably attired ladies.

Among the early gold seekers was a young couple newly arrived in Denver, H. A. W. Tabor, his wife Augusta, and their baby. The Tabors cut a road through the mountains for their wagon, taking three weeks to make the trip from Golden to Idaho Springs. They used a pine tree fastened to the back of their wagon as a brake and often had to sleep on the steep mountainside, their feet wedged against a log to keep from rolling down

The fit members of any town's hose cart company represented strength, valor, and Victorian sex appeal. *Courtesy Denver Public Library Western History Department.*

Two youths pose with their burro before the firehouse. *Courtesy Denver Public Library Western History Department.*

The water wheel is Idaho Springs's best known tourist attraction. *Kendal Atchison*

the hill. When they arrived in Idaho Springs, Augusta Tabor, the first white woman in camp, opened a bakery while her husband prospected, making enough to keep them through the winter. An old prospector warned Tabor to take his wife to Denver for the winter because of the danger of avalanches. Tabor did so, only to find when he returned in the spring that the prospector had jumped his claim.

More successful in Idaho Springs than the Tabors was William Doe, who staked a claim on the Dictator Mine and later became a banker and a member of the state legislature. Doe invested in Central City as well, sending his son Harvey to keep an eye on Doe's interest in the Fourth of July Mine. Harvey's wife, Baby Doe, later became Tabor's second wife.

Founded as a placer mining camp in 1859, Idaho Springs had become a major center for lode mining by the mid-1860s. For a brief time, from 1861 to 1867, it was Clear Creek County seat, and often attracted important visitors. Ulysses S. Grant, who was enamored of Colorado's mining camps and attempted to invest in several mines, was driven over the harrowing Virginia Canyon route from Central City to Idaho Springs, the notorious "Oh-My-God" road, at extraordinary speed. His daughter Nellie, in the coach behind, clutched her throat and timidly questioned the driver, who reassured her: "Look here, Miss, don't forget that I am right here, and if trouble comes I am as likely to get killed as you are, and I want you to know that I think as much of my neck and life as you do of yours, even if you are Miss Grant, daughter of the greatest man of the day," reports Ethel Morrow Gillette in *Idaho Springs.*

By the end of the century, Idaho Springs was a prosperous Victorian community with substantial brick business blocks and tidy gingerbread houses set on sloping green lawns. On the Fourth of July the fire department sponsored hook-and-ladder races with a $250 first prize. The pony race, "open to any old thing," according to an 1899 program, paid $25 to the winner; the relay race paid $40, and the slow burro race paid only $5.

The favorite form of recreation for Idaho Springs residents, however, was "taking the waters" at the hot and cold mineral springs discovered by Jackson in 1859. Idaho Springs was

Independence is being stabilized by Aspen volunteers. *Kendal Atchison*

only a few years old when attempts were made to capitalize on the springs, and by 1866 there were two bathhouses in operation. It was not until after the turn of the century when a mammoth resort was built that Radium Hot Springs, as it came to be called, attracted wealthy health seekers. Private railroad cars regularly deposited fashionable guests such as Jay Gould's daughter to take the cure.

In 1893 work began on the Newhouse tunnel. Built by mining entrepreneur Samuel Newhouse, the tunnel, now the Argo Tunnel, located at the east end of Idaho Springs, was driven 20,000 feet through the mountain to Central City to tap some of the richest veins in the area. The tunnel, finished in 1910, kept Idaho Springs mines alive well into the twentieth century.

Crime also prospered in the twentieth century. In the 1920s, Royal R. Graham, an Idaho Springs judge, was charged with stealing from the estates of widows and orphans. Graham denied the charges, but he committed suicide.

And in the 1940s, a crusading minister attempted to rid Idaho Springs of slot machines, which he claimed were leading small children with nickels and dimes into sin. Popular *Rocky Mountain News* columnist, Lee Casey, erstwhile champion of sin, pilloried the outraged preacher, pointing out that revenue from the machines supported recreational facilities used by those tempted juveniles. "Protect us from gambling, to be sure," wrote the columnist. "But also protect us, O Lord, from the more dangerous evil of fanaticism."

Independence

COUNTY: *Pitkin*
LOCATION: *17 mi. southeast of Aspen*
MAP 6
No P.O.

The Independence Mine was discovered on July 4, 1879, and bestowed its name on the collection of cabins that were built nearby. The town thrived briefly on a mountainside just below Independence Pass, the thoroughfare between Leadville and Aspen, under a variety of names, including Chipeta. In 1882 the *Rocky Mountain News* noted: "The name of the town known generally as Independence has been changed again and is now Sparkhill. This is about the fourth change. It is expected to hold good for a week or ten days."

By any name, it did not last much longer. In 1889 the *San Francisco Chronicle* reported

Not a single soul is now living [in Independence]. Hundreds of deserted houses are standing tenantless, and some of them quite pretentious. A newspaper was once published in the corporate limits of the city, and the arm of the Washington handpress on which it was printed is now sticking out of the office window. The proprietor was too much disgusted to take it away.

Independence's fortunes have picked up in recent years, and the town's cabins are being rebuilt and stabilized.

Independence

COUNTY: *Teller*
LOCATION: *2 mi. north of Victor*
MAP 14
P.O. est. May 12, 1899; discont. July, 1954

Sprawled between Altman and Goldfield, Independence played a decisive role in the 1904 labor war in Cripple Creek. At 2 A.M. one June morning, Harry Orchard, a terrorist allied with the Western Federation of Miners, blew up the Independence depot, killing thirteen men waiting

Thirteen men died when the Independence depot was bombed during Cripple Creek's labor war. *Courtesy Denver Public Library Western History Department.*

on the platform and mutilating several others. In the daylight, horrified miners and mine owners sorted through the carnage, collecting parts of bodies. One of them picked up a severed leg with a boot still attached. The incident hastened the end of the labor war.

Independence, named for the Independence Mine, Winfield Scott Stratton's great discovery, was within walking distance of many of the mines in the district. It was a jumble of miners' cottages, stores, and saloons that once accommodated a population of fifteen hundred. Because the town, now deserted, was occupied into the 1950s, Independence is one of Colorado's best preserved, if thoroughly picked over, ghost towns.

Ironton

COUNTY: *Ouray*
LOCATION: *8 mi. south of Ouray*
MAP 9
P.O. est. May 2, 1883; discont. Aug. 7, 1920

In 1882, John Robinson, who had discovered the Guston Mine a year earlier, staked a claim he called the Yankee Girl. He apparently sold the claim, because the next year the *Denver Republican* reported: "Two men mined enough ore to keep 70 pack animals going all winter. The ore produced by the two that winter paid the $125,000 purchase price of the mine." As the Yankee Girl and other mines began to produce, railroad builder Otto Mears spent $1.2 million improving the Ouray-Ironton route, turning it into a toll road later dubbed the "Million Dollar Highway."

Ironton, with its long main street crowded with buildings that still stand, was a more godly place than nearby Red Mountain. When Red Mountain turned down a church, a minister went to Ironton, where he convinced the school board members to put up $10 to $30 each to build a church. The land was donated by Colorado's lieutenant governor, and pews came from a minister in Ouray. Silverton sent a contribution of $100, and Ironton and Ouray split the final cost of $159.

A resurgence of interest in gold, copper, and lead brought several families to Ironton in 1898, but the second boom was short, and by 1899 a *Denver Times* reporter described Ironton as

Independence (Teller County), with Bull Hill in the background *(top). Courtesy Denver Public Library Western History Department.* The same scene, 1981 *(bottom). Kendal Atchison*

Above: Ironton during its hey-day. *Author's collection.*
Left: One or two Ironton houses still stand in a landscape
of gentians, wild strawberries, and aspen trees. *Kendal
Atchison. Below:* Most Ironton buildings have either
crumbled or been vandalized. *Kendal Atchison*

"the most dull portion of the district." Population had dropped from a peak estimated at two thousand to less than two hundred and fifty. A few people stayed on until the railroad was removed in the 1920s.

Irwin

COUNTY: *Gunnison*
LOCATION: *8 mi. west of Crested Butte*
MAP 8
P.O. est. Sept. 12, 1879; discont. June 5, 1900

For a few short years, when the Forest Queen, the Bullion King, the Ruby Chief, the Howard Extension, the Venango, and the Lead Chief turned out $2 million in silver, Irwin was a booming town of five thousand persons and twenty-three saloons. It lasted only five years, though. Founded in 1879, it was deserted by 1884, and before long all that was left were a few disconnected fire plugs.

The Forest Queen and the Ruby King were discovered in 1879 by a man named Fisher, who gave one of the mines to a man who had helped him pull his team out of the mud. The Lead Chief was discovered by a Missouri farmer whose horse had died. While he waited for a replacement, he hammered away on rocks, discovering the mine.

Prospectors crowded into Irwin and nearby Ruby (which later was absorbed by Irwin) as soon as they heard of the first strike, and many stayed the winter. Working in the snow, they felled trees for cabins, and when the spring thaw came, they discovered they had left fifteen-foot stumps. As the snow had piled up on their roofs, they added lengths of stovepipe, finding in the spring that some chimneys were twenty feet high.

The town's first mayor was Edward Travers, a southerner addicted to cards and liquor. One Fourth of July he suspended an ordinance prohibiting shooting in town, and he and an Irish saloonkeeper celebrated the holiday by taking turns placing their hands on the wall, fingers spread, while the other shot, aiming the bullets between the fingers.

When Ulysses S. Grant visited Irwin, legend says, a local lawyer discovered a plot to kill the former president while he was giving a speech. As a southerner, Mayor Travers cursed the for-

Irwin was a promising town in 1881. *Courtesy Denver Public Library Western History Department.*

mer Yankee general, fervently hoping for his death, but he did not wish it to occur in Irwin, so he banned speeches during Grant's visit.

Irwin's short life was spirited. It had the only brass band in Gunnison County—two in fact, one playing at each end of the main street. Along with selling liquor, saloons were equipped with singers whose songs were "sandwiched between drinks," according to the *Gunnison Review,* as well as with all kinds of gambling devices, and

The town of Irwin has crumbled into a mountain marsh. A few logs on the outskirts remain. *Kendal Atchison*

108
I

games went on day and night. When a local preacher attempted to hold services next door to a saloon, the proprietor refused to stop the gambling but obligingly passed the hat for the preacher.

A combination of foul weather and poor transportation doomed Irwin, which quickly sank into the marshy timberline bog on which it was built, all but the fire hydrants, which lasted for years. Today, they too are gone. All that is left is a pretty cemetery with fifty graves, a mile down the road from the townsite.

Jamestown

COUNTY: *Boulder*
LOCATION: *13 mi. northwest of Boulder*
MAP 3
P.O. est. Jan. 8, 1867

We have no mails and but very few females. . . . Our supply of reading matter has dwindled down to one number of the *Colorado Transcript* and a copy of the Governor's message. . . . We have not sodcorn enough to "exhilerate" us. We have not even a doubled barrel shot gun with which to shoot jay birds who come provokingly near our front door—our only one. Our chimney smokes horribly. Our gal has gone to Montana, and we are happy.

Thus wrote a contented Jamestown miner to the *Rocky Mountain News* in 1867.

Only the year before Jamestown had been christened by the United States Post Office. Originally called Jimtown because it was located at the confluence of the Jim and Little Jim creeks in Boulder's rich tellurium belt, the town was officiointly renamed Jamestown by the Post Office Department, the beginning of a running disagreement between the town and the Post Office Department. A hundred years later the federal government attempted to replace the old post office, located in a mercantile store, with a free-standing building, but the townspeople protested the waste and won.

There was a "total absence of town lots," the 1867 *News* correspondent wrote. "Any pilgrim who may chance to stray so far from his road as to visit this locality is compelled to buy a slice from some mill-site or homestead on which to build, or go on his way rejoicing." Lot sales were brisk, however, in part because sellers were accommodating—at a price. At an early town

Jamestown's post office and general store is identical to a deserted building in Ward. *Kendal Atchison*

meeting miners addressed the thorny question of whether a town lot could be sold for a keg of beer. The town's best legal mind concluded: "No doubt a lot had been sold for a keg of beer, but the beer was drunk, and drunk or sober, the title was just as good as if the consideration had been money."

Jimtown prospered through several booms. And while none of the mines ranked as bonanzas, they were respectable producers. The biggest were the Golden Age, the John Jay, and the Buena.

The promoters did even better. At its peak, Jimtown was packed with two or three miles of tents, half of them dance halls, saloons, gambling parlors, and cribs. There were gamblers, card sharks, liquor sellers, and prostitutes who lived in lower Jimtown, called Bummerville. None made the mark of a onetime local boy who later became an actor—Douglas Fairbanks, Sr.

Jamestown was hit by a series of floods. The most devastating occurred in 1894 when water swept down the Jim and the Little Jim, taking the road, houses, businesses, and the church,

Jasper today looks much like it did in this photograph, probably taken in the early part of the century. *Courtesy Denver Public Library Western History Department.*

Glass insulators and purple bottles decorate the windows of this hewn-log cabin. *Kendal Atchison*

which swept downstream majestically, its bell tolling doom. In 1969 a flood again destroyed part of the town, wreaking its worst devastation on the site proposed for the unwanted post office.

Jasper

COUNTY: *Rio Grande*
LOCATION: *32 mi. southwest of Monte Vista*
MAP 11
P.O. est. Nov. 20, 1882; discont. Feb. 15, 1927

The little town of Jasper, originally called Cornwall, was settled in 1880 by a group of mining entrepreneurs that included Alva Adams, later a Colorado governor.

By 1897 the town boasted the Hotel Jasper with fourteen rooms, a collection of stores, and "the usual necessity—a saloon," reported the *Denver Republican.* The saloon apparently was even less productive than the mines, and in 1902, when Jasper experienced a brief revival, the *Denver Times* noted: "Jasper has not a saloon

in the town. It's a twentieth century camp with the gunfighters and killers left out."

The mines in the area were never major producers, though the miners had such great hopes for one that they sent a shipment of ore to Denver to be refined. The smelter burned down with the ore, and Jasper never did learn the results.

Jefferson

COUNTY: *Park*
LOCATION: *16 mi. northeast of Fairplay*
MAP 4
P.O. est. Sept. 3, 1861

Located on a windswept meadow in South Park about 1860, the town of Jefferson was named, prematurely as it turned out, for the state of Jefferson. The state, of course, was eventually named Colorado, but the town kept Jefferson anyway.

Jefferson was organized as a supply center for Hamilton and Tarryall to the south and Georgia

Jefferson, 1981. *Kendal Atchison*

Gulch to the west. Still, Jefferson claimed a modest gold strike of its own. In 1862 a resident digging a well spotted a gold nugget, and a few days later a second homebuilder, using dirt from the well to plaster his house, found five gold nuggets worth as much as $1.25 each.

In 1861 a letter writer to the *Rocky Mountain News* reported a young man named James Clark, newly arrived from Gregory Gulch, "died here last night, but little is known of him here. We buried him in our new cemetery, the first interred there." James Clark was one of thousands of hopeful gold seekers who came west only to die among strangers.

Eventually a way station on the Denver, South Park & Pacific, Jefferson was a bleak town, dreary in winter when winds swept through the treeless streets. It was an uneventful place except in 1901 when a Jefferson woman, Mrs. Ella Vallie, was charged with murdering her husband. She was hauled off to jail in Denver—on the same train that carried her husband's body—and the *Denver Times* hinted darkly that Mrs. Vallie and her lover had murdered the husband. The lover's blood-stained overalls, it reported, were found with Mrs. Vallie's soiled linen. But a week later charges against Mrs. Vallie were dropped. "No evidence whatsoever was introduced to connect her with the crime," the *Times* reported, never for a minute retracting its earlier allegations.

Jefferson's depot has been restored since this photograph was taken in the 1960s. *Sandra Dallas*

Keystone's buildings have been incorporated into a science school. *Kendal Atchison*

Keystone

COUNTY: *Summit*
LOCATION: *7 mi. east of Dillon*
MAP 4
No P.O.

Keystone was a Denver, South Park & Pacific way station, a loading point for ore as well as lumber. Railroad officials had ambitious plans to continue the railroad east over the Continental Divide, but Keystone became the terminus of the line. The rails were taken out about 1937.

More than thirty years later the Keystone ski area was built near the old town, which today is part of the Keystone science school.

Lake City

COUNTY: *Hinsdale*
LOCATION: *55 mi. southwest of Gunnison*
MAP 8
P.O. est. June 18, 1875

Surveyor Enos Hotchkiss scouted the San Juans in 1874 for a wagon road and spotted rich float, some of which assayed out at $40,000 in gold per ton. He promptly quit road work and staked the Hotchkiss Mine (later the Golden Fleece) and spent the winter in Lake City with his crew.

By spring, when the Lake City rush got under way, the settlement had thirteen cabins, and by fall there were sixty-seven buildings, four hundred people, a newspaper named the *Silver World* (begun with three subscribers), a restaurant that seated four, and an American flag made from white handkerchiefs, a blue flannel shirt, and red drawers. It did not have any dance halls, doctors, deaths, or church services.

All that changed in the next year with the development of the Ute and the Ulay mines, the Hotchkiss, the Belle of the West, and the Ocean Wave. The population doubled along with the price of town lots, and at the end of 1876, Lake City supported seven saloons, four Chinese laundries, four hotels, and fifteen lawyers.

By Lake City's second winter the town had begun to look permanent with an influx of women. Some thirty-five married women gave a Christmas supper for 311 people, virtually the entire camp, that was followed by a dance. The *Silver*

Lake City during prosperous times. *Courtesy Colorado Historical Society.*

A group of the faithful at the Baptist Church in 1898. *Courtesy Colorado Historical Society.*

World boasted the celebrants had decorated the first Christmas tree on Colorado's western slope.

The arrival of families meant a civilizing influence. Frame houses with gingerbread trim replaced log cabins. Schools and churches went up, and balls, suppers, raffles, and skating parties were popular entertainments. After telephones were installed in the area, Lake City initiated telephone concerts in which residents from Lake City to Capitol City picked up the party line at an appointed time to sing, play the zither or banjo, or just listen. At a leap year dance in 1876, the *Silver World* reported, women arranged "the 'swapping' of husbands,"

Hardly as elegant as its New York City namesake, Lake City's Delmonico's nonetheless featured tablecloths, wood floors, and a gaslight. *Courtesy Denver Public Library Western History Department.*

M. J. McNamara & Co. Kid Gloves, Laces, and Ribbons.
Cor. Larimer & 15th Sts., Denver.

LAK   244   LAK

DELMONICO RESTAURANT.

W. W. JONES,   -   PROPRIETOR.
Sleeping Rooms Attached.
Lake City,   -   Colorado.
REFRESHMENTS AT ALL TIMES DURING THE SEASON.

During the 1920s and 1930s, Lake City's economy depended on fishermen and occasional tourists. *Courtesy Denver Public Library Western History Department.*

an apparently innocent exchange that lacked the connotation of later years.

Not everyone was impressed with the ladies of Lake City. Fractious David Day, editor of Ouray's *Solid Muldoon,* noted: "the jeweled garter craze has not yet reached Lake City. This information is entirely superfluous as the average Lake City woman's style of architecture requires no artificial stays or fastenings. They simply cut a hole in their stockings and button them over their knee caps."

Whatever their appearance, the women of Lake City apparently took themselves seriously. Along with Lake City's male population, they turned out en masse to attend a women's rights lecture by Susan B. Anthony. The talk attracted such a large crowd, in fact, that the lecture was moved from the courthouse to the yard to accommodate listeners, and Anthony was persuaded to stay and talk the following day. Her lectures did little good, however. When Colorado men voted on the question of female suffrage, Hinsdale County turned it down by a vote of almost two to one.

Lake City was more egalitarian than most mining towns. The owners of tonier saloons were members of polite society and lived in fine houses on Gunnison Avenue and Silver Street. Moreover, the Reverend George Darley regu-

larly preached at funeral services for Lake City's gamblers and prostitutes, generally with more sympathy than censure. "My eyes filled with tears as I thought of the fate of him who dealt faro till midnight Saturday, and was dead on Monday morning," he wrote after the death of gambler Benjamin House. After services for Magg Hartman, he wrote: "As the 'girls' came in from the 'dance halls' I took each one by the hand and spoke a kind word."

Compassion did not sway the Reverend Darley from duty, however. He passionately opposed gambling and drinking and inspired many a miner to sign a temperance pledge. Most signed in the winter when money was scarce and signed off in the spring, but the temporary abstinence probably did them good, the minister noted.

Darley's opposition made only slight inroads into Hell's Acre, as the gambling and red-light district was called. It was a haven for horse thieves, rumpots, card sharks, and murderers. Among the foulest dives was the San Juan Central, a dance house owned by George Betts and James W. Browning, a disreputable pair of cutthroats who shot and killed Lake City Sheriff E. N. Campbell in 1882 while they were robbing a house.

Incensed citizens yanked the pair out of jail and strung them up on the Ocean Wave bridge, where they promptly were "hurled to hell," according to the *Gunnison Review,* which noted approvingly: "The lynching is endorsed by almost everybody."

Nearly as heinous was the murder in 1896 of a customer of Clara Ogden's elegant bordello, the Crystal Palace, by one of the inhabitants. The woman, Jessie Landers, shot her fiance when she spied him talking to a pimp. She was sent to prison, Clara Ogden left town, and the red-light district was nearly closed down. Four years later Jessie Landers returned to Lake City, where she died of tuberculosis. The Baptist minister agreed to perform a funeral service, but a trustee blocked the door, and the service was held instead near the prostitute's grave. Some time later, friends of the dead woman spotted the trustee driving in his buggy and waylaid and horsewhipped him.

Lake City went through a series of economic fluctuations. After an initial boom in the 1870s, mining slowed down until the arrival of the railroad in the 1880s. The silver crash caused another recession, but Lake City compensated by producing gold as well as increasing silver output.

By the turn of the century, however, Lake City was on the decline. Camping, fishing, and hunting helped to revive Lake City as a summer community. Its greatest appeal, at least to history buffs, is the ghoulish legend of Alferd Packer, who was convicted in a Lake City trial of killing several companions and eating their choicest parts.

Packer was hired in 1874 to guide a group of five prospectors through the San Juans. Several weeks later Packer surfaced at the Los Pinos Indian Agency claiming he had lost his companions and nearly starved to death. He appeared well fed, however, and had plenty of money to spend. After Packer disappeared, a search party found the miners—four of them killed from ax blows, the fifth shot. All had been nicely butchered.

Nine years after the crime, Packer was captured in Wyoming and tried for murder in the Lake City courthouse. He was sentenced to death, but that was commuted to a term in prison. Several years later he was pardoned following an emotional series of articles by *Denver Post* sob sister Polly Pry.

While there is no truth in the story, legend insists the Lake City judge sentenced Packer to

Lake City storefronts, 1982. *Kendal Atchison*

death because "they was seven dimmycrats in Hinsdale County and ye et five of 'em."

Packer's cannibalistic exploits have inspired a following of groupies far beyond Lake City. Students at the University of Colorado named their cafeteria the Alferd Packer Grill, and a group of supporters, citing new evidence that the cannibal acted in self-defense, asked Colorado Governor Richard D. Lamm to grant Packer a posthumous pardon. Lamm, however, demurred: "Unfortunately, the proof was in the pudding, and Alferd ate that." Packer supporters persevere, though, and have formed "The Friends of Alferd E. Packer." The club's motto: "Serving our fellow man since 1874."

La Plata

Boarded-up school at La Plata. *Sandra Dallas*

The retail economy of Lawson, shown in 1966, was curtailed after an interstate highway bypassed the town. *Sandra Dallas.*

COUNTY: *La Plata*
LOCATION: *9 mi. north of Hesperus*
MAP 9
P.O. est. July 24, 1882; discont. Dec. 23, 1885

Hundreds of gold seekers, most of them men, crowded into La Plata, where today only a two-story log structure, a fine weathered school, and a few cabins stand. "Here beauty and grandeur have kissed each other," gushed a local clergy-man.

Here beauty and grandeur also made a profit. "The Convent" was a local brothel once dubbed "Jessie's Convent" for the madam who took refuge there with her girls. The girls moved on, but the name stuck, and later histories report piously that La Plata had a convent of nuns.

Prostitutes were not the only enterprising women in La Plata, which had a female freighter who hauled goods between Durango and La Plata.

La Plata—the name is Spanish for silver—outlasted the silver panic of 1893, but by the turn of the century it was on the decline.

Lawson

COUNTY: *Clear Creek*
LOCATION: *7 mi. west of Idaho Springs*
MAP 1
P.O. est. June 29, 1877; discont. 1967

Lawson was settled in 1877 when rich quartz mines were discovered on nearby Red Elephant Mountain. The town originally was called Free America by jingoistic immigrant John Coburn, who came to Colorado from Ireland in 1870 and built a home in the area in 1876. Coburn, who operated a toll road near his house, renamed the town Lawson, for his son-in-law, though whether it was because of affection for the young man or faltering nationalism is unknown.

Within a few years the town had five hundred residents, most employed in the Red Elephant mines, which were then among the state's great producers—the Saint James, the Free America, the Young America, the Dexter, and the Lulu.

Red Mountain could be bitterly cold. The temperature in November, 1880, was minus 31

By 1891, Lawson's best days were behind it. *Courtesy Denver Public Library Western History Department.*

degrees, and the *Rocky Mountain News* reported: "The face and ears of Charles Whitney were severely frosted Tuesday evening while he was fetching them down to Lawton from Georgetown."

Part of the town was sliced away when Interstate 70 was built in the mid-1960s, and some of Lawson's best houses were destroyed, including the Coburn house and another belonging to Anson Stevens, who operated a mill in Lawson and owned several mining properties. Stevens was so wealthy that one legend says when he was stumped over what to give his wife for Christmas, he handed her $1 million.

The highway destroyed Lawson's roadside economy, but the town still thrives. It contains several frame houses with wooden quoins, a closed general store, and a boarded-up school where a dilapidated merry-go-round creaks and rotates drunkenly in the school yard.

Leadville

COUNTY: *Lake*
LOCATION: *103 mi. southwest of Denver*
MAP 5
P.O. est. July 16, 1877

Built on a dreary hill, surrounded by threatening mountains and buffeted by fierce snowstorms, Leadville is an ominous place, stark and cold. But hidden beneath the grime and bilious paint encrusted on the buildings like a patina are the remains of the wildest, gaudiest, most raucous mining camp in Colorado, the most glamorous, glittering silver town in the West. From the time silver was discovered in Leadville in 1875 until the collapse of the silver market in 1893, Leadville fascinated the world with its instant millionaires and villainous ways. It was known as both the wickedest city in the world and the most progressive mining town in Christendom.

As silver production increased, Leadville became a substantial city. Brick blocks replaced log cabins and flimsy frame structures. *Courtesy Denver Public Library Western History Department.*

After the silver crash, Leadville, shown just before World War II, kept its economy going by diversifying into gold, molybdenum, and even bootleg whiskey. *Author's collection.*

Architect George King had a decided preference for mansard roofs, which he used in the Tabor Grand Hotel *(above)*, *courtesy Colorado Historical Society,* the Delaware Block *(below left), Kendal Atchison,* and his own home *(below right). Kendal Atchison*

The area was first settled in 1860 as Oro City, when prospector Abe Lee picked at the nuggets he found in his gold pan and called out: "Boys, I've got all California here in this pan." Between $5 million and $10 million in gold was taken out of California Gulch before the miners deserted it a few years later.

Then, in 1875, two prospectors, one of them a metallurgist, tested the heavy sands that clogged the sluice boxes of the gold seekers and discovered they were rich in silver. When the news became public, some two hundred prospectors a day poured over the divide into Leadville, sleeping in alleys or in dry goods boxes, paying fifty cents to sleep in a tent or $1 to roll up in their coats under a gaming table. One saloonkeeper rented floor space to anyone but reserved table tops for regular customers. He rang a bell in case of fire.

The combination of cold, high altitude, and poor food and shelter killed many of the men, but even the risk of death seemed worth it. The three Gallagher brothers discovered the Camp Bird Mine and sold it for $225,000. George Fryer hit a silver mine behind his cabin on Fryer Hill. A group of pallbearers dug a grave, discovered pay dirt, and left the body of their dead friend in a snowbank. Several discouraged miners agreed to sell their claim for $10,000, and while the buyer went to fetch the money, the owners hit silver. When he returned, the price was $60,000. And two worthless prospectors, grubstaked by storekeeper H. A. W. Tabor, dug in the easiest spot they could find and struck ore at the only place on the hill the vein came close to the surface.

Even barren mines produced. Chicken Bill Lovell salted a prospect hole called the Chrysolite with ore stolen from Tabor's Little Pittsburg and sold the mine to Tabor. The silver king refused to admit he had been bilked and ordered his men to keep digging; they struck silver.

Ghost house in Leadville, the "Cloud City." *Kendal Atchison*

H. A. W. Tabor. *Courtesy Colorado Historical Society.*

Baby Doe Tabor. *Courtesy Denver Public Library Western History Department.*

The H. A. W. and Augusta Tabor house in Leadville. *Courtesy Denver Public Library Western History Department.*

NO ONE exemplified the hope, the exhilaration, the despair of the western prospector as much as Horace Austin Warner Tabor, the stonemason who became a bonanza king and died in poverty. With his beautiful and adoring young wife, his mansion in Denver, and his extravagant ways, Tabor was the inspiration of every gold and silver seeker in the West.

Tabor arrived in Colorado in 1859 with his first wife, Augusta, and infant son, Maxcy, and for the next nineteen years prospected for gold in a succession of camps from Idaho Springs to Oro City. He operated a series of stores, but it was Augusta who kept the family together, by baking pies and taking in boarders. In 1878, Tabor grubstaked a pair of improbable prospectors, who by sheer luck discovered the Little Pittsburg near Leadville, and from then on everything Tabor touched turned to silver.

Tabor spent the money almost as fast as it came in. He built opera houses in Leadville and Denver. He outfitted the Tabor Hose Company and the Tabor Light Cavalry. He ordered silk nightshirts with diamond buttons and indulged in champagne and oyster suppers at Leadville's elegant Saddle Rock Cafe. It was there that he met divorcee Elizabeth McCourt Doe, and in a scandal that rocked Colorado, he divorced the faithful Augusta, who had grown old and bitter from overwork and too many mountain winters. In 1883, Tabor, who had been named to fill a thirty-day term in the United States Senate, married Baby Doe in the Willard Hotel in Washington. President Chester Arthur attended the wedding, along with the city's most prominent men, though their wives snubbed Baby Doe and stayed away.

If Baby Doe was ignored, Tabor was tolerated because of his money. "A fouler beast was never depicted," one senator confided to his wife. "Such a vulgar, ruffianly boor you never beheld; uncouth, awkward, shambling, dirty hands and big feet turned inward; a huge solitaire diamond on a sooty, bony blacksmith hand . . ."

Tabor's money and gullibility made him a victim of investment sharks, and he threw away millions on worthless mines and exotic schemes, while Baby Doe squandered money on peacocks for the lawn and thousand-dollar dresses for the Tabor daughters, Elizabeth Bonduel Lillie and Rose Mary Echo Silver Dollar.

The combination of poor investments and the silver crash depleted Tabor's fortune, and he died penniless in 1899, exhorting Baby Doe to hold onto his Matchless Mine. She did, living in exile at the mine shaft, deserted by her daughters. Lillie moved to the Middle West to live with relatives, and Silver Dollar became a prostitute and was scalded to death in Chicago.

In 1935, Baby Doe's body, dressed in rags, was found at the Matchless. She had frozen to death among the mementos of the bonanza years, including scrapbooks filled with yellowed clippings and tattered ribbons that told the incredible saga of the Tabors.

Those who did not become silver kings made money too. Charles Boettcher's hardware store was the basis of an extraordinary fortune that made Boettcher, who controlled the Great Western Sugar Company, the Ideal Cement Company, and the Brown Palace Hotel in Denver, the most powerful man in Colorado. David May turned a successful dry goods store into the May Department Stores Company. And a family of Philadelphia lace merchants named Guggenheim purchased the A. Y. and the Minnie mines, then risked their capital on a smelter, forming the American Smelting and Refining Company (now Asarco, Incorporated). Leadville claimed that in a ten-year period it had created more millionaires than any city in the world. "Not only your banker, but your baker and grocer and the man who saws your wood, has some cash interest in the silver diggings," noted a *Scribners Monthly* reporter in 1879.

But rich men and their instant wealth were easily parted. Leadville was gaudy with saloons, gambling dens, dance halls, and other fleshpots reeking of bartered virtue. "Gambling saloons are more than five times as numerous as churches, and are twenty times as well patronized," wrote an 1879 visitor, who counted twenty-one regular gambling houses and noted faro equipment in drugstores, groceries, and offices. By 1883 Leadville had ninety-seven saloons, along with twenty-three restaurants, fifty-one boardinghouses, two sausage makers, one soap manufacturer, and countless gambling halls, variety theaters, concert halls (so called because they offered music, boxing matches, and waiter girls), and other dens of iniquity.

Writers for Leadville's six newspapers, as well as visiting journalists, made the *de rigueur* tour of Leadville's resorts—all in the interest of informing their readers, of course. They watched the frayed women and hardened men under the gaslights of the Bon Ton, the Odeon, the National, the Comique, the Pioneer, the Bella Union, and dozens of other establishments, and chronicled greed and lasciviousness and the petty ways of the denizens. They relished the cat fights, treating women as pitiful but amusing objects. When the women from two State Street dance halls battled over which wore shorter skirts, the Leadville *Chronicle* covered the event gleefully. Drunk on whiskey mixed with gunpowder, the women of the Red Light attacked their rivals at the Bon Ton. "The fight was short and bloody. The air was thick with wigs, teeth, obscenity and bad breaths," the *Chronicle* noted.

The favorite spot for the underworld was Pap Wyman's Saloon where a Holy Bible was chained to the counter with a sign, "Please Do Not Swear." Wyman refused to let married men gamble, but other places were only too happy to take advantage of the unwary. A newcomer lost his $800 stake first, and then his $300 horse, and his watch, mule, rifle, and dog. Intending to shoot himself, the dupe put his hand into his pocket for his gun and found instead his meerschaum pipe, which he hocked. He rejoined the game, and by daylight he was $4,800 ahead. Collecting his winnings, the man called for a Bible and swore on it never to gamble again.

There were occasional temperance movements, but they never amounted to much. The Grocers and Butchers Protective Association studied the weighty problem of regulating gambling halls and saloons. The members concluded that saloons—which served free lunches—were legitimate, but they came out against gambling halls.

The grocers and butchers were not the only ones to make money off the resorts. Saloon-keepers, gamblers, madams, and occasionally even prostitutes and dance hall girls got rich, though generally they spent the money as quickly as they made it. Maude Deuel, who was living on a $7.50-a-month pension in 1935, recalled that some dance hall girls made $100 a week, and that she took in as much as $200 as the most popular girl at the Pioneer Dance Hall. She spent $200 a week, however. "I always believed in keeping money in circulation," she said.

Very few of the women who hustled drinks or their own bodies came out ahead. Most ended like Mabel Johnson, a tired, aged dance hall performer who collapsed amid the catcalls and jibes of her drunken audience. She was carried to her shack in Tiger Alley where the whores and dance hall girls, described as "hard enough to cut up for harrow teeth," brought in bread and cakes and set up a death watch. When it was over, the women passed the hat to raise enough for a rosewood coffin with silver handles.

"It was a blessed death," sighed one of Mabel's women friends. For many of the hopeless women of Tiger Alley and the more infamous Stillborn Alley, where the foulest of the cribs were located, death was indeed blessed.

Easy money inevitably produced lawlessness with footpads and cutthroats lurking everywhere. Anyone who flashed a roll of bills was doomed. Businessmen walked in groups down dingy corridors to their hotel rooms, and when forced to go out alone at night even a brave man walked down the center of the street with a cocked pistol in each hand.

There were scofflaws in high places, too. Three leading banks "fell into ruin through profligate management, and two of them were shipwrecked by the dishonesty of the controlling powers," wrote historian Frank Hall. When the First National Bank of Leadville folded in 1884, one Leadville paper ran a headline accusing its president, Frank W. DeWalt, of running out, noting: "Reasonable Suspicion That There is Something Rotten."

"DeWalt had gambled away $50,000, most of it depositors' money, in a mere six months and was reported to have bankrolled Winnie Purdy's byzantine bagnio, "the most remarkable house of wickedness in Leadville," according to a reporter. DeWalt eventually served a prison term for his part in the bank's failure. "Oh, he was

a beautiful gambler, but a chump of a bank president," said a sporting man.

Despite its wicked ways, Leadville was an elegant Victorian city high in the clouds with an active civilizing class of people. If churches and schools lagged behind saloons and variety halls, they were built nonetheless. Father John Dyer, Father Henry Robinson, and Parson Tom Uzzell brought comfort to the godly and exhortations of hell to others. Hell was not far away. One sinner remarked: "If one wants to see hell uncovered, let him go through one of the many gambling houses."

Religious societies, fraternal orders, and women's clubs dominated upper-class social life with masked balls and 'possum suppers, skating parties and picnics. For the cultured, there was the Tabor Opera House, where entertainers from Jack Langrishe to Oscar Wilde performed. Wilde's lectures were roaring successes, not because of their languid subjects but because Wilde had captivated Leadville by drinking a group of miners under the table. Just as elegant as the opera house was the Tabor Grand Hotel, which opened in 1885. Its lobby floor was set with silver dollars. So many fashionable people paraded about Leadville that a visiting reporter was astonished to discover he had "seen more handsome and really tasteful costumes here than I saw in Omaha."

During its heyday Leadville produced more than $200 million in ore, mostly silver. But the 1893 silver crash closed most of the mines for good, throwing Leadville into a depression that was relieved only slightly by gold production at the Little Jonny Mine. Owned by big-spending John Campion, known as "Leadville Johnny," the Little Jonny was managed by industrious James J. Brown, whose wife, Margaret, craved admittance to Denver society. Her social betters, called the "Sacred Thirty-six," snubbed her until she emerged as the heroine of the *Titanic* disaster, and they were forced to admit "the Unsinkable Mrs. Brown" to their homes.

In an attempt to muster civic pride and to stem economic and population losses, Leadville

A popular dance hall girl at the Pioneer could make as much as $200 a week. *Kendal Atchison*

Lenado was not very big during any of its booms. *Courtesy Denver Public Library Western History Department.*

leaders in 1896 built a glittering ice palace. Made of huge blocks of ice cut and hauled to the Leadville site, the ice palace with its ballrooms, skating rink, restaurant, and lounge, was lit by electric lights. Their glow reflected off the ice and glittered like stars.

The ice palace, which had cost nearly $40,000, proved a costly extravagance. A rare warm chinook blew in, and in March, only two months after it opened, the ice palace slowly melted away.

So did Leadville. By the turn of the century, mine production had dropped to a fraction of its high in the 1880s. Houses were torn down for firewood. Dogs slept undisturbed in the middle of Harrison Avenue, once so busy that pedestrians could cross only if they "drifted with the current as it moved," Hall noted. Stills operated

out of old mine shafts as Leadville became bootlegger to Colorado. Illicit whiskey, in fact, was the county's major source of income during the period of prohibition. By 1930, Leadville's population, once twenty thousand, had dropped to less than four thousand.

Unlike the gentler, prettier mining towns, Leadville, with its dreary winters and quick summers, never appealed to those seeking a second home. For the past three-quarters of a century, it has lived catch-as-catch-can, unhampered by inflows of capital and such niceties as historic preservation. Its once stylish buildings are cluttered with neon signs and distorted by cheap remodeling. Still, through the grime of a hundred years there lurks a faded splendor, a haunting reminder of a long-gone era when silver was king and silver kings owned the world.

Lenado

COUNTY: *Pitkin*
LOCATION: *17 mi. northwest of Aspen*
MAP 6
P.O. est. Feb. 4, 1891; discont. Jan. 2, 1907

Lenado's repetitive boom-and-bust existence began in the 1880s with discovery of two rich ore deposits, the Leadville and the Aspen Contact, which contained lead, silver, and zinc. The town died with the silver crash of 1893, but was resurrected at the turn of the century. After a few years it folded again, then was started up when lead and zinc were needed during World War I. Another boom came in the 1930s when timber production was begun. Finally, in the post-hippie days, Aspen dropouts discovered Lenado as a less hectic alternative to peripatetic Aspen and moved into Lenado's cabins. Their vegetable and flower gardens are a pleasant relief to the yellow mine tailings.

Lincoln

COUNTY: *Summit*
LOCATION: *4 mi. northeast of Breckenridge*
MAP 4
P.O. est. June 28, 1861 as Paige City; discont. July 10, 1894

In the 1860s, Harry Farncomb discovered splendid specimens of wire gold—thin strands of high-quality crystallized gold—in French Gulch near Breckenridge. Farncomb quietly bought up claims in the "wire patch" on Farncomb Hill. When news of his discovery and consequent land grab leaked out, jealous prospectors aided by Denver financiers fought Farncomb in a lengthy battle that lasted ten years and ended in a shootout. Forty men were involved in the fight, according to Summit County historian Mary Ellen Gilliland, and three of them died. Eventually an outside party purchased Farncomb's holdings.

French Gulch, named for a French Canadian prospector, and Farncomb Hill were extraordinarily rich in gold. Colorado's largest gold nugget was found in a placer claim in French Gulch in 1887 by Tom Groves and Harry Lytton. Groves was so proud of the nugget, which he cradled like an infant, that the 136-ounce specimen was dubbed "Tom's Baby." Despite its fame, the nugget disappeared after a few years, and historians assumed it had been broken up or melted down. But in 1971, officials of the Denver Museum of Natural History, prodded by historian Mark Fiester, discovered Tom's Baby stored in a box in a vault. Guards had believed the box contained dinosaur bones.

Lincoln was settled by miners on Farncomb Hill and later was home for employees of the Wellington Mine in French Gulch, as well as for workers on the French Gulch dredges. Among its early residents was the Methodist preacher

Many Lincoln residents worked at the Wellington Mine. *Courtesy Glenn L. Gebhardt*

The remains of a dredge near Lincoln. *Kendal Atchison*

Father John Dyer, who concluded he could not pay board and room out of his meager collections and therefore purchased a cabin on French Gulch.

Wrote Dyer:

My bedstead was made of pine poles, even to the springs. The bed was hay, with blankets for covering. I slept well, and rested as well as though I had been in a fine parlor-chamber. My furniture was primitive and limited—a table, and a couple of boards against the side of the wall for a cupboard, six tin plates, half a set of knives and forks, with a few other indispensables; a coffee-pot, a tin cup, and a pot for boiling vegetables—when I had them—and a frying-pan.

Dyer and others did not stay long in Lincoln, which originally had a population of hundreds of miners. By 1882 its population was two hundred and fifty, and by 1891 the number of residents had declined to fifty.

By 1889, Lulu was a ghost town. *Courtesy Denver Public Library Western History Department.*

Lulu

COUNTY: *Grand*
LOCATION: *30 mi. north of Granby*
MAP 12
P.O. est. July 26, 1880; discont. Nov. 26, 1883

Lulu, named for Lulu Brunett, the daughter of the town surveyor, sprang up overnight when silver was discovered north of Grand Lake in 1879. Miners quickly staked the Georgiana, the North Star, the Battle Creek, the Southern Cross, and the Wolverine.

There were almost as many schemers as mines. One told a reporter his mine was "cheap at a million dollars," and another, Brick Pomeroy, prince of the promoters, arrived with a crew to look things over. "Brick, with his usual luck, will undoubtedly strike it rich here," predicted the *Rocky Mountain News.*

Brick's usual luck ran out, and so did everyone else's. The town, which may have had as many as a thousand residents for a few weeks in 1881, was virtually deserted a year or two later. A hundred years later all that is left of Lulu—located at the end of a pleasant three-mile walk in Rocky Mountain National Park— are the foundations of two cabins. One acts as a planter for a half dozen full-grown evergreen trees.

Magnolia

COUNTY: *Boulder*
LOCATION: *7 mi. southwest of Boulder*
MAP 3
P.O. est. May 16, 1876; discont. Dec. 31, 1920

In a version of one of the West's favorite folk tales, Hiram Fullen discovered tellurium ore as he idly struck a rock outcropping with his pick while he was eating lunch. He named the mine the Magnolia, and the town that sprang up nearby in 1875 took the same name. The discovery caused miners who had been unfamiliar with tellurium ore to scramble through mine dumps in search of riches. The area had several paying mines, including the Dunraven, the Mountain Lion, the Keystone, and the Ben C. Lowell.

Magnolia was a quiet town because residents in 1876 voted 173 to 27 to forbid saloons.

The Ben C. Lowell and several other mines kept Magnolia going for a time. *Courtesy Denver Public Library Western History Department.*

The schoolhouse is like a lonely sentinel marking the once prosperous Malta area. *Kendal Atchison*

Malta

COUNTY: *Lake*
LOCATION: *4 mi. west of Leadville*
MAP 5
P.O. est. Oct.26, 1875; discont. 1955

"The Maltanese are trying to persuade themselves that *this*, and not Leadville, will be the carbonate city of the future," *Crofutt's Grip-Sack Guide of Colorado* reported in 1885. No such luck. Malta, which once boasted a population of four hundred, was a railroad switching point and smelter center for its lustier, wealthier neighbor to the east.

Oro City, the first California Gulch settlement, was founded in 1860 near the site of Malta, but after a brief boom the area declined until the discovery of Leadville silver. Once known as Swilltown, Malta had its seamier side. A pair of footpads attempted to rob a newspaper boy at Malta. Realizing his youth, they then argued whether they should take his money. In the meantime, the newsboy ran away.

During racing season, Leadville's sporting crowd packed into the $5,000 Malta racetrack to watch the local horses compete against champions from Denver, Colorado Springs, and Central City.

Malta began to decline long before the silver crash and today is only a pretty red schoolhouse and a few ruins beside a railroad track.

Manhattan

COUNTY: *Larimer*
LOCATION: *4 mi. north of Rustic*
MAP 12
P.O. est. March 19, 1887; discont. Dec. 31, 1900

A rich strike near the Cache la Poudre River in the mountains west of Fort Collins in the mid-1880s sent prospectors scurrying over the hills in search of gold, and for a time Manhattan, the center of their activities, boomed. Manhattan had a hotel, homes, stores, and a saloon called the Ace of Clubs, located in a pretty meadow that today contains only a few old boards. There was but little gold in the Katy's Pet, the Little Tipsy, or the Laugh-a-lot, and despite a prediction in 1897 by the *Denver Post* that "there is no doubt Manhattan is on the eve of a boom," the town never amounted to much.

At Manhattan's peak, some three hundred miners crowded into the settlement, fighting for space in the few cabins or at tables in the Ace of Clubs, which was named for the shape of the collection of buildings that were put together to form the saloon. Its construction was none too sturdy, and when a fight erupted during a card

Manhattan has almost completely crumbled into the ground. *Kendal Atchison*

game, one man was slammed through the window, taking part of the wall with him.

Manhattan did have one curious connection with fame. In 1901, Lady Cecil Moon, who already owned property in the vicinity, purchased a ranch at Manhattan for $2,500. Once a washerwoman near Fort Collins, Katie Lawder married Moon, an English remittance man, who later inherited an English fortune and a title. As Lady Moon, the onetime Colorado domestic led a hard life as a would-be member of English society. Her mawkish trials and tribulations inspired a soap opera that ran for years on radio, "Our Gal Sunday."

Marble

COUNTY: *Gunnison*
LOCATION: *28 mi. south of Carbondale*
MAP 6
P.O. est. March 19, 1890; discont. November, 1942

It was not gold or silver but marble, the finest quality marble in the world, that brought settlers and entrepreneurs to a remote town on the Rock Creek (later the Crystal River). A geologist, Sylvester Richardson, discovered the stone in 1873

while scouting the Crystal River valley. Although the high quality of the stone and the vast deposits were quickly noted, because of its remote location the marble remained mostly a curiosity.

There were no serious attempts to find commercial markets until the mid-1880s, and it was not until after the turn of the century that regular shipments of marble left the little community. The town was launched in 1906 when a railroad reached it, and the following year Marble's quarries received their first major order—for a courthouse in Cleveland. The town of Marble boomed.

Marble originally was settled not only to serve the marble quarry but as a supply center for prospectors. Its location was so far from the railroad that the town's first piano was packed in on burros. By the time it arrived, noted Muriel Sibell Wolle in *Stampede to Timberline*: "When you started to play on it, it sounded like a crash of thunder mixed with falling bricks, tin pans and horns."

By the time the quarries began shipping marble in earnest, Marble had hundreds of workers, many of whom lived in tiny company cottages, a high school with a marble foundation, marble paved streets, and a number of saloons—which were abolished in 1908 when the town went dry.

Marble also had its own newspaper, the *Marble City Times*, operated by Sylvia Smith, who delighted in charging the Colorado-Yule Marble Company with stock manipulation and other frauds. Her crusades were lonely ones, because most of the town was dependent on the company, and few townspeople agreed with her. When Marble residents dismantled her printing press and forced her to leave town, she sued most of the town, forcing several merchants out of business when the court later ruled in Smith's favor and they could not pay their fines.

Marble provided the stone for some of America's grandest buildings—the Cheesman Park pavilion and Daniels & Fisher, both in Denver, the Otis Building in Chicago, and the Washington Memorial, the Lincoln Memorial, and the Tomb of the Unknown Soldier in Washington, D.C.

Marble was awarded the contract to supply the stone for the Tomb of the Unknown Soldier in 1930 because it was the only quarry that could cut the enormous chunk of marble required—124 tons when it was quarried, fifty-six after it

The Marble mill during the days the Colorado town shipped out the finest marble in the world. *Courtesy Denver Public Library Western History Department.*

was trimmed. It took seventy-five men working more than a year just to quarry the marble.

Despite such prestigious contracts, the marble quarries of Marble were in trouble. Winter blizzards sent avalanches down on the town, the marble mill, and the railroad, which was named the Crystal River & San Juan but was dubbed the "Can't Run and Seldom Jumps." In addition, the marble company was overextended, creating a precarious financial situation. In 1941 operations at Marble were closed.

They never reopened. Today Marble, whose population swells in the summer, is home to a few year-round residents. A quarry a few miles above town is a tourist attraction, and the mill, which appears like the wreck of an ancient marble temple, is a national historic site.

The gravestones in Colorado's mining town cemeteries tell stories of short lives and tragic deaths. *Sandra Dallas*

Churches, houses, and mills were built with marble foundations or walls. *Kendal Atchison*

Masontown

COUNTY: *Summit*
LOCATION: *½ mi. south of Frisco*
MAP 4
No P.O.

Built part way up Royal Mountain above Frisco, right at the end of an avalanche path, Masontown grew up around the Victoria Mine, discovered by a General Buford in the 1860s. In 1872 a group of Masontown, Pennsylvania investors built an extensive processing facility and named the community for their hometown.

While the town was neither large nor particularly prosperous, it was persistent. Most of it was destroyed in 1912 when an avalanche crashed down Royal Mountain, smashing the town. Legend says no one was hurt because local residents had gone to Frisco to a party.

Masontown's greater glory came during prohibition, when bootleg liquor poured more money into the Masontown economy than mining ever did.

Maysville

COUNTY: *Chaffee*
LOCATION: 11 mi. west of Salida
MAP 13
P.O. est. July 28, 1879; discont. Dec. 23, 1893

First called Feathers Ranch, not for any wanton doings but because the site was a ranch owned by a man named Feathers, Maysville was founded in1879 as a smelter town. Feathers, an itinerant salesman, purchased the site from its original owner for $150 and a sewing machine, then prospered by selling lots for up to $75 each.

Only a year later, "the streets are filled with loaded teams and prosperity everywhere abounds," the *Inter-Ocean*, a magazine, reported. By the next summer, there were thirty-four mines taking out ore and sixty-three com-

This shabby house is a reminder of better times in Maysville. *Kendal Atchison*

panies active in the district. By 1882, Maysville was the largest town in the county with two smelters, a number of stores and hotels, and a population of a thousand.

Prosperity did not last long, in part because the smelters were inefficient. By 1890 population was down to forty.

Midway

COUNTY: *Teller*
LOCATION: *4 mi. north of Victor*
MAP 14
No P.O.

Never much of a town, Midway, in the Cripple Creek mining district, had only a handful of residents, but hundreds of miners, on foot or on the streetcar, passed through it on their way to work each day.

In 1901 the *Denver Times* reported: "Midway is rapidly forging to the front as a shipping point for ore." Coal for nearby mines was shipped through Midway, and as many as thirty carloads of ore were transported out each day on the two railroads that ran through the town. Most important, Midway served as a watering spot for

tired miners who forgot their toils at the Grand View Saloon. The Grand View is about all that is left of Midway.

Montezuma

COUNTY: *Summit*
LOCATION: *7 mi. southeast of Keystone*
MAP 4
P.O. est. June 15, 1871

Montezuma grew up near the site of Colorado's first silver discovery, in 1863. The early town was crude. "We slept in the common garret, with perhaps eight or ten others, hardy, tired miners and prospectors, some of whom snored loud enough to wake the dead," William H. Brewer, an 1869 traveler wrote about Montezuma's only hotel.

But things picked up, and Montezuma became an important mining camp for several silver producers, including the Tiger, the Silver King, the Queen of the West, and the New York.

By 1885, Montezuma had two stores, a post office, two hotels, a weekly paper, and a sawmill, along with businesses that *Crofutt's Grip-Sack Guide of Colorado* did not mention. Whore-

The Grand View, 1981. *Kendal Atchison*

Montezuma about 1908. *Author's collection.*

Mountain City, where Central City gold was first discovered. The Gregory Store, slightly altered, still stands. *Courtesy Denver Public Library Western History Department.*

houses were an accepted part of the town's economy, and so were prostitutes, as long as they kept their distance. The gaudy local madam, an avid baseball fan, was welcome to attend Montezuma's ball games as long as she sat by herself at the end of the stands.

Montezumans had their standards. When a destitute former resident showed up with a sad story, residents organized a benefit for her. But when they saw her entering a saloon with a disreputable mine manager, and then blatantly heading for the red-light district, they sent for the stage driver, who made a special run to take the brazen woman to the depot at Dillon.

Transgressions were not limited to Montezuma lowlife. The town banker was arrested for speculating with school funds.

Like most mining camps, Montezuma had its ups and downs, and as early as 1877, a newspaper lauded the residents who had "bravely held the fort through a decade of light times." While the other camps around it died, Montezuma, today a pretty mountain town, remained

alive through periods of low prices for the metals and disastrous fires.

Mountain City

COUNTY: *Gilpin*
LOCATION: *½ mi. east of Central City*
MAP 2
No P.O.

When prospector John Gregory discovered gold in early 1859 on a lonely mountainside later known as Mountain City, he justified the beliefs of scores of prospectors who had joined the 1858 rush to the Rockies and fired the dreams of thousands more. The discovery at Gregory Diggings proved gold was not just elusive float to be panned out of streams but was hidden in veins in the mountains, waiting to be discovered.

Despite its preeminent position in Colorado history, Mountain City was quickly eclipsed by its more elegant neighbors, Central City and Black Hawk. Annexed by Central City, Mountain City today is a few dilapidated buildings, some rock embankments, and a solitary monument inscribed "Gregory Diggings" that marks the spot that changed history.

Thousands of men flocked to the diggings, among them editor William N. Byers of the *Rocky Mountain News*, Henry Villard of the Cincinnati *Commercial*, author Albert D. Richardson, and the influential Horace Greeley. All put their editorial stamp of approval on the gulch. Even the inconveniences of camp life failed to daunt their enthusiasm. Six men slept in a tent ambitiously called the Mountain City Hotel, Richardson wrote, "lying so close that none of us could turn over separately." But instead of complaining, he noted they slept

Snug
As a bug
In a rug.

Their enthusiasm was due, in part, to the extraordinary riches being gouged out of the diggings. One miner took out $972 in three days, then sold his claims for $21,000. And, in fact, when they couldn't find gold in three days, Greeley noted, the prospectors gave up in disgust.

For several years Mountain City was the blustery heart of Colorado mining. Almost any occasion was reason for a celebration, particularly

the Fourth of July when Green Russell, who had led the first gold party to the Pikes Peak country in 1858, gave the traditional oration to the cheers of hundreds of prospectors, many of them drunk. The miners did not need a Fourth of July to drink and often drank themselves into stupors on foul-tasting, over-priced whiskey. Sickened from the effects of too much liquor, mountain cold, and freezing streams, many died in the lonely cabins sprawled across the mountainside.

Nathrop

COUNTY: *Chaffee*
LOCATION: *8 mi. south of Buena Vista*
MAP 7
P.O. est. Sept. 8, 1880

The town of Nathrop originally was located a mile and a half up the valley from its present site, but when the Denver & Rio Grande roared to a stop at its junction with the Denver, South Park & Pacific in 1880, the enterprising townspeople of Nathrop packed up their town and moved it closer to the railroads' stone depot. A few months later Nathrop was so ambitious it tried to get the county seat.

While there were low-grade silver deposits in the area, commerce kept Nathrop going. The town, which had several stores and saloons as well as a charming $2,700 school by 1882, acted as a railroad junction and supply point for the mines of Chalk Creek.

Nathrop was named for merchant and entrepreneur Charles Nachtrieb, a fitting tribute, since Nachtrieb owned the townsite and built the railroad's Gothic hotel, replete with verandas and sharp gables, near the depot. Nachtrieb, a hot-tempered, thrifty man, did not live to see his town prosper. In 1881, at the age of forty-eight, he was murdered by a cowboy in a wage dispute.

Nederland

COUNTY: *Boulder*
LOCATION: *16 mi. west of Boulder*
MAP 3
P.O. est. Sept. 13, 1871 as Middle Boulder

Nederland boomed because of tungsten. Populated in the early 1870s, Nederland, which was

The school at Nathrop. *Kendal Atchison*

Above: Teams haul an electrical transformer to Barker Dam construction site near Nederland about 1910. *Courtesy Public Service Company of Colorado. Right:* Nederland garage, 1981. *Kendal Atchison*

first called Brownsville and then Middle Boulder, was a supply town for Caribou, the silver town several miles away, as well as for the Caribou Mill, located just outside Nederland. By 1874, the town had a sawmill, several saloons, meat markets, and thirty houses and boardinghouses.

When the price of silver dropped, the population of Nederland dwindled, but it began to grow again at the turn of the century with the discovery of what one newspaper called "the greatest deposit of tungsten in the U.S." One prospector, who had discovered tungsten ore in 1860 but tossed it aside as worthless, returned to the spot in 1900 and opened a mine.

By 1915, Nederland was booming with an annual tungsten production valued at more than $1 million. Miners slept in pool halls, and shopkeepers complained about down-and-outers who crowded around their stoves. Long lines of

Those who ventured out on this cold day in 1889 stopped to pose obligingly for the photographer in Nevadaville. *Courtesy Denver Public Library Western History Department.*

men waited for slap-dash meals, "40 percent an edible product and 50 percent plain grease," noted a reporter who failed to account for the remaining 10 percent.

In an effort to control the boisterous element, the town closed the saloons in 1916, forcing most of them to become pool halls. But nothing prevented drunks from stashing away their own supply of liquor and reeling down the street without enriching the coffers of the town merchants.

The tungsten boom peaked shortly after that; by 1918 the population was down to five hundred. More than fifty residents died from influenza that year.

Nevadaville

COUNTY: *Gilpin*
LOCATION: *1 mi. southwest of Central City*
MAP 2
P.O. est. Jan.12, 1861 as Nevada; discont. Oct. 15, 1921

Nevadaville was one of the Gilpin County towns that sprang up in the enthusiasm of John Greg-

ory's discovery of gold at Mountain City. Prospectors by the hundreds roamed Quartz Hill and Bald Mountain (Nevadaville once was known as Bald Mountain), and by 1861, when Nevadaville was scarcely a year old, it had some twenty quartz mills, a number of stores and hotels, dozens of private dwellings, and hundreds of residents, many of them Irish and Cornish.

"Everywhere near Nevada people could be seen picking at the ground. Men and women spent hours digging up bits of earth and washing it in a basin or washtub," recalled Mrs. H. E. Ford, who arrived in 1860 and was interviewed forty years later. "At night they would go home disheartened and weary; but in the morning, they were just as hopeful . . . they were all going to strike it rich."

Those who did not strike it rich worked in the mines—the Casey, owned by illiterate Irishman Pat Casey, the Kansas, the Ophir, and the Hidden Treasure. The pay was good, $3 to $4 per day, giving the miner "almost as much here for one day's work as he could [make] in Massachusetts for a week of toil," proclaimed the *Rocky Mountain News.*

Nevadaville in 1931 *(above), courtesy Denver Public Library Western History Department,* and in 1982 *(below).*
Kendal Atchison

The John Manhervis butcher shop offered the latest in Victorian decor. Sanitation was another matter. *Courtesy Denver Public Library Western History Department.*

The Masons, the Odd Fellows, the Foresters, and the Red Men all had chapters at Nevadaville and often gave balls. In 1899 the *Denver Times* noted Nevadaville had just held its second masquerade ball of the season, which had followed a masquerade parade through Black Hawk and Central City. Nevadaville residents organized a baseball club and, in addition, they liked whippet racing and cricket, which was introduced by the Cornish. The Mountain Daisy Cricket Club was so confident of its skill that it offered a fine silver pitcher to anyone who could beat it.

Water, which sold for forty cents a barrel in the early days, was a problem for Nevadaville, and fire was a constant threat. Despite several fires, it was weather that ate away at the town, leaving only mine dumps, a few round-arched, fine brick buildings, and a tiny frame structure that once housed the city hall.

North Empire

COUNTY: *Clear Creek*
LOCATION: *2 mi. north of Empire*
MAP 1
No P.O.

Miners who worked the mines on Silver Mountain above Empire settled the town of North Empire. Never more than a collection of houses and a few business establishments, North Empire had only the roughest accommodations for visitors. One 1863 traveler took shelter in a boardinghouse and later complained that a group of miners coming off shift stretched out on the floor, put their boots under their heads for pillows, and covered themselves with buffalo robes. One, however, knelt in what the visitor called "closet prayer," which did the viewer more good "than the elocutive exhibitions of an army of modern artful evangelizers."

North Empire's boom was brief, though the town did not die until the 1940s. Miners stayed on working at the Conqueror and other mines until the federal government closed them down during World War II.

North Star

North Empire mine structure, 1981. *Kendal Atchison*

COUNTY: *Gunnison*
LOCATION: *1 mi. southeast of White Pine*
MAP 8
P.O. est. Oct. 11, 1889; discont. May 18, 1894

Miners who were tired of the mile-long uphill walk from White Pine to the North Star and adjacent mines formed the community of North Star in 1883. While North Star claimed the richest mines in the district, it never equaled its neighbor in size, and White Pine quickly eclipsed its newer rival.

Besides serving the North Star Mine, which was discovered in 1879, the town also provided housing for miners of the mighty May-Mazeppa just below it. At its peak the town had a population of a hundred or so. The figure dropped to half that with the demonetization of silver in 1893, and before long North Star was deserted. Today there are only a few rotted log shacks with tattered wallpaper clinging to the walls.

North Star today. The building on the left still has remnants of wallpaper and painted wainscoting. *Kendal Atchison*

Tattered cheesecloth hanging from the ceiling of a caved-in building frames the view of a deserted cabin in North Star. *Kendal Atchison*

Ohio City

COUNTY: *Gunnison*
LOCATION: *28 mi. northeast of Gunnison*
MAP 8
P.O. est. June 15, 1880 as Ohio

Miners who rushed over the mountains from Leadville in search of gold founded the Gold Brick mining district and settled the town of Ohio City (originally called Eagle City) on the banks of Gold Creek (originally called Ohio Creek) in 1880.

Within a couple of weeks some fifty log cabins and tents had been erected to serve as saloons, assay offices, stores, restaurants, and occasionally as houses for the hundreds of miners who rushed to the town. Everyone who visited Ohio City was caught up in the silver excitement as mines such as the Sultan, the Chicago, the Mary May, and the Way-up were discovered. There was so much demand for promising mines that the miners passed a law allowing a claim to be jumped if it was not properly marked within four days. Even a detached journalist, a Mr. Atchison of the *Chicago Journal of Commerce,*

was swept away and spent $1,000 for a ten-foot hole and called it a mine.

Mines were not the only things that were bought and sold. During a ten-day period in 1881, some one hundred lots changed hands.

The mining furor eventually brought crime. A miner who had argued with another man one evening approached the tent where his antagonist slept and fired into the tent. The second man, aroused by shouts, returned the fire. When the shooting was over, both men were dead, shot through their hearts.

There were other fatalities attributable to Ohio City's hard life. A visitor approached a grave and noted an epitaph entitled "Dear Friend":

> *Death went prospecting,*
> *and he was no fool,*
> *Here he struck faithful Pete,*
> *the emigrant mule.*

Ohio City was a long-lived camp. When the 1893 silver crash came, Ohio City's mines turned to gold production, and though activity gradually decreased as the twentieth century wore on, the last mine did not shut down until World War II.

Fishing and hunting have helped keep Ohio City going since World War II when mining ended. *Kendal Atchison*

144
o

Ophir

COUNTY: *San Miguel*
LOCATION: *14 mi. south of Telluride*
MAP 10
P.O. est. May 17, 1878; discont. June 3, 1922

Named for the biblical site of King Solomon's mines, Ophir was two locations. The original Ophir, sometimes called Old Ophir, is a couple of streets of nondescript houses and old wood barns in a high mountain meadow. Ophir Loop, two miles to the west of Old Ophir, was a railroad station.

By 1879, Old Ophir had a population of fifty with another two hundred and fifty working in the vicinity. Ten buildings were under construction, including a hotel that could accommodate forty. "It will be at no distant day a far more pretentious town than it is now," predicted the *Ouray Times.*

And indeed it was. By 1885 when George Crofutt visited Ophir, it was a town of two hundred and contained a stamp mill and two arastras for working free gold. The Ophir mines—the What

Cheer, the Butterfly-Terrible, the Klondike, and others—produced steadily, and in 1901 there was "not a vacant house in town to live in, and many occupied by two or more families," reported the *Denver Times.* "At least twenty-five modern tenements could be rented readily at a figure that would make their construction a good investment."

The town was decidedly pro-union. In 1901 when a new schoolteacher named Wogan refused to join the miners' union, he was confronted by an angry group of miners who insisted he resign. The proprietor of the hotel where Wogan lived, threatened with a boycott, evicted the teacher. Wogan succeeded in renting a house but was accosted by a group of thirty miners, including a member of the school board, who gave him five minutes to join the union or resign.

Wogan fled to Telluride, where the county superintendent of schools agreed to pay him a year's salary and promised to provide guards if he wanted to return to Ophir. Wogan never went back.

In winter Ophir was in constant danger of

Burros loaded with timbers, probably headed for a mine. *Courtesy Denver Public Library Western History Department.*

A deserted Ophir shack in a field of dandelions. *Kendal Atchison*

avalanches that swept away buildings and made travel treacherous. A Swedish mail carrier, Swan Nilson, who carried the mail between Silverton and Ophir, disappeared in December, 1883, while taking Ophir's Christmas mail from Silverton over Ophir Pass. The trip, which Nilson made wearing snowshoes (long skis) was so hazardous in winter that he was paid a salary of $200 a month.

With sixty pounds of mail strapped to his back, Nilson left Silverton in a blizzard, against the advice of the Silverton postmaster. When he failed to arrive and a search party turned up no trace of him, local residents grumbled he had absconded with their Christmas mail. Nilson's brother searched for the mail carrier's body all winter, through the summer and fall, and into the next winter. Finally, in August, 1885, he discovered the frozen body of Swan, buried in a snowbank, the water-soaked mail pouch with its rusted lock still strapped to his back.

Ophir's population declined steadily from early in the twentieth century. In 1940 the U.S. Bureau of the Census announced Ophir was tied with towns in Arkansas and Maryland for the lowest population in the country—two. In 1960 the Census Bureau announced Ophir was one of four incorporated towns in the United States with no residents. (One of the four was Eureka, Colorado.) The Census Bureau was wrong. The town had one resident, who was out of town the day the census taker came by.

Orient

COUNTY: *Saguache*
LOCATION: *12 mi. southeast of Villa Grove*
MAP 13
P.O. est. Oct. 15, 1894; discont. May 15, 1905

The discovery of lignite coal at Iron Mountain in Saguache County led to the 1880 establishment of Orient City, the Orient Mine's company town. At its peak Orient had a population approaching four hundred with one-fourth working at the mine and cashing their paychecks at the general store at Valley View Hot Springs. A messenger who carried money to meet the payroll hid it in a paper sack stashed under a buggy seat for the ride from Saguache to Valley View.

The Orient Mine was operated on and off for some fifty years by the Colorado Coal & Iron Company, which finally abandoned the workings in the 1930s and dynamited the mine entrance.

Concrete foundations of Orient are scattered through the sagebrush and chamisa. *Kendal Atchison*

Teamsters and Packers Union float, Ouray, July 4, 1906. *Courtesy Denver Public Library Western History Department.*

Ouray

COUNTY: *Ouray*
LOCATION: *36 mi. south of Montrose*
MAP 9
P.O. est. Oct. 28, 1875

The awesome mountains that trap Ouray in a box canyon disgorged the wealth that made Ouray the most elegant mining town of the San Juans. The splendid Gothic Beaumont Hotel with its divided stairway and three-story rotunda, and with a special entrance for ladies, was host to turn-of-the-century luminaries including young Herbert Hoover, a mining engineer. Thomas Walsh gave the town a 7,500-volume library, though local residents claim he was illiterate. Gold from the mountains near Ouray made Tom Walsh a multimillionaire and provided the cash for his daughter to purchase the Hope Diamond.

Under the incandescent lamps and arc lights of Ouray, miners made the rounds of the cribs and the parlor houses, such as the Bon Ton and the Clipper, the thirty saloons, and the many gambling halls. Newsboys hawked papers in dimly lighted faro palaces where inebriated gamblers paid them with $5 gold pieces instead of nickels.

Ouray also was the scene of violence, not merely the saloon brawls and labor confrontations that most mining towns witnessed, but irrationally violent acts. In 1884 when authorities learned a 10-year-old orphan girl had died mysteriously, they dug up the body and discovered the child, who had been suffering from severe frostbite, had been beaten and raped. She died from a blow to her head. When the couple who had abused her was put in jail, incensed citizens stormed the jail and hanged the pair, the only lynching of a woman in Colorado's mining camps.

Above: Floods have plagued Ouray throughout its history. The latest disaster was in 1982. *Courtesy Denver Public Library Western History Department. Below:* Ouray's remote setting was spectacular, but isolation caused problems for the town. *Courtesy Denver Public Library Western History Department.*

The Beaumont Hotel, photographed in the 1890s, was the most elegant hostelry in the San Juan Mountains. *Courtesy Denver Public Library Western History Department.*

In July, 1875, two prospectors found pay dirt near Ouray and named their strike the Mineral Farm because of the claim's rows of parallel veins. Shortly afterward a pair of anglers discovered two deposits they called the Trout and the Fisherman mines. By early 1876, Ouray was shipping ore.

First called Uncompahgre City, Ouray was a thriving town where what little money there was changed hands frequently. Two would-be merchants put up a cracker box for a counter, turned a metal stove into a safe, and set up business selling their stock, which was primarily dried apples and shoestrings. Early church services were held in a saloon with worshippers sitting on beer kegs. "There were no society lines drawn then, and the town not cursed with gossips," the *Ouray Times* reported.

The first Christmas, the miners gathered in a cabin for dinner. Discovering there was no liquor available in town, they doctored a bottle of vinegar, christening the site of the cabin "Vinegar Hill." The following Christmas three hundred people crowded into a butcher shop for a holiday banquet and ball.

By the winter of 1877, however, Ouray was on hard times. Roads were so poor that there was little transportation into Ouray, particularly in the winter, and the inhabitants lived for a time on coffee and bread. "A hot biscuit swallowed then would blister a man's backbone," the *Denver Times* recalled a few years later. Ouray endured periodic shortages. In 1878 when the population was close to eight hundred and the town bragged of three churches, two newspapers, and a millinery shop, a 100-pound sack of flour sold for $10 and sugar for twenty-five cents a pound. In 1879, diners carried their own butter to Ouray's three hotels, carefully unwrapped it to cut off a precious slice, then saved the rest for the next meal. As late as 1880 hungry miners with empty syrup cans and market baskets gathered around wagon teams to buy provisions as soon as they were unloaded.

Without adequate roads, the mines springing up in the Red Mountain, the Uncompahgre, and the Mount Sneffels mining districts could afford to ship only high-grade ore, and the goods freighted in were exorbitantly priced. Mail arrived erratically, delivered by dog sled driven by a man named Daniels, whom the *Times* described as "a good fellow, but an awful liar."

If transportation was a problem for Ouray, it was a challenge for Otto Mears, a diminutive Russian orphan who came to the United States alone at the age of ten. At eleven he joined the California gold rush. Along with his other accomplishments, Mears, a Civil War veteran who had fought Indians under Kit Carson, spoke Ute fluently and was a close friend of Chief Ouray, for whom the town of Ouray was named.

By the time he reached Ouray, Mears was the state's major roadbuilder. He had built a toll road over Poncha Pass, connecting the San Luis valley with Leadville, and a second toll road from Saguache to Lake City. But it was the Ouray roads that made him famous, giving him the title "Pathfinder of the San Juan." In 1881 he built a toll road from Dallas, just north of Ouray, to Telluride. Then he hacked out a road from Ouray to Mount Sneffels and the rich Virginius Mine. His most ambitious road was the twelve-mile "Rainbow Route" from Ouray to Red Mountain, built at a cost of $10,000 per mile. One section cost Mears $1,000 per foot. The narrow shelf road, with sheer dropoffs that even today terrify tourists, enabled the Red Mountain mines to ship the lower-grade ore they had been tossing onto the dumps, justifying Mears's charges for use of the road of $5 per wagon and $1 per saddle horse. While Mears went on to bring railroads into the San Juans, his wagon roads, which are still used as major thoroughfares, were his major contribution.

In 1879, David Frakes Day began publishing the most irreverent newspaper in the West, the *Solid Muldoon.* He wanted a paper that was as solid and honest as the greatly admired prizefighter Bill Muldoon, Day told his wife, explaining the name. (Another version says the paper was named after an early day con, a "petrified" man of cement, dubbed "the Solid Muldoon.")

Day was illiterate when he enlisted in the Union army as a boy; he learned to read and went on to become a writer with wit and biting sarcasm. "The coarse, remorseless scathing wit of the *Muldoon* has made it a terror to pretentious humbugs in politics," noted the *Great Divide* in 1890. "The courage of the Muldoon ... has made it the chief defender of the faith."

Day's favorite targets were politicians. Sena-

Even with 5-cent phone calls and 10-cent beer, tourists were few and far between in 1942. *Courtesy Denver Public Library Western History Department.*

tor Thomas Hart Benton, he noted, "lacked several cogs of connecting." Colorado Senators Henry M. Teller and Thomas M. Bowen proved "the office of United States senator is not too sacred to be prostituted." Day's victims were outraged, but though he once fought forty-seven libel suits at one time, he never paid out a penny.

He castigated Silverton as the scourge of the San Juans. "A novel suit will be tried before Justice Cobb on Saturday. A former landlord sues one of the scarlet daughters of prosperity for a month's rent, and she brings a contra bill for wear and tear. This is getting to be as hard a town as Silverton," Day wrote.

He was not above creating stories to fool his readers. On a trip to England, he sent back breathless dispatches of his meeting with Queen Victoria, who, he assured readers, was devoted to him and wept with grief when he left. If it had not been for Day's wife, he wrote, he might then be the prince consort. "There is reason to suspect . . . that this bold assertion is false," the *Great Divide* warned.

The silver panic of 1893 brought a depression to Ouray, but it lasted only a few years until Thomas Walsh discovered the great gold-producing Camp Bird, a few miles from Ouray.

The Beaumont was kept alive by summer tourists in 1965, but it is no longer in operation. *Sandra Dallas*

Camp Bird wealth combined with tourism kept Ouray alive for another half century.

Pandora

COUNTY: *San Miguel*
LOCATION: *1 mi. east of Telluride*
MAP 10
P.O. est. Aug. 5, 1881; discont. Oct. 15, 1902

The town of Pandora was named for the Pandora Mine, discovered in the 1870s, but it was the immense Smuggler-Union Mill that domi-

nated the community. The mill processed ore from the combined Smuggler and Union mines high in the mountains beyond the town. Total output of the Smuggler-Union before it closed in the 1970s, was well over $50 million.

Despite its unprepossessing appearance today, Pandora has a dramatic history of snowslides, fire, and union violence. In 1902 a manager of the Smuggler-Union Mine, Arthur Collins, was murdered while he sat in his Pandora home. The assassination was blamed on the Western Federation of Miners, which had called a strike the year before to protest wages of less than $3 a day.

Collins was replaced by Bulkeley Wells, a wickedly handsome man whose father-in-law owned controlling interest in the Smuggler-Union. Wells, who moved into the manager's house with his butler, had equally stormy relations with the union, and in 1908 he barely survived an attempted assassination when a time bomb placed under his bed destroyed the house but threw Wells out into the yard uninjured.

Wells, who ran the Smuggler-Union from 1902 to 1923, had an intimate friendship with Mrs. Crawford Hill, leader of Denver society. Mrs. Hill, whose husband was a prominent mining man, hung a life-size portrait of Wells in her Denver home. When Wells, who had been divorced in 1918, remarried in 1923, Mrs. Hill threatened to ruin him. From that point Wells's fortune declined, and eight years later he committed suicide. Pandora's future was equally black. Today it is mostly a mobile home camp.

Rocks outline the graves in the Parkville cemetery. *Kendal Atchison*

Parkville

152
P

COUNTY: *Summit*
LOCATION: *10 mi. northeast of Breckenridge*
MAP 4
P.O. est. Dec. 13, 1861; discont. Oct. 22, 1866

Now buried under tons of mining debris, the town of Parkville was once the county seat of Summit County, a contender for the territorial capital, and the site of one of the first three Masonic Lodges in Colorado. All that remains today is a cemetery, its graves outlined by stones and marked with stick crosses.

Parkville's short, intense life began in 1860 with discovery of gold at Georgia Gulch. Within months, the hillsides were stripped of timber to build houses, saloons, stores, billiard halls, and even a mint. Most of the two thousand residents were miners, though some specialized in "loafing, saloon-keeping and peddling," according to a newspaper account. For excitement, the miners flocked to see actress Mlle. Rose Haydee, or the theatrical company of Mike Dougherty and Jack Langrishe, or watched Confederate and Union sympathizers fight it out.

Elections were equally entertaining. Tom Miller, a Kansan who was a candidate for county attorney, told a Parkville crowd that as attorney for a Kansas county he had won convictions in every case but one, which he lost on a technicality.

"What was the technicality?" shouted a rival for the office.

Miller studied his opponent for a moment then replied: "The mob broke into jail and lynched him." Miller won.

Pearl

COUNTY: *Jackson*
LOCATION: *19 mi. northwest of Cowdrey*
MAP 12
P.O. est. Jan. 19, 1889; discont. Aug. 30, 1919

The discovery of copper ore with traces of gold and silver sent miners scurrying to Pearl, a town just south of the Wyoming border in northwestern Colorado. Outcroppings were first spotted in the 1890s, but the rush did not begin until after the turn of the century when the Pearl Mining and Townsite Company established the town of Pearl.

Within a year or two, Pearl had a population of several hundred, three saloons, a newspaper, and a hotel, as well as the backing of Denver capitalist Charles Boettcher. "Why should not Pearl be an outstanding success! Why should not a townsite like this double and double again in its money value?" asked a brochure printed by the townsite company. Why not? Poor ore.

Perigo, looking up Gamble Gulch. *Courtesy Denver Public Library Western History Department.*

Perigo

COUNTY: *Gilpin*
LOCATION: *4 mi. southwest of Rollinsville*
MAP 2
P.O. est. March 2, 1895; discont. March 15, 1905

In the winter of 1859, a prospector named A. D. Gambell thawed out a promising shovelful of dirt over a fire and panned out a few flakes of gold. He collected a sizable amount of dust, and when he went to Denver in the spring and bought supplies with the gold, a group of prospectors followed him back to Gambell (now Gamble) Gulch to start the town of Perigo.

The Perigo and the Gold Dirt were the two major mines, with ore assaying at close to $18 per ton. The ore was "something marvelous," noted writer Frank Fossett.

At the turn of the century when most of the mines in the area were played out, Perigo still had a population of a hundred. The miners left soon after that, letting the town that once housed several hundred decay into a few foundations and a sway-back building.

Pieplant

COUNTY: *Gunnison*
LOCATION: *15 mi. north of Tin Cup*
MAP 8
P.O. est. Aug. 24, 1904; discont. May 14, 1906

Shortly after the turn of the century, the Woods Mining Company established a 200-ton-per-day stamp mill for gold ore near a little settlement in Taylor Park called Pieplant for the rhubarb plants that grew wild along Pieplant Creek. At one time Pieplant had one hundred residents, but today a cow camp stands on the site.

Pitkin

COUNTY: *Gunnison*
LOCATION: *6 mi. northeast of Ohio City*
MAP 8
P.O. est. Sept. 1, 1879

"We have three women, eight children, three fiddlers, 180 dogs, two burros, and one cat, and need a newspaper and a sawmill," wrote an early resident of Pitkin about 1880. A year later the

A lonely cabin remains in Pieplant, now a cow camp. *Kendal Atchison*

The Pitkin town hall was built in 1900. *Kendal Atchison*   Pitkin Community Church, 1966. *Sandra Dallas*

A bunch of the boys in front of a Placerville saloon. *Courtesy Denver Public Library Western History Department.*

town boasted 1,500 residents, a number of stores, the *Pitkin Independent,* and women to meet every need, from homemaker to hooker.

Founded as Quartzville, the community changed its name in 1879 to Pitkin, ostensibly in honor of Governor Frederick W. Pitkin, though the real reason for the change undoubtedly was to win whatever political plums the governor cared to bestow on his namesake.

For a time political patronage was unnecessary. Pitkin thrived on rich mineral deposits—the Little Tycoon, the Nest Egg, the Little Roy, and the Fairview mines.

Crime went unchecked. "Nowhere has prejudice and avarice and jealousy done so much mischief as here," lamented the *Rocky Mountain News.* After a railroad worker shot a teamster over a card game, the murderer was "jerked to Jesus," according to a newspaper, in the first legal hanging in the county. Even the respective editors of the *Independent* and the *Pitkin Mining News* sparked dissension by calling each other thugs and blackguards in print, questioning each other's ethics and parentage.

The mines did not last for long. Ore bodies proved to be poorer than expected, and demonetization of silver in 1893 dealt a blow from which Pitkin never recovered.

The town also was hit by disastrous fires. A

fire in 1898 wiped out the business portion of the city, leaving $100,000 worth of property in ashes. "The horses in the livery stable . . . screamed like children as the heat roasted their flesh to a crisp," noted the *Denver Times,* which called the fire suspicious and said authorities were following a "clew."

Five years later another fire wiped out an entire block. The "clews" there were obvious. A drunk with a candle had set the fire.

After the mines closed, logging and the state fish hatchery and eventually land development kept the town of Pitkin going.

Placerville

COUNTY: *San Miguel*
LOCATION: *17 mi. northwest of Telluride*
MAP 10
P.O. est. April 22, 1878

In 1876 a group of prospectors under the direction of S. H. Baker left Del Norte to pan the San Miguel River. They found float, starting a rush that led to the establishment of a settlement called Placerville. In the 1880s a hill near the town was placer mined by hydraulic pressure.

Despite the initial good showing, the placer

deposits played out, and the town declined until the Rio Grande Southern laid tracks for its Telluride-to-Ridgway route. When the railroad built its depot a mile upstream, the population of Placerville moved the town to the station. Placerville became a transportation center, first for the mines and later for the ranchers who made the town a major western slope cattle-shipping point.

Platoro

COUNTY: *Conejos*
LOCATION: *13 mi. southwest of Jasper*
MAP 11
P.O. est. March 12, 1888; discont. April 30, 1919

Named for the Spanish *plata* (silver) and *oro* (gold), Platoro never quite lived up to its ambitious name. The town, which flourished in the 1880s and 1890s, had modest production from the Puzzler Chief, the Puzzler Number One, the Last Chance, and the Pass-Me-By.

In 1893 the *Denver Republican* reported a general merchandise store, "Crosswy [*sic*] &

Williamson," had been attached by a creditor who was owed $463.10. "The cause of the failure is the prevailing hard times," noted the paper.

Platoro does slightly better today when its rows of neat cabins are rented during the summer for the *plata* and *oro* of Texas tourists.

Poncha Springs

COUNTY: *Chaffee*
LOCATION: *5 mi. west of Salida*
MAP 13
P.O. est. April 22, 1868 as South Arkansas

For a bucolic little town, Poncha Springs had its share of calamities. A series of fires, several set by arsonists, plagued it from the beginning. In an attempt to make the town a pleasant place, Poncha Springs elected to keep the Denver & Rio Grande's railroad shops out, only to discover the town's economy followed the railroad to nearby Salida. When the town was only two years old, Poncha's founder, James True, was charged with murder, dividing the sentiments of the residents.

Platoro has changed little since this photograph was taken in 1913. *Courtesy Denver Public Library Western History Department.*

The Poncha Springs school, shown in 1885, still stands though it has been many years since any classes were held in it. *Courtesy Public Library Western History Department.*

The Jackson Hotel. Its registration book lists the names of Billy the Kid (William Bonney) and H. A. W. Tabor. *Kendal Atchison*

A Querida smokestack. *Kendal Atchison*

True laid out Poncha Springs in 1879 and stayed on to become a banker. A falling-out with his business partners made him wary, and when his bank caught fire and he found an old adversary fighting the flames, True accused the man of arson and shot him.

There was no question the fire was arson, because the town marshal later discovered a coal-oil-soaked gunny sack in the burned building. The question was who set the fire. True blamed the murdered man. The man's friends charged True, claiming he had set the fire to cover up bad management and losses. The jury believed True and acquitted him.

That was high crime for a town that viewed itself as a pleasant resort. Entrepreneurs built lodgings to attract invalids to the dozens of hot springs in the area, claiming miraculous cures. The most famous of these hotels was the Jackson, which still stands.

The Jackson, a way station rather than a resort, claimed a run of prominent guests, including Susan B. Anthony and Evalyn Walsh McLean, and the names of Frank and Jesse James and William Bonney (Billy the Kid) are on the register, though the signatures are suspect. H. A. W. Tabor was a regular guest, who, legend says, slept in a nightshirt with diamond buttons, which he handed to the proprietor each morning to be kept in a safe.

Querida

COUNTY: *Custer*
LOCATION: *9 mi. east of Westcliffe*
MAP 13
P.O. est. Jan. 12, 1880; discont. May 14, 1906

When Edmund Chase Bassick, an inquisitive miner, assayed an abandoned prospect hole that piqued his curiosity each day as he passed it on his way to work, he found he had a bonanza. The ore was so rich that "high graders" stole it to salt other mines, and legitimately mined ore was transported to Westcliffe with six guards carrying sawed-off shotguns.

Bassick took some $500,000 in gold and silver from his Bassick Mine before selling out to a syndicate in 1879. He retained a small interest in the new mining company.

The town that grew up around the mine was called Bassickville, but the name was changed to

Redcliff, after the turn of the century. *Courtesy Denver Public Library Western History Department.*

Querida, apparently at the instigation of David Livingstone, known as "Little Dunk," who claimed to be the nephew of the African explorer, Dr. David Livingstone. "He was suited to the early struggling days that tried men's souls and stomachs, when pioneers had to live on faith and venison (principally venison)," noted O. L. Baskin in his 1881 *History of the Arkansas Valley, Colorado.*

Livingstone was one of five hundred residents who lived in Querida at its peak in the early 1880s. In 1885 the Bassick, plagued with poor management, went into receivership. The mine was under litigation for fourteen years, until it reverted to Bassick's heirs. By then, Querida was well on its way to becoming a ghost town. Mining activity picked up in the early 1900s, but Querida never regained its former glory.

Redcliff

COUNTY: *Eagle*
LOCATION: *22 mi. north of Leadville*
MAP 5
P.O. est. Feb. 4, 1880 as Red Cliff

After a Leadville hunter bragged he had spotted outcroppings with iron stains similar to Leadville's rich ore, a group of Leadville miners grubstaked two hearty prospectors, who set out in the winter of 1878 to file a claim. They returned in time to celebrate Christmas with their partners, toasting the discovery of their Little Ollie Mine. In March the men set out again with sleds and snowshoes, followed by a good portion of Leadville. By late spring there was a rush of miners to what was called the Battle Mountain mining district and the little settlement named Redcliff for the nearby red quartzite cliffs.

Nearly as numerous as mining claims were Redcliff saloons. The *Leadville Herald Democrat* reported nineteen saloon men in operation, mostly working out of tents, with bars improvised from barrels, boxes, and even sleds, "dealing out lightning and essential oils of fearful and wonderful concoction."

Many of the miners returned to Leadville during the winter of 1879-80 because of the fearsome snows, which as late as the 1960s were causing avalanches in Redcliff, and because of the lack of lumber. But they returned in force in the spring, and the Star Hotel was jammed with miners and capitalists who paid handsomely to sleep in rooms delineated by cloth partitions. The establishment of a sawmill led to a building boom. Before long Redcliff had a brass band, a jail, and a newspaper, the *Eagle River Shaft,* whose editor published the truth despite horse-whippings and—even worse—the lack of newsprint. When the snow prevented him from receiving a load of newsprint, he printed on wallpaper.

Redcliff grew steadily despite fires—three in one month in 1883—and other setbacks. The population, which was 250 in early 1880, rose to 400 by the mid-1880s after Redcliff was named Eagle County seat (a designation it lost to the town of Eagle in 1921).

Never a very elegant town, despite boasting a bank and three hotels—the Star, the Southern, and the Mountain House—Redcliff nevertheless was a permanent town, depending on mining for nearly a hundred years. In 1977, New Jersey Zinc Company closed the last mine in the area.

Red Mountain

COUNTY: *Ouray*
LOCATION: *13 mi. south of Ouray*
MAP 9
P.O. est. Jan. 29, 1883; discont. Feb. 28, 1913

Red Mountain was located on Saturday, January 6, 1883. On Sunday the first load of sales merchandise was shipped to the site, and by Monday ten commercial lots had been sold and six houses were under construction.

The settlement was part of the Red Mountain mining district, which included the towns of Ironton and Guston and a number of rich mines, including the Yankee Girl, which produced some $3 million in silver.

Red Mountain, which had a population of a thousand or more, was the roughest town in the district. Saloons did triple duty as courtrooms and theaters as well as drinking establishments. When the Florence Hayden Dramatic Company performed in Red Mountain in 1891, curtains closed off the glasses and bottles in the saloon where the production was held, and

"Springtime" in Red Mountain in the 1890s. *Courtesy Denver Public Library Western History Department.*

Red Mountain mining structures. *Kendal Atchison*

kegs and barrels were moved out of sight in deference to the ladies attending the performance. The play was the temperance production, "Ten Nights in a Bar-Room."

"Red Mountain was the mecca for all who were allured into the San Juan by the fickle goddess of fortune," wrote the *Denver Times*. With demonetization of silver, "the hard-fisted, big-heart miners hit the trail," the paper continued. Population dwindled to forty by 1896.

In 1901 a few "big-heart" miners returned when the National Belle, the Guston, and a dozen other mines were consolidated. "Unprecedented prosperity is in store for Red Mountain," predicted the *Times*. "Red Mountain will now bloom as she did when we had silver at the old time prices." But she never did.

Redstone

COUNTY: *Pitkin*
LOCATION: *16 mi. south of Carbondale*
MAP 6
P.O. est. May 19, 1898; discont. Aug. 1, 1962

Among nineteenth-century robber barons, John Cleveland Osgood was an original—an indus-trialist who built a utopian village for his workers then acted as apologist for coal interests after the infamous Ludlow massacre of coal workers' families near Trinidad. He was an intensely private man of Victorian sensibilities who married a series of headlines-grabbing women. Osgood's first wife, who fictionalized their marriage in torrid novels, was nearly thrown out of the Hotel Colorado in Glenwood Springs for improper behavior.

Osgood formed the Colorado Fuel Company —later the basis of CF & I Steel Corporation— in 1884 to exploit rich coal deposits along the Crystal River. By the turn of the century he was a feudal lord, master of the village of Redstone, which housed his workers. Tempered in part by his second wife, a mysterious foreigner who was tinged with scandal but whose kindness caused her to be dubbed "Lady Bountiful," Osgood was a benevolent despot. Instead of a grimy coal village where employees were bound to the coal company by means of excessive rents and a usurious company store, Redstone was a utopian town of neat pastel-colored cottages built for families and a fine clubhouse for unmarried men. Osgood provided a theater, a library, an inn with a clock tower, and a bar, which went dry

Cleveholm sits in baronial splendor behind an enormous expanse of lawn. *Kendal Atchison*

Massive gates separate the Cleveholm estate from the village of Redstone. *Kendal Atchison*

Every mining camp with any pretensions had a restaurant named either Delmonico's or the Bon Ton. This one was in Rico. *Courtesy Denver Public Library Western History Department.*

for a time when Osgood decided demon rum worked to the detriment of his employees. Later they persuaded him a mug of beer was not such a bad thing after a day in the mines. In addition, Redstone had Lady Bountiful, who dispersed presents to village children at Christmas.

Egalitarianism had its limits, of course. The Osgoods could not be expected to live among their retainers. They built for themselves an impressive manor house, called Cleveholm, a mile from the village. It was a $2.5 million English Tudor country home with a massive expanse of land rolling down to the Crystal River. There they lived in baronial splendor with Tiffany lamps and elephant-hide wall coverings, entertaining guests such as Theodore Roosevelt and John D. Rockefeller, Jr.

Osgood lost interest in Redstone about the time his marriage to Lady Bountiful was dissolved, and boarded up the house in 1913, coming home only to die in 1926. Eventually most of the mines were closed, the village was sold off, and the third Mrs. Osgood, some fifty years her husband's junior, rid herself of Cleveholm. The estate remains in private hands.

Rico

COUNTY: *Dolores*
LOCATION: *36 mi. northeast of Dolores*
MAP 10
P.O. est. Aug. 25, 1879

Nearly $50 million in ore was taken out of the Enterprise, the Grand View, the Johnny Bull,

the Puzzle, the Parole, the Uncle Ned, the Hog Back, and other mines of the area around Rico, which in 1879 was named, appropriately, after the Spanish word for "rich."

In 1878 prospectors struck pay dirt near Rico and the boom was on. Miners crowded into Rico during 1879, and in a single month more than a hundred cabins and twenty-nine commercial buildings, a fourth of them saloons, were built. The first murder took place in August, 1879, when "Kid" McGoldrick killed a man called Frenchy. Frenchy was the first to be put to rest in the new cemetery, but he was not alone for long. A few days later a local saloonkeeper accidentally shot and killed himself and was buried near Frenchy. More than thirteen men were murdered in one infamous alley.

When news of a Ute uprising reached Rico, the women were moved into a log cabin while the men were assigned guard duty around town. Several of them courageously protected Lovejoy's Saloon, barricading it with beer kegs and bales of hay. When a pack train arrived in town after dark, one well-fortified guard was so startled by the sound of hooves that he shot a burro. The only human casualty was the guard, who was badly beaten by the packer.

In January, 1880, Rico was snowbound, and the miners ran out of whiskey and tobacco. They turned to food, and within a few weeks, the town was faced with a famine. Meals were selling for up to $5. The first packer who reached town in April sold hundredweight sacks of flour as fast as he could unload them from his jacks, at $35 each.

Teams haul freight to Rico mines. *Courtesy Colorado Historical Society.*

Only the strongest and fleetest young men were allowed to join the fire department to save the town from conflagrations and to defend local honor in hose cart races, such as this one in 1886. *Courtesy Colorado Historical Society.*

A Victorian relic from mining days. *Kendal Atchison*

By summer Rico was booming with four hundred houses and another four hundred under construction. There were six general stores, four butcher shops, three blacksmith shops, one tent church, two dance halls, and too many saloons to count. Lots that sold a few months earlier for $75 were going for $2,000.

The boom leveled off in the mid-1880s as production fell, but picked up again with the 1887 discovery of the Enterprise by David Swickhimer. A onetime sheriff whose wife, Laura, ran a restaurant, Swickhimer was convinced the Enterprise contained ore, but he lacked the money to develop it. As he was about to give up, his wife won several thousand dollars in a lottery and gave her husband the money to continue with the mine.

He struck silver, and the Swickhimers made millions from the Enterprise. Laura Swickhimer later lost her money in Denver real estate, while her husband backed the Rico State Bank, which failed in 1907, and his fortune went to pay off depositors. The two, who eventually were divorced, ended up with little more than they had had before the Enterprise discovery.

At the turn of the century, most of the mines in the area were consolidated into the United Rico Mining Company. By the 1920s the population, which once reached six thousand, had dropped to three hundred. Rico's remote location made it a hangout for horse thieves as late as 1920. Posses in cars and on motorcycles eventually routed them.

Ridgway

COUNTY: *Ouray*
LOCATION: *11 mi. north of Ouray*
MAP 9
P.O. est. Oct. 1, 1890

Ridgway, built at the junction of the Denver & Rio Grande's Montrose-to-Ouray line and the Rio Grande Southern's Telluride route, was named for D & RG official R. M. Ridgway.

Ridgway was, of course, a transportation center, supplying the mines with equipment and hauling out ore and concentrate. Founded in 1890, Ridgway was a prosperous town of substantial stone and brick buildings and Victorian houses, but there were saloons and pool halls

Ridgway school, 1891. *Courtesy Denver Public Library Western History Department.*

Ridgway buildings, 1981. *Kendal Atchison*

as well, where suckers could be fleeced through fixed horse races or enticed into lion hunting. A mountain lion was tethered behind one Ridgway saloon and released once a week for a lion hunt. Once the lion was captured, he was hauled back to Ridgway for another week's captivity.

Not all of Ridgway's con men were in the saloons. In 1931, Ridgway bank president C. M. Stanwood invested the bank's deposits, along with negotiable securities he found in safety deposit boxes, in stocks. When the market dropped, Stanwood and the bank's patrons were wiped out. Depositors later recovered some of their money, but those whose securities were stolen got nothing.

When the mining dropped off Ridgway declined. In an effort to use its rails more economically, the Rio Grande Southern introduced the "Galloping Goose," a centaur-like amalgamation of automobile front and boxcar behind that swooped down the rails between Dolores and Ridgway. Both the Goose and the tracks were dispensed with about 1950.

Today the business blocks are boarded up, and mobile homes coexist with deserted houses overrun with cascades of yellow and orange rose bushes gone wild.

Rollinsville

COUNTY: *Gilpin*
LOCATION: *14 mi. north of Black Hawk*
MAP 2
P.O. est. Jan. 31, 1871

Pioneer John Q. A. Rollins built a hotel of sorts on the road from Central City to Middle Park in the 1860s, and established the town of Rollinsville. The town was to become a center for mining, farming, and railroad activity.

Rollins was no slouch. Along with operating the Rollins House, which catered to travelers as well as to social-climbing Central City residents, he acquired mining claims and ranch land. By 1885, when George A. Crofutt visited the area, Rollinsville had 170 residents, a stamp mill, and a concentrator. The area boasted 1,100 acres of tilled land, another 1,000 acres of timberland, and 400 acres of patented placer-mining land.

Within a few years, however, things began to slide. In 1889 the *San Francisco Chronicle* reported that Rollinsville "was a very becoming place in 1871, and town lots were at a premium. Hundreds of people were proud to call it their home, and it was thought to be founded on rock.

The Perigo Mine office *(left)* and the Gooch Hotel in Rollinsville in the 1880s. *Courtesy Denver Public Library Western History Department.*

Romley's tattered structures are painted red. *Kendal Atchison*

Today the rock is still there, but the population has fled." Things picked up again after the turn of the century when the Moffat Short Line laid tracks adjacent to the town.

At one time early in its history, Rollinsville prohibited saloons and liquor sales. Today such activities appear to be the town's major support.

Romley

COUNTY: *Chaffee*
LOCATION: *3 mi. south of Saint Elmo*
MAP 7
P.O. est. Jan. 15, 1886; discont. Oct. 30, 1924

First called Murphy's Switch, then Morley, then —possibly because of a typographical error— mysteriously transformed into Romley, this little way station was the shipping point for the silver-rich Mary Murphy Mine a mile away. The Mary Murphy, legend says, was named by a grateful miner for the nurse who restored him to health, though there is no explanation for the name of the nearby Pat Murphy Mine.

The Mary Murphy, which produced millions of dollars in ore was sold in 1904 to an English

syndicate. The mine, which peaked before World War I, operated intermittently until World War II.

Tragedy stalked Romley. In 1908 a fire, started by sparks from a Colorado & Southern Railway engine, destroyed most of the town. It was rebuilt and the buildings were painted bright red. Then in 1912 food poisoning, possibly from canned spinach, killed five men at the Mary Murphy boardinghouse. When the remains of the dinner were thrown on the Murphy garbage dump, five burros died.

Rosita

COUNTY: *Custer*
LOCATION: *12 mi. southeast of Westcliffe*
MAP 13
P.O. est. July 8, 1874; discont. 1967

Rosita "did not amount to much of a town until 1874 when it went up with a rush," noted O. L. Baskin's *History of the Arkansas Valley, Colorado.* By then it had "dropped and become duller," Baskin wrote, but in the mid-1870s Rosita was a bustling, hell-raising town of fifteen hun-

Rosita in 1888, after it became "duller." *Courtesy Denver Public Library Western History Department.*

Rosita, 1981. *Kendal Atchison*

Laundry on the clothes lines indicates it was wash day at Russell Gulch. *Courtesy Denver Public Library Western History Department.*

dred inhabitants, who included three assayers, three lawyers, three ministers, six doctors, and one real estate agent, but fortunately, noted the *Golden Transcript,* "no sewing machine or insurance man."

The town, once the seat of Custer County, was founded in 1873 by three prospectors, and within six months, it had a population of five hundred fighting for space in sixty log cabins and a hotel. Space was more readily available at the many saloons, which before long were supplied with beer from a local brewery. Rosita had class. When a vigilante group hanged a pair of town toughs, legend says, it sent out printed invitations.

The Pocahantas was Rosita's most infamous mine. Part-interest in the mine once was purchased for a $20 freight bill. During its heyday the mine became the center of a squabble among its various owners, one of whom was the local banker. The banker, who turned out to be a con man with an impressive record, eventually looted the Rosita bank, leaving only eighty cents.

Much of the town was burned in 1881, but enough was rebuilt to give Rosita a curious rebirth in the 1950s as a movie colony. Metro-Goldwyn-Mayer rearranged several of the town's buildings, refurbished a carpenter Gothic mansion as a rooming house, and filmed a Robert Taylor movie, *Saddle the Wind,* in Rosita.

Movie making proved more illusive than mining. No more movies were filmed at Rosita, which today is comprised of a few sloping structures and yellow mine dumps.

Russell Gulch

COUNTY: *Gilpin*
LOCATION: *3 mi. southwest of Central City*
MAP 2
P.O. est. Sept. 29, 1879; discont. June, 1943

William Green Russell led a group of prospectors to the confluence of the South Platte and the Cherry Creek to pan gold—a settlement that later became Denver. When he heard of the gold discoveries made by his fellow Georgian, John Gregory, at Mountain City, Russell hastened to

that community. He settled a few miles above Gregory Diggings in Russell Gulch and began to placer mine the rich earth.

By the end of 1860 the town of Russell Gulch had a school with more than a dozen students and a church with services almost every Sunday. A *Rocky Mountain News* correspondent wrote: "Last Sabbath the Rev. Dr. Rankin delivered a sermon to a crowded audience—crowded because the house was so small, not because there were so many present."

More successful was a grand ball held two years later when the settlement had grown to include several stores, a billiard saloon, and a blacksmith shop. Balls continued to be popular even when mining was not. In 1899 a group of Italian and Austrian miners held a dance to replenish the coffers of the fraternal American Alpine Society, and the next year a group of amiable young ladies called the Merry Milkmaids threw a dance at the Elks Club.

Russell Gulch peaked early with a population of 2,500. Its mines were meager and played out quickly, though there was some mining into the twentieth century. In the 1920s, bootlegging replaced mining in Russell Gulch's economy when scofflaws used abandoned mines to produce their moonshine.

Above: A Russell Gulch school class in the late 1890s. *Courtesy Denver Public Library Western History Department. Below:* Masonry walls at Russell Gulch. *Kendal Atchison*

Saint Elmo in 1964 looked much as it did when the Stark family lived there. *Sandra Dallas*

Saint Elmo

COUNTY: *Chaffee*
LOCATION: *17 mi. west of Nathrop*
MAP 7
P.O. est. June 23, 1880; discont. October, 1952

With its doors still locked against intruders and its windows boarded up to hide the contents inside, Saint Elmo is the most haunting of Colorado's ghost towns. An eccentric pair of brothers and their sister—Roy, Tony, and Annie Stark—ran the sour-smelling general store until the last of the trio died in the 1950s. There, amidst faded tins of outdated food and stale tobacco, they railed against author Muriel Sibell Wolle for inferring in *Stampede to Timberline* that Saint Elmo was a ghost town. It was Mrs. Wolle,

they claimed, not the musty smelling Starks or their tattered store, that drove away business.

The Stark clan, who built the first house in Saint Elmo, once had been part of Saint Elmo's elite, a high-class group that attended church regularly. One member of Saint Elmo society, Fred Brush, was so upstanding that when his drugstore and post office burned, he grabbed the mail and let the liquor and cigars perish. Even the town's name showed class. Originally called Forest City, the settlement, because of post office objections, was renamed Saint Elmo, after the title of a romantic nineteenth-century novel.

Founded in 1880 and laid out in six feet of snow, the town provided for the miners who worked in the nearby mines. When the Alpine tunnel was under construction, Saint Elmo, as

The thirty minutes has long since passed. *Sandra Dallas*

the largest town in the area, was the scene of raunchy Saturday night sprees. The town was always crowded, and accommodations were scarce. An 1880 traveler recalled he and his companions "put up at the best hotel the place

could afford, which was, in fact, the only one, at three dollars per day. . . . When we asked about a bed and a room by ourselves, the land-lord told us the best he could do was to give us a bed and draw a chalk mark around us for a room."

Accommodations were more abundant later in the year when the *Denver Tribune* reported three hotels, five restaurants, two sawmills, and several stores.

Population peaked at nearly two thousand in the mid-1880s, when the decline began. Fire destroyed the business section in 1890, and the town was never entirely rebuilt. The population dwindled to sixty-four in 1900, to seven in 1930, and finally to one in the 1950s. When the last of the Starks died, Saint Elmo, with no one left to protest the designation, became a true ghost town.

Saints John

COUNTY: *Summit*
LOCATION: *1 mi. southwest of Montezuma*
MAP 4
P.O. est. Aug. 8, 1876; discont. Feb. 1, 1881

Silver was discovered in Colorado in 1863 near Saints John by John Coley, and the town that grew up around the discovery was first called

Saints John, 1981. *Kendal Atchison*

Coleyville. But Freemasons renamed the site Saints John in 1867 after their patron saints, John the Baptist and John the Evangelist.

Saints John was bizarre for a remote Colorado mining camp. It had a 350-volume library, no saloon, and the mine manager's house was furnished in elegant English furniture. The high moral atmosphere was a reflection of the Saints John mine ownership, the Boston Mining Company. Saints John was a one-company town, and its fortunes paralleled those of the Boston company. The decline of silver meant the demise of Saints John.

Nearly as devastating was the weather. Avalanches ripped out cabins. One Saints John resident sawed off a tree where it stuck out of the snow only to discover when the snow melted that the stump was more than twelve feet high. The altitude caused other problems. Beans for Sunday dinner had to be started by Friday noon.

Salina

COUNTY: *Boulder*
LOCATION: *8 mi. west of Boulder*
MAP 3
P.O. est. Nov. 19, 1874; discont. Jan. 1, 1925

In 1874 a group of men from Kansas discovered ore in Gold Run Gulch and named their Camp Salina, for their Kansas home. Within a year the town boasted a chlorination works, a post office, a blacksmith shop, an assay office, one store, three boardinghouses, and more than a dozen homes. By the time guidebook writer George A. Crofutt visited Salina in the early 1880s, the town also had a toll gate with a charge that Crofutt noted was excessive.

There were several camps of Chinese who worked the gravel beds of Four Mile Creek near Salina. Anglo miners worked in the Black Swan Mill, whose ruins stand below the town.

Salina residents erected a substantial church, which still holds services, and a schoolhouse. "There are not many children in Salina," reported the *Sunshine Courier* in 1875. "But if the citizens are diligent, I think we will be able to keep the school marm busy."

The Salina String Band tunes up at the Model Laundry. Note the unusual instrument leaning against the house. *Courtesy Denver Public Library Western History Department.*

Silver Cliff

COUNTY: *Custer*
LOCATION: *1 mi. east of Westcliffe*
MAP 13
P.O. est. Oct. 30, 1878

Discovery of horn silver in the Wet Mountain valley in 1878 led to the founding of Silver Cliff, a splendid town with a fine reputation for rich and raucous living.

Silver Cliff feasted off the productive mines around it—the Bull Domingo, the Racine Boy, the Plata Verde, and the Milkmaid. Within weeks of Silver Cliff's founding, miners were fighting over the two hundred dwellings that had been hastily erected, as well as tents and even wagon covers. A 25- by 100-foot lot went for $500. The town, the third largest in the state and a contender for the state capital, had 5,083 residents in 1880, and "it is a remarkable fact that Silver Cliff is the only city in the state that proved to have, by actual count, the population claimed," puffed one of the Cliff's eleven newspapers.

Silver Cliff residents, in addition, had their pick of twenty grocery stores and two banks, and visitors chose between "three excellent hotels and seven inferior ones," according to the *Golden Transcript.* If they were fastidious, they could stop at the Eureka Bath Rooms in the basement of the Joplin Drugstore before being tempted at the three dance halls and twenty-five saloons.

"A blast in the Racine Boy mine yesterday threw a large rock very high that fell with considerable force in front of the Little Chief saloon,

Above: Silver Cliff, probably during a Fourth of July parade. *Courtesy Silver Cliff Museum. Below:* Finish line of a Silver Cliff footrace. *Courtesy Silver Cliff Museum.*

Above: Hose carts decorated for a holiday. *Courtesy Silver Cliff Museum. Left:* The old firehouse is now a museum. *Kendal Atchison*

barely missing Harry Dougan," reported the *Daily Prospect* in 1880. It was enough to keep Harry Dougan and his friends safely inside the swinging doors.

One of Silver Cliff's hapless miners was Captain Joseph Raphael DeLamar, a onetime ship's captain who invested in the Terrible and other mines in the Silver Cliff district. His investments failed in the early 1880s, and with debts piling up, the captain skipped out.

In Idaho his luck changed. He bought up mining claims in an area south of Boise, eventually called DeLamar, and made a fortune. When he died in 1918, he left a thirty-million-dollar estate. But before that, when the money began to come in, DeLamar sought out the Silver Cliff merchants left holding his bills and paid them off.

Silver Cliff boasted two fire companies, the Robinson Hook and Ladder Company and the McAuley Hose Company. The McAuley Company claimed to have set a world record for

Silver Plume

COUNTY: *Clear Creek*
LOCATION: *2 mi. west of Georgetown*
MAP 1
P.O. est. April 7, 1871 as Brownsville

Saint Patrick's Church in Silver Plume is a combination of two buildings. *Sandra Dallas*

The search for silver along Clear Creek in the 1860s led to the settlement of Silver Plume, whose cluster of sloping, weathered buildings give it an air of bygone splendor today. The town was named for a plume-like shadow of ore on a mine dump (or for a plume-like formation of silver, or for Charlie Plume, an early prospector).

From the early 1870s when the silver mines began producing until the 1893 collapse of silver, Silver Plume boomed. At night hundreds of men swarmed out of the mines and made their way to the saloons and billiard halls on Main Street, their lanterns twinkling along the hillsides like falling stars. Nine saloons were lined up in a row on Main Street, where even in the morning "groups of stalwart men sit around in social circles. The reader must not confound these men with hoodlums, as they are miners who have been working on the night shift, and thus spend their few leisure hours between working and sleeping in discussing the topics of the day," reported the *Colorado Miner.*

In addition to a generous selection of saloons, the two thousand residents of Silver Plume had access to three Chinese laundries, three shoe stores, two barbershops, a weekly newspaper called the *Jack Rabbit,* and two churches, Methodist and Catholic.

In 1884, Silver Plume was hit by fire, which started in a saloon and killed the proprietor. The town formed a bucket brigade of men passing leather sacks of water. The women and children knelt in front of the Catholic church asking for divine intercession. When the fire, which destroyed most of the business section, stopped just short of the kneeling supplicants, grateful residents enlarged the church and later sent to Italy for a pair of splendid hand-carved doors.

Silver Plume's fine brick school building— today a museum—owes its existence to another fire. Designed by Denver architect William Quayle, it was built in 1894 after fire destroyed the first one. The new school was decidedly larger than its predecessor, which had been too small

pulling a hose cart five hundred feet and hooking up the hose. But even the fire companies could not prevent Silver Cliff's disastrous 1881 fire. The business district was wiped out, and from then on it was downhill for Silver Cliff. "When a mining camp ceases to go ahead, it at once begins on a rapid decline," the *Denver Times* noted in a 1909 story on Silver Cliff.

The fire was not the only cause of the decline. Repeal of the Sherman Silver Purchase Act doomed Silver Cliff. Two of its churches were moved to nearby Westcliffe, and the Saint Cloud Hotel was hauled off to Canon City. Lots that once sold for $500 dropped to $12 and eventually were sold by the sheriff for twenty-five cents.

Silver Cliff's buildings, "once filled with an active and prosperous people, are tumbling down and decaying, the windows broken out, the roofs caved in and the walls toppling to destruction," the *Times* described Silver Cliff in 1909. Today the town has improved slightly.

Above: These weathered false-front buildings have been stabilized. *Below:* Knights of Pythias Hall *(left)* on Main Street. *Kendal Atchison*

and too poorly equipped to handle the burgeoning population. Students had had to bring their own chairs and put them wherever they could find space.

Children abounded. "Everywhere we see numbers of children," the *Miner* noted in 1878. "The benedict miner, cognizant of the absurdity of attempting to raise fruit and vegetables at an elevation of over 9,000 feet, utilizes his spare moments by raising all the babies he can."

When not procreating, the miners skied, played bocce ball or baseball, or participated in drilling contests and band concerts at the little bandstand built in 1904. Several mines sponsored their own bands—there was the Terrible Silver Cornet Band and the Payrock Band—and

Above: Silver Plume in the foregound with Georgetown beyond. *Below:* There were once nine saloons along Main Street. The buildings on the near right are among the false-fronted ones being stabilized. *Courtesy Denver Public Library Western History Department.*

Silver Plume residents enjoyed their short summers by attending outdoor get-togethers. *Courtesy Denver Public Library Western History Department.*

By 1905, school crowding had abated. *Courtesy Denver Public Library Western History Department.*

A lonely day in Silverton in the 1880s. *Courtesy Denver Public Library Western History Department.*

one mine operator supposedly hired his men as much for their musical ability as for their mining skill.

Over the years Silver Plume mines produced millions in silver. Among the major mines were the Pelican-Dives, the Snowdrift, the Terrible, and the Seven-thirty, whose owner started the first shift at 7:30 A.M. instead of the more traditional 6:30.

The Seven-thirty was owned by Englishman Clifford Griffin, whose fiancée, legend says, died the night before their wedding. Despite his success as a mine operator in America, the unhappy Englishman could not forget the woman he loved, and each evening he played mournful songs on his violin in his cabin high above Silver Plume. One night after he finished playing, Silver Plume residents heard a gunshot and rushed to Griffin's cabin to find him dead. In his hand was a suicide note asking that he be buried where he lay. Today a granite monument marks the grave.

Located only two miles west of Georgetown, Silver Plume is 1,000 feet higher, presenting a dilemma for the Union Pacific, which found it impossible to negotiate the steep grade. The problem was solved when an engineer designed an ingenious system of switchbacks to allow the train to climb the mountain. Reported George A. Crofutt: "First they run into the 'Devil's Gate,' turn back, *cross* over the 'Bridal Veil,' make a 'three ply,' 'horse shoe,' a 'double ox bow,' but *never* for a hundred feet do they make a tangent on the whole distance." The Georgetown Loop, as the series of switchbacks was called, not only was a marvel of engineering genius but also was a successful tourist attraction that continued to bring visitors even after the silver mines played out. The track was dismantled in 1939, but has been rebuilt and operates in the summer as a tourist attraction.

Silverton

COUNTY: *San Juan*
LOCATION: *49 mi. north of Durango*
MAP 9
P.O. est. Feb. 1, 1875

"We may not have gold, but we have silver by the ton," yelled a prospector, thereby naming the hopeful settlement in the San Juan Mountains. Actually, Silverton had gold as well as silver, and copper and lead too. In 1899 total production in San Juan County, where Silverton is county seat, amounted to $2.5 million, with

Above: Silverton, 1881. *Courtesy Denver Public Library Western History Department. Below:* When prohibition closed their Iron Mountain Saloon, the Giacomelli family opened a confectionary. *Courtesy San Juan County Historical Society.*

The Grand Imperial Hotel, 1965. Sandra Dallas

nearly half of that from gold. The major producers in the Silverton area were the Silver Lake, the Iowa, the Gold King, the Royal Tiger, and the Sunnyside.

The area was first prospected in the early 1860s by a group of gold seekers led by Charles Baker, who nearly was lynched by his companions when they found his claims of easy riches were grossly exaggerated. Prospectors continued to come into the area, known as Baker's Park, even though the land was owned by the Ute Indians, who were fierce fighters. In 1874 the Brunot Treaty was signed, forcing the Utes to give up the land, and the area was opened to prospecting. By 1876, Silverton had a population of five hundred, thirty-seven buildings, and four hotels, and the women were complaining that the water from Cement Creek was so heavy with minerals it was unfit for washing clothes.

Locked in a mountain valley, accessible only by traveling over high mountain passes, Silver-

ton could afford to mine only the richest ore. The ore had to be transported out by burros that brought in supplies on the return trip. In winter the mail was carried by a postman on skis, while water was delivered by dog sled. Not until the narrow-gauge Denver & Rio Grande, the first of four railroads that eventually served Silverton, arrived in 1882 did the town flourish. The railroad did not always guarantee ready access to the outside world, however. In early 1884 heavy snow blocked the tracks, and Silverton residents were snowbound for seventy-three days. Crews of men digging from both directions eventually plowed through an 84-foot snowslide, allowing the train to reach Silverton, where it was met by cheering and weeping Silverton residents who were down to their last few cups of flour.

Unlike many of the early mining camps of Red Mountain, which were built to provide only temporary residences for fortune seekers, Silverton was a substantial town built to last. By 1882,

Advertisement for the hotel when it was known as The Grand. *Courtesy Denver Public Library Western History Department.*

Motorcycles have replaced burros for mountain transportation. *Kendal Atchison*

Silverton had four hundred buildings, two banks, a $5,000 church, and several hotels available only to paying guests. A Silverton resident recalled the proprietor of one of them questioning newcomers: "Yes, we have a room for you, but have you the cash to pay for our accommodations? If not, we don't want you."

For those who could afford the finer things, Silverton was a pleasant place. White miners played in a silver cornet band, and the blacks formed a band of their own. The Silverton Club provided social outlets such as a library to keep young men from being tempted into sin. There was a jockey club and a racetrack, which was used for hook and ladder contests as well as for horse racing.

Silverton's main street was elegant with high-style Victorian buildings crowded with investors, bankers, drummers, and gamblers. The town's showplace was the Grand Hotel—later the Grand Imperial—a three-story brick palace with mansard roof and grand trappings.

Just as fine was the extravagant mansion built by Lena Stoiber, whose husband, Edward, owned the Silver Lake Mine. Dubbed "Captain Jack" for her prowess with horses and epithets, Mrs. Stoiber also was known as a Lady Bountiful when at Christmas she hitched her team to a sleigh filled with toys for Silverton children. Edward Stoiber sold the Silver Lake for more than $2 million to the Guggenheim brothers, and the Stoibers moved to Denver, where Mrs. Stoiber built an even finer home.

Fine buildings failed to make Silverton a town of consequence, one critic contended. David Frakes Day, editor of the *Solid Muldoon* in Ouray, Silverton's rival, frequently chided the town in his newspaper:

"Silverton has a boom," Day noted in 1883. "We saw it going by, a few days since—three gamblers, two women and a 'yaller dog.'"

Later Day wrote: "Over in Silverton last week the society gentlemen attended a grand ball, and after they had escorted their ladies home, cut loose and rounded up 'the scarlet daughters of prosperity,' repaired to the same hall and made Rome howl until daylight. . . . Talk about your hard towns! Silverton is the morning-glory [weed] of the Colorado bouquet."

Silverton had plenty of scarlet daughters and other sins from which to choose. Blair Street,

Silverton's main street. *Kendal Atchison*

named for a prominent citizen, was ablaze with the gas lamps of dozens of saloons, as well as the red lights of the parlor houses where some sixty prostitutes worked.

In 1884 the *Rocky Mountain News* reported Blanche Deville, a leader of the demimonde, had skipped town after being charged with a $50 theft. The stage driver who spirited her away was charged with stealing Miss Deville's trunk.

Silverton's decline began at the turn of the century as the mines began to play out. Some mines stayed opened until World War II, however, often subject to the conflicts of a generation earlier. In 1939 a doctor named Razor seized control of the union's hospital and refused to treat union miners and members of their families. The papers reported Dr. Razor "would not treat a 'damn' one of our people . . . and that he considered the CIO simply another way of spelling bolshevism," a labor leader charged.

Silverton's revitalization came at the end of the war when tourists discovered the Denver & Rio Grande's narrow-gauge train, which made the spectacular trip from Durango to Silverton along a route that had been blasted out of the

mountains. The trip, made each day during the summer, accounts for a major part of Silverton's economy today.

At about the same time, Hollywood found Silverton, with its antique train and nineteenth-century storefronts, an ideal site for filming. A host of movies, including *Ticket to Tomahawk, The Naked Spur,* and *Around the World in Eighty Days*, were filmed in Silverton. Film companies were attracted by the authenticity of Silverton's streets, but at the same time they made changes that would have made Silverton's oldtime denizens chuckle: One film company built a church on Blair Street.

Sneffels

COUNTY: *Ouray*
LOCATION: *6 mi. southwest of Ouray*
MAP 9
P.O. est. Oct. 31, 1879 as Mount Sneffels; discont. Oct. 6, 1930

In the fall of 1875 a group of prospectors worked their way from Silverton to Mount Sneffels hunt-

Work was going on in the Revenue-Virginius in 1981. *Kendal Atchison*

ing for gold. They built a cabin and spent the winter in bleak loneliness, blizzards howling about them at an altitude of more than 10,000 feet, little realizing another group of gold seekers was camped on the site of Ouray, only a few miles below.

The camp was in a fortuitous location. Within two years some of the area's richest mines, including the Wheel of Fortune, the Yankee Boy, the Ruby Trust, and the richest of them all, the Virginius, were discovered.

The town of Sneffels—named for Mount Sneffels, which in turn was named for the mountain in the Jules Verne novel, *A Journey to the Center of the Earth*—served as a camp for the various mines and for the Revenue Tunnel. In the mid-1890s, it had a population of eight hundred, nearly all miners. There were fewer than fifteen schoolchildren.

Completed in 1895, the Revenue Tunnel burrowed nearly 7,500 feet into the mountain to intersect the rich Virginius vein. The tunnel, 2,000 feet lower than the Virginius outcrop, was built at Sneffels' 10,500-foot elevation at the end

of a shelf road. Beyond its sheer drop today are spectacular waterfalls and the remains of old mines.

The blizzards that howled about the first settlers on Mount Sneffels continued to be a scourge for miners. More than once, rescue parties sent to find the bodies of men killed in avalanches were themselves avalanche victims. On one occasion a team of miners pulling a wounded man on a sled to Ouray failed to meet a relief party of four men from the Virginius, so they pulled the wounded miner all the way to Ouray themselves. The bodies of those in the relief party were found the next day, buried under a snowslide.

Spar City

COUNTY: *Mineral*
LOCATION: *14 mi. south of Creede*
MAP 11
P.O. est. Aug. 16, 1892 as Spar; discont. Aug. 23, 1895

Spar City is a privately owned fishing camp. *Kendal Atchison*

Discovery of silver south of Creede in 1892 started a rush to the little settlement named Fisher City. Within a few weeks the town, whose name was changed to Spar City for the huge boulders of feldspar the miners found in the area, had a population of five hundred, most of them living in tents and log cabins set on generous 50- by 150-foot lots on streets 80 feet wide. "Buildings are going up solid on both sides of the thoroughfare," the *Denver Republican* reported.

Mining was short-lived in Spar City because the mines failed to produce paying ore in any quantity. By the turn of the century Spar City was nearly deserted. There was an attempt at reopening the most promising mine, the Emma, but it failed, and the town eventually was sold to a group of vacationers who maintain it as a private fishing camp of tidy log cabins.

Stringtown

COUNTY: *Lake*
LOCATION: *1 mi. south of Leadville*
MAP 5
No P.O.

Raw and ugly, strung out in a crooked line south of Leadville, Stringtown was a blue-collar extension of Leadville. It was made up of a few neat cottages, unpainted shacks, tenements, and a sparse number of businesses. Stringtown was a rough place. In 1903 a rowdy was sentenced to up to twenty years in prison for the murder of a man in a Stringtown saloon.

The Leadville poorhouse was located between Stringtown and Malta. The Leadville *Chronicle* charged that the poorhouse, rife with mismanagement, spent more money on liquor for the inhabitants than on food. The poorhouse was shut down in 1937, though not for lack of poor people; the building was too decrepit to be safe.

Summerville

COUNTY: *Boulder*
LOCATION: *10 mi. west of Boulder*
MAP 3
No P.O.

Summerville was never more than a group of cabins perched on the hillsides of Gold Run Gulch midway between Salina and Gold Hill, much as it is now. The town boomed briefly in 1899 when the Victoria Mine came on stream.

When lease operators discovered rich gold and silver ore in the Victoria, the *Denver Times* called the discovery one of the richest strikes ever made in Boulder County. Said the *Times*: "Charles Davis, owner of the mine, has been lying at the point of death for some days past, but is now somewhat improved." Alas for poor Charles Davis. Only a month later the *Times* reported the sale of the Victoria for $125,000—by the widow Davis.

Summitville

COUNTY: *Rio Grande*
LOCATION: *26 mi. southwest of Del Norte*
MAP 11
P.O. est. Nov. 17, 1880; discont. April, 1948

More than $7 million in gold (most of it at $20 per ounce) was taken out of the timberline mines of Summitville, once the highest of Colorado's major gold camps. Summitville had three booms and has been trying for a fourth. The biggest boom of them all was the first one, which made a millionaire out of poker-playing Senator Thomas M. Bowen.

The treacherous winters at Summitville—thirty-one feet of snow in thirty-one days one winter—were so bad that the area was worked for five years before anyone stayed through the winter.

Gold was discovered in Summitville in 1870 when John Esmund, a rancher, found a ledge he claimed was nearly half gold. He visited the location each summer, taking out high-grade ore, but never did the necessary work to prove up his claim. When he visited the site in 1873, he found someone else had established a mine, the fabulously rich Little Annie, on his site, so he wandered to another part of the mountain and discovered two new mines, the Esmund (Aztec) and the Major. That was easy enough to do, since South Mountain, where Summitville's major mines were located, was one giant gold mine.

By the time Tom Bowen, a brigadier general in the Union army, arrived in Del Norte, 30 miles away, Summitville was a roaring camp. At its height, Summitville had a population of fifteen hundred, with nearly two-thirds working in the mines and mills. To help its miners pass the long winter evenings, one company built a pool hall above its corporate offices, and pool sharks from all over the state traveled to Summitville to match their skills against the miners.

Summitville was shut down during World War II, though the Anaconda Company was exploring the area in the 1980s. *Kendal Atchison*

The chimney on the pumphouse building in the foreground gave access in winter. *Kendal Atchison*

Elected a judge in 1876, Bowen came to know the mining camps of Rio Grande County well, both as judge and as poker player. His skill and his luck were legendary. He once lost shares of a mining company in a game only to have the winner tell him the next day he didn't want the stock. Bowen redeemed the stock for a nominal amount, and it later made him rich. Legend says he also played the champion poker player of Lake County for all the gambling IOUs in the two counties, which the two men had cornered. Bowen won.

Bowen applied the same luck to mining, and in 1880 he quit the judgeship to concentrate on his holdings, a group of mines so rich they were called "Bowen's Bonanza." In 1883, when Colorado had two senatorial seats to fill, one for six years, the other for thirty days, Bowen was elected for the longer term. The short term went to Leadville silver king H. A. W. Tabor.

Summitville's first decline was rapid. In 1885 the Little Annie announced it could not meet its payroll. The other mines, too, appeared to be played out, and by 1889, there were only twenty-five residents in Summitville.

A second boom came in the late 1890s when A. E. Reynolds, who owned the Virginius Mine at Sneffels, acquired control of Bowen's Bonanza. The third boom came in the late 1930s, but the mines were closed by the government during World War II, and attempts at large-scale production since then have failed. In 1976, while the area was under lease to Asarco, Incorporated, an employee discovered a 114-pound boulder containing $350,000 worth of gold, lying by the side of a road.

Anaconda Copper Company leased the Little Annie, the Little Ida, the Iowa, and other mines on South Mountain from the Reynolds heirs in 1979 but decided against full-scale mining.

Above: The Sunset station. *Courtesy Denver Public Library Western History Department. Below:* Summer day in Sunset. *Kendal Atchison*

Sunset

COUNTY: *Boulder*
LOCATION: *14 mi. west of Boulder*
MAP 3
P.O. est. Sept. 25, 1883; discont. Nov. 15, 1921

Passengers on the Colorado & Northwestern's "Switzerland Trail" sometimes were startled at midday when the conductor called: "Sunset on your right." The reference was to the town of Sunset, a tiny mining community whose population never exceeded 175.

The railroad was lifeblood to Sunset. The Greeley, Salt Lake & Pacific ran an excursion train from Boulder to Sunset. The trip took a little less than two hours. Passengers arrived at noon and alighted to have lunch, to hunt for rocks, and to pick wildflowers. They spent another two hours backing down the canyon because there was no trackage that allowed the train to turn around.

Originally called Penn Gulch, Sunset was started as a lumber camp, then became a mining town with the discovery of promising mines. For a brief time Sunset was a summer resort, until its hotels burned down.

Sunshine

COUNTY: *Boulder*
LOCATION: *8 mi. west of Boulder*
MAP 3
P.O. est. Feb. 26, 1875; discont. Aug. 31, 1913

Sunshine was named for the Sunshine Mine, a major discovery of tellurium ore west of Boulder. The name Sunshine, bestowed on the mine by a grateful discoverer in honor of his good fortune, extended to the first child born in the town—Susie Sunshine Turner.

Susie Sunshine's father founded the town in 1874. Prosperity came quickly, and within a few months the town boasted four stores, two butcher shops, two shoe shops, a reading room, and various other buildings, all worth $85,000. Butter sold for fifty cents a pound, eggs for fifty cents a dozen, bacon, twenty cents a pound, and meat, ten cents a pound, while board and lodging for a week cost seven dollars.

Class came with the eastern-born mother of three college-educated mining men who refused to allow her to live in a miner's hut. They built her the first substantial house in town, from which she exercised moral control over Sun-

The drab appearance of the town belies its sunny name. *Courtesy Colorado Historical Society.*

The dog appears to be protecting this dilapidated Sunshine cabin. *Kendal Atchison*

Swandyke, 1981. *Kendal Atchison*

shine. "The good works and sincere prayers of this mother in Israel have no doubt contributed largely to the healthy moral condition of the society of Sunshine," wrote the *Sunshine Courier*.

The Sunshine boom did not last long, though there were several revivals of mining activity. Shortly after an 1897 flood, four prospectors spied a gold vein that had been uncovered by the rain and leased the site for a year. They took out $1,100 a month from the mine, named the Tilly Butzel; it was not a fortune but still a tidy sum when top wages were $3 a day.

The town boomed again in the depression era when an old miner discovered a body of ore that he claimed ran $35 to the pound of ore or $70,000 per ton. It was located directly under the old schoolhouse.

A later stone school still stands, its desks and a stove intact, though the two outhouses long since have fallen into disrepair.

Swandyke

COUNTY: *Summit*
LOCATION: *13 mi. northeast of Breckenridge*
MAP 4
P.O. est. Nov. 30, 1898; discont. Sept. 30, 1910

Swandyke, today two wasted cabins and the crumbled remains of a third, was predicted to

be "one of the bonanza camps of the state" by the *Breckenridge Bulletin*. Some three hundred people lived in Swandyke about 1899 when the post office was established. Many families camped out during the summer, though they hurried for cover with the first snow. Located just below the timberline, Swandyke, on the Middle Fork of the Swan River, experienced bitterly cold winters.

The hills surrounding Swandyke were "seamed with veins carrying gold, silver, lead and copper," the *Bulletin* reported, and the hills were dotted with mines—the Cashier, the Michigan Belle, the Ground Hog, the Three Kings, the Lone Jack—many mining ore bodies that were close to the surface.

Swandyke was "a typical mountain town where the prospector alone holds sway," concluded the *Bulletin*. Today it is a typical, crumbling ghost town.

Telluride

COUNTY: *San Miguel*
LOCATION: *50 mi. west of Ouray*
MAP 10
P.O. est. July 26, 1880

"To hell you ride!" the Rio Grande Southern conductor yelled to startled passengers headed

Nestled in a bowl surrounded by high mountains, Telluride found its isolation a problem. *Courtesy Denver Public Library Western History Department.*

for Telluride. Despite its splendid setting in a box canyon guarded by towering mountains that are splashed with eternal snow and spectacular waterfalls, there was more than a little hell in Telluride. Ragged prospectors and boiled-collar swells rubbed shoulders in the three dozen saloons and gambling dens that never closed. Or they picked from 175 women who worked the line or operated out of extravagant bordellos—the Pick and Gad, the Silver Bell, the Whitehouse. Drunken brawls and saloon fights, gun battles and wanton murders were common, and the most lawless of all sometimes was the law.

Robert Meldrum, a swarthy lawman with a dozen killings to his credit—he always shot his victims in the stomach—ambled into a Telluride saloon, looked over the awed crowd, and announced: "I'm Bob Meldrum. You can always find me when you want me. Now if any son of a bitch has anything to say, spit it out; otherwise, I'm going to take a drink—and alone."

Then he turned his back to the room and ordered a drink. If anyone said anything, Meldrum did not hear it. He was deaf as a stone.

What set Telluride apart from other hardrock camps was the length and ferocity of its labor strife, which ranked only with Cripple Creek in intensity. There was some truth in the boast by town wags that the name Telluride was indeed a contraction of "to hell you ride."

Gold was discovered in Marshall Basin above Telluride in 1875 when a prospector filed a claim on the Sheridan vein. Two claims, the Sheridan and the Union, were producing profitable ore when a devious mining man, J. B. Ingram, measured the claims and discovered they were oversized. He promptly filed on the excess land and called his claim, appropriately, the Smuggler.

Perched above the Smuggler-Union were the Japan, the Liberty Bell, and the Tomboy, which was sold to the Rothschilds in 1897 and operated until the late 1920s.

Main Street, Telluride. The New Sheridan Hotel *(left)* catered to San Juan swells. *Author's collection.*

Mines depended on pack trains to bring them supplies, particularly in winter. *Courtesy Denver Public Library Western History Department.*

Telluride was founded in 1878 as Columbia. Growth for the first decade was steady if unspectacular. By 1881, with corner business sites going for twenty-five dollars and residence lots for seventy-five cents, Telluride had a population of nearly a thousand people, two grocery stores, and thirteen saloons. Telluride always had "more than a sufficiency of saloons," noted Frank Hall in his history of Colorado, "features common to all mountain towns, where extreme dryness induces thirst." By 1890, when the railroad finally reached Telluride, dryness had induced such a mighty thirst it took three dozen saloons operating day and night to quench it.

In the early 1890s, with silver pouring out of the mines that ringed Telluride, the town glittered with wealth. When the price of silver dropped in 1893, throwing most silver camps into a depression, Telluride's mines obligingly began turning out gold ore.

Mining magnates disported themselves in style, gambling at tables in the Telluride Club, hosting elegant picnics in the mountains with wine chilled in icy streams, or attending fancy balls at the New Sheridan Hotel. A few even shipped in polo ponies. Their wives, dressed in gowns from Daniels & Fisher in Denver or imported from Paris, held "at homes," nibbling on pastries from the New Sheridan or ices made at Baur's in Denver and shipped to them on the Rio Grande Southern. Once a week they listened to musicales performed by alcoholic musicians who normally played at the brothels but for a price would play uptown as well.

Society was rigid in Telluride, even though some of the upper crust were only a few days removed from sowbelly and beans and moved their lips when they read—if they could read at all. When a proper Boston lady considering a move to Telluride wrote to a town official asking about the town's society, the official, legend says, sent the following reply:

As for sowciety it is bang up. This is a mighty morrell town considerin that theres 69 saloons and two newspapers to a poppylation of 1,247. . . . Only two men has been killed since Monday. . . . Cheatin at gamblin is punished by linchin. . . . Ladies is universally respected and I sell them beer at half price when they buy at my place . . .preachin every Sunday that the preacher dont have ter stay ter home on account of the big rush at his bowlin alley. Dont hezzytate about comin here on account of sowciety. This a morrel town.

Proper women did not mix with the wives of the gamblers who lived in what historian David Lavender, a third-generation Telluride resident, called a nether world of "shuttered houses." The gamblers' wives spent their time in stultified boredom, rejected by the upper class, disdainful of the prostitutes, and none too friendly with each other.

The prostitutes had their own social strata, with those who worked in the cribs at the bottom. The bordellos, with their orchestras and

Above: Telluride saloon. Note the brass spittoons and footrail that required constant polishing. *Courtesy Denver Public Library Western History Department. Below:* By the late 1920s, things had begun to slow down in Telluride. The motion picture playing is *7th Heaven. Author's collection.*

Pack train headed for the mines, 1898. *Courtesy Denver Public Library Western History Department.*

Refurbished Main Street buildings. *Kendal Atchison*

wine rooms and gaudy parlors, ranked higher than the disease-ridden cribs. So rich and powerful were the madams that in 1906 when Harriet Fish Backus arrived in Telluride as the bride of a mining engineer, she watched a funeral cortége followed by two lines of solemn male mourners and concluded the funeral was for a prominent member of the community. She discovered later the casket contained the body of the town's leading madam.

Telluride's vast middle class belonged to the Elks or the Masons, played in the silver cornet band, and attended the annual ball thrown by the muleskinners and packers. Invitations for the dance arrived in the form of miniature horse blankets. The hall was decorated with quirts and blacksnake whips, and bales of hay covered with Navajo blankets were used for seats. At one muleskinners' ball guests consumed thirty-five cases of champagne.

But the most important event of the year was

THE union strife that swept through the West's mining camps in the early twentieth century brought destruction and death to Telluride. Because Telluride was isolated at the end of a box canyon, the conflict was more virulent than elsewhere. No one in Telluride was unaffected.

The confrontation began in May, 1901, when the Smuggler-Union introduced the fathom system of wages in which miners were paid for the amount of ore they removed rather than on a shift basis. The new system reduced pay by 40 percent, and the Western Federation of Miners urged a strike. In the ensuing violence several men were killed, and in two months the Smuggler-Union capitulated, agreeing to a three-year contract at the prevailing $3-per-day wage.

The seething resentment felt by both sides flared up little more than a year later when Arthur Collins, the Smuggler-Union's manager, was murdered. He was replaced by Bulkeley Wells, the dashing, fearless son-in-law of the mine's majority shareholder. Wells, patently antiunion, shut down the mine for a month as a warning. Not long afterward, an antiunion shopkeeper displayed in his window the skull of a scab who had been murdered by the union in 1901.

In September, 1903, the union called a strike. Colorado's antilabor Governor James Peabody declared martial law, sending in the National Guard and putting Wells in charge of a citizens' militia. For fifteen months Telluride was in a state of siege. Union members were beaten and deported and militiamen and mine owners were threatened. The same trains that brought in frightened scabs, many of them foreigners who did not know they were strikebreakers, hauled out strikers, who were hastily rounded up and pushed onto the train without coats and sometimes shoes, then dumped in the winter snow. The mine owners built a military facility, called Fort Peabody for the governor, on the mountain pass between Telluride and Ouray, to keep strikers from returning. The union sent in its biggest guns—Big Bill Haywood, Charles Moyer, and the notorious Harry Orchard, who was behind union bombings in Cripple Creek later on. Both sides committed murder, and for years afterwards skeletons of unidentified men turned up in isolated mountain gulches.

Finally, in December, 1904, after the Smuggler-Union had lost millions, Wells agreed to reinstate the $3-per-day wage. It was a hollow victory for the WFM, though. The Smuggler-Union and other mines refused to hire any man who had belonged to the union.

the Fourth of July, the only day besides Christmas when the mines shut down. Parades and fireworks, hose-cart races and horse races, the obligatory reading of the Declaration of Independence, and a grand ball were crammed into the three-day celebration.

Telluride was spared the conflagrations that hit other mining camps, though small fires broke out periodically. A fire in a sporting house called the Club threatened the Pick and Gad, but "by strenuous efforts of the firemen," the *Rocky Mountain News* reported, the building got by with only a scorching—nothing new for Telluride's most infamous brothel. The firemen were equally heroic when the Pick and Gad itself caught fire. "The fire company was prompt in responding," reported the *Denver Times*.

More devastating was the weather. A woman was drowned and her body washed a block and a half down the street when Cornet Creek overflowed, and the town was isolated for weeks when a dam washed out and flooded Telluride. With heroism matching that of the firemen fighting the whorehouse fire, a freighter managed to get through to the town from the outside, bringing relief in the form of a mule train loaded with beer.

The snow that piled up in the mountain bowls was Telluride's greatest threat. Each winter hapless travelers were swept away by avalanches and melted out in the spring. In 1902 a snowslide hit the Liberty Bell, killing several miners. The rescue party was hit by a second and then a third slide. When the avalanches stopped, nineteen men were dead.

Telluride's lawlessness was not limited to the city's miners and sporting element. Some was imported. In 1889 three men held up a Telluride bank in broad daylight. They escaped toward Rico with a posse in such close pursuit that they could not take time to switch to the fresh horses they had hidden outside Telluride. Weeks later the skeletons of the horses were found tied to a tree, legend says. The gang escaped, however, and the men went on to bigger holdups. It was the first bank robbery for their leader, Butch Cassidy.

Telluride's most spectacular robbery was an inside job. In 1929, Charles Delos Waggoner, president of the Bank of Telluride, defrauded six New York banks of a total of $500,000, which

The once infamous cribs are an official historic site in Telluride today. *Kendal Atchison*

he used to cover losses in his own bank. Using a special banking code, Waggoner telegraphed the banks to deposit funds to his account and signed the messages with the names of major Denver banks. Waggoner then drew out the money and used it to repay depositors of the Bank of Telluride. The bank was floundering because a number of loans were in default, caused by the area's faltering economy. The press gleefully reported the success of the little country banker in taking the New York giants, and his attorney portrayed Waggoner as a Robin Hood, but the banker spent several years in prison.

By the time of the Waggoner fraud, Telluride was well into a decline that had begun during the labor confrontations of the early part of the century.

One by one the mines shut down until, in the late 1920s, even the huge Tomboy exhausted its paying ore. The Smuggler-Union, renamed the Idarado and eventually acquired by Newmont Mining Corporation, hung on until the late 1970s, when at last it too closed.

By then, Telluride had developed "white gold" —skiing—which has brought a new boom. Today in Telluride nouveaux Victorian houses mix with classic nineteenth-century gingerbread, and cocaine busts are replacing gambling and prostitution crackdowns. Time has brought a patina and even a veneration for the quaint vices of an earlier age; in 1979 the cribs of Pacific Avenue were purchased by the National Trust for Historic Preservation and given landmark status.

Tiger

COUNTY: *Summit*
LOCATION: *6 mi. northeast of Breckenridge*
MAP 4
P.O. est. Dec. 26, 1919; discont. November, 1940

The prospector who discovered the Tiger Mine was so enthusiastic about its possibilities that only a few days after filing the original claim, he returned to the Breckenridge courthouse and amended the claim to read "Royal Tiger Mine."

Tiger, about the time of World War I. *Courtesy Denver Public Library Western History Department.*

When the Royal Tiger and other mines in the area were consolidated, the Royal Tiger Mines Company built the company town of Tiger.

The town thrived from about 1918 until the mine was shut down in the 1930s. Some of Tiger's buildings were lost to dredging operations on the Swan River, though the real destruction came in 1973 when the United States Forest Service and the Bureau of Land Management, in an effort to rid the area of hippies who had taken over Tiger, burned down the town.

Nothing remains of Tiger today except for traces of mining on the mountainside.

Tin Cup

COUNTY: *Gunnison*
LOCATION: *26 mi. north of Pitkin*
MAP 8
P.O. est. July 22, 1879 as Virginia; discont. Jan. 31, 1918

In 1860 a prospector named Jim Taylor stooped by a mountain stream and dipped out water in his tin cup. Mixed with the cold liquid were flakes of gold. Despite those indications of mineral wealth, the area was not settled until nearly

Tiger, about 1970, before the Forest Service and Bureau of Land Management burned it down. *Sandra Dallas*

Tin Cup was once the wickedest town in the Gunnison country. *Courtesy Colorado Historical Society.*

twenty years later when the Gold Cup Mine was discovered. The settlement was named Virginia City at first, but miners, loyal to Jim Taylor, insisted the name be changed to Tin Cup.

By any name, Tin Cup, at one time, was the wickedest town in the Gunnison country. By 1882 it had three thousand residents and twenty saloons, the most notorious of which was Frenchy's, which dubbed itself "the Old Reliable." It also had four cemeteries.

One newcomer awoke one morning to find eight bullet holes in his tent, while another claimed that justice, which was dealt out by a judge operating in Frenchy's, could be purchased by the man who set up the most drinks.

Tin Cup bragged it had eight marshals in its early years, only one of whom finished out his term. The first, known as Old Man Willis, was

told: "See nothing. Hear nothing. Do nothing, and the first arrest you make will be your last." Willis followed orders only to discover that his employers also intended to do nothing. When he went unpaid, he quit. His successor, Tom Lahay, was a bully, a former border ruffian who arrested men to show off his fearlessness, then let them go once they reached jail. Town fathers, afraid Lahay would be lynched by irate townsmen, let him go too. Lahay himself disposed of the third lawman by gunning him down in a shootout.

The fourth sheriff arrested so many men the court had to work overtime to hold their trials. He was shot by a gambler he supposedly had disarmed, and was replaced by Jack Ward, a tough, who quit to become a preacher. The fifth marshal, Sam Micky, was committed to an

A more discreet Tin Cup, 1982. *Kendal Atchison*

insane asylum where he spent his time pacing the floor, believing he was back on the Tin Cup beat. The seventh marshal was shot, and the eighth managed to last out his term.

In the early days miners often risked their lives to ski out for provisions. In 1878 one miner, who snowshoed to Saint Elmo for supplies, found when he returned that he could sell flour for $15 a hundredweight, eggs for $1 a dozen, and dried fruit for $2 "per grab." Prices remained high. A freighter in 1881 hauled 3,500 pounds of flour and a brass bedstead to Tin Cup and sold the flour for $14 a sack before he could unload. He failed to report the market for brass bedsteads.

By 1884 the boom was over. There were flurries of excitement after that, and Tin Cup remained an active town for years. In the 1890s it got telephones and fire hydrants.

In the 1950s, Tin Cup had a curious revival. Denver radio personality Pete Smythe hosted a morning show that he claimed originated from a general store in East Tin Cup, Colorado. The program sent hundreds of listeners to visit the mountain community, which even today is a prosperous little summer town with a number of log houses, a pretty white church or community center, and a general store that sells tin cups.

Turret

COUNTY: *Chaffee*
LOCATION: *13 mi. north of Salida*
MAP 13
P.O. est. Feb. 28, 1898; discont. November, 1939

The frenzy of mining activity that took place in Turret in 1897 belied the disappointing mineral discoveries of mines optimistically named Golden Wonder and Last Chance. Only a few weeks after the first discoveries, a hundred people were living in tents and shacks and a few log cabins along Cat Gulch, and more arrived every week on the Salida stage.

At the height of the excitement, evangelist and temperance hawker Billy Sunday arrived in Turret to visit an old friend, who closed his business in deference to the guest. The friend ran a Turret saloon.

The newcomers built a substantial village and even decorated the log cabins with gingerbread trim in anticipation of prosperity that proved to be short-lived. The Gold Bug played out almost immediately, and the Vivandiere did not live up to expectations, either. Population peaked after 1900. The *Denver Times* reported optimistically in 1901 that "there has been a sharp in-

Turret had begun to decline when this photographer showed up to record the sights. *Courtesy Denver Public Library Western History Department.*

A prizefight at the Woods Saloon, 1905. *Courtesy Denver Public Library Western History Department.*

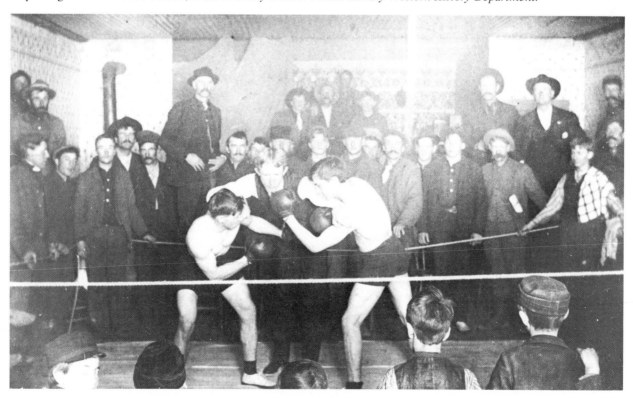

Turret, 1981. *Kendal Atchison*

quiry for Turret City lots for business purposes in anticipation of a coming boom." Turret hung on for a number of years, but the boom never came.

Twin Lakes

COUNTY: *Lake*
LOCATION: *21 mi. south of Leadville*
MAP 7
P.O. est. Oct. 16, 1866 as Dayton

Twin Lakes was an anemic mining camp, but its spectacular setting and good fishing made it a popular resort. As early as 1868, traveler Samuel Bowles noted that he sat down to dinner in Twin Lakes (then called Dalton) to a white tablecloth, a lady and a gentleman for hostess and host, and raspberry shortcake "to kill."

Bowles, like other travelers, remarked on the extraordinary scenery at Twin Lakes, though another visitor noted: "The people, with singular perversity, have selected the only spot where a view of the beautiful lake is shut out from them." With the discovery of rich mines at Lead-

ville and Aspen, Twin Lakes, located on the road between the two camps, became a crowded resort.

The Inter-Laken was the most popular of several hotels and drew so many guests that one entrepreneur built a steamboat called *Idlewild* to take them on lake cruises. While the Inter-Laken was ostensibly a rustic log hotel, its guests lived in luxury with a paneled dining room, gaming hall, ballroom, and indoor privy.

"It is the most charming summer resort in Colorado," George A. Crofutt wrote in 1885, though resort activities were not limited to summer. In winter there were sleigh rides and skating parties.

Twin Lakes attracted guests, many of them wealthy, until after the turn of the century. John Campion, Leadville's mine owner, built a house for his bride on the lakes, with a bluegrass lawn for the peacocks, a kennel of dogs, and a tally-ho to transport guests.

High-toned resort goers like the Campions stopped coming in the early 1900s when the lakes were turned into a reservoir, spoiling their beauty for many vacationers.

Twin Lakes was a resort for Leadville and Aspen residents who stayed at hostelries such as the Campion, pictured here. *Below:* The interior of the Campion. *Courtesy Denver Public Library Western History Department.*

Twin Lakes school. *Kendal Atchison*

Valley View Hot Springs

COUNTY: *Saguache*
LOCATION: *12 mi. southeast of Villa Grove*
MAP 13
No P.O.

Valley View Hot Springs was one of a dozen or more blue-collar resorts for Colorado miners. While their betters took the waters at Glenwood or Wagon Wheel Gap, the miners eased their pain and soothed their hangovers in the lesser waters of Trimble Hot Springs outside Durango or Valley View, near Villa Grove.

Originally a ranch, Valley View—named for the spectacular view of the San Luis valley—thrived as a resort when the Orient Mine, a mile and a half away, was in operation. Never very elegant, Valley View nevertheless became a popular auto resort during the 1920s, when most of its cabins were built, and it is a private club today.

Vicksburg

COUNTY: *Chaffee*
LOCATION: *13 mi. west of Granite*
MAP 7
P.O. est. May 3, 1881; discont. July 30, 1885

Traces of gold had been spotted in the Vicks-burg area as early as the 1860s, but it was not until 1879 that miners explored the site seriously. By 1882, Vicksburg, named for early resident Vick Keller, had two hotels, a boardinghouse, a school, two billiard halls, and two saloons, along with its first sale; the Swiss Boy was sold to a Leadville man for $2,000. The mine became a major producer.

Though it never amounted to much, Vicks-burg has a sense of permanence. Someone planted balm of Gilead trees along the ditches that run on both sides of the main street, trees that a century later shade the row of cabins and the two small museums that are all that is left of the town.

Victor

COUNTY: *Teller*
LOCATION: *6 mi. southeast of Cripple Creek*
MAP 14
P.O. est. June 7, 1894

Victor was a lusty gold camp. Its buildings were as elegant, its saloons and whorehouses as wicked, its fire as disastrous as Cripple Creek's. As youths, both radio personality Lowell Thomas and Colorado Governor Ralph Carr worked for Victor newspapers. Prizefighter Jack Dempsey mucked in the Portland Mine. Vice-president Theodore Roosevelt laid the cornerstone of the YMCA. Victor's mines were the richest in the West, so rich, in fact, that Victor was called the "City of Mines." But the mine owners and the big spenders lived in Cripple Creek. The financial and political clout was in Cripple Creek, and Cripple Creek attracted the newspaper reporters and writers. Victor was destined to live in the shadow of Cripple Creek's legend.

The basis of Victor's wealth was Battle Mountain, a hillside peppered today with the yellow rot of mine dumps. The Portland, the Independence, and the Ajax mines were located on Battle Mountain, just north of Victor, though one of the area's richest mines, the Gold Coin, was discovered in the middle of town. An assayer tested rock he picked out of a hole being dug for a hotel foundation, and when the owners discovered they were excavating pay dirt, they relocated the hotel and commenced mining. Two miles of tunnels of the Gold Coin and other mines are threaded beneath Victor's streets.

A tightrope walker performs in Victor, 1895. *Courtesy Denver Public Library Western History Department.*

Victor never fully recovered from its disastrous 1899 fire. *Courtesy Denver Public Library Western History Department.*

The "City of Mines." *Courtesy Denver Public Library Western History Department.*

Victor during its depression. The three-story house *(fourth from left)* was weathering badly. *Courtesy Denver Public Library Western History Department.*

After Winfield Scott Stratton discovered the Independence Mine, the area's first bonanza, two enterprising brothers and their father formed the Woods Investment Company in 1893. They bought a 160-acre site, named it Victor, and in what turned out to be more than hyperbole, touted the lots as gold mines.

While the Independence was the district's most fabled mine, the Portland was the wealthiest, producing some $60 million in gold. It was discovered by three Irishmen on a tiny plot of land surrounded by larger claims. The three miners stealthily shipped their ore at night and saved their money to fight lawsuits they knew would be filed as soon as word of their discovery became public. When it did, Stratton offered financial help to the three in return for an interest in the venture. The Portland fought off thirty-seven lawsuits before getting title to the mine.

Within a few years of its founding, Victor was as raucous and wide open as Cripple Creek. Gold seekers jammed into town, paying as much as a dollar to sleep an eight-hour shift on a cot in a tent. The minute one man left, another took his place. Saloons were open day and night, and murder and suicide were so common in Victor that news of such atrocities ran as filler in big city newspapers. "Lillie Stanley, a dance hall girl, quarreled with her lover last evening, after which she took a dose of morphine and died at 11:20 o'clock," the *Denver Times* noted in 1899.

Several railroads and two electric lines served the rich mines and the teeming populace of Victor. Banks and mercantile stores, cribs and shanties sprawled across the mountainside, most of them hastily constructed of wood and jammed together.

The inevitable fire began in a crib in Paradise Alley on August 21, 1899. The crib's denizens, the *Times* reported, had been smoking opium. Despite the fire departments that rushed to the scene from all over the district, the fire burned for four hours, sending up billowing smoke that could be seen in Colorado Springs and destroying fourteen blocks. Some eight hundred buildings worth $1.5 million were burned, leaving fifteen hundred people homeless. The heaviest loss was suffered by the Woods Investment Company, whose $50,000 insurance covered only a portion of the value of its buildings, which were worth hundreds of thousands of dollars.

The fire, in fact, led to the demise of the Woods brothers' company; one of the brothers died a pauper.

While the ashes were smoldering, Victor began rebuilding. The banks and saloons were back in business in three days. About a thousand men began removing debris as the property owners made plans to rebuild with stone and brick and iron instead of wood. Capitalists from Denver arrived on every train to offer money, and the town's major problem was not capital but getting enough construction materials. By the following year, when the firemen held a ball to observe the first anniversary of the fire, nearly a million dollars' worth of new buildings were standing in Victor. Among them was the Gold Coin Club, a stunning $40,000 clubhouse complete with bowling alley, swimming pool, and library.

The Gold Coin Club and the other buildings erected after the fire represented a more sophisticated and more mature community than the flimsy shacks of early Victor. The town developed a patina of respectability and ordered the removal of a dance hall located too close to the high school. An attempt to close the gambling halls lasted only a week, however.

Despite its pretensions, Victor remained a working-class town that eschewed culture for tests of strength. Drilling contests, hose-cart

The same house shown on page 208 is deserted. Note the ghost marks of an outside stairway on the first-floor porch. *Kendal Atchison.*

races, and greased pig competitions (with the winner keeping the pig) were favorite Fourth of July events. The women participated in a talking contest and a fat women's race.

But the favored sport was boxing, and the favorite boxer a onetime mucker who trained in a gymnasium above the Victor town hall. William Harrison Dempsey, fighting for his ailing brother under his brother's name Jack (which he kept), beat the local favorite, George Coplen, in a gruelling fight. The fight was ferocious, legend says, because the two were vying for the attentions of a Cripple Creek dance hall girl, but Dempsey later said that was just hype.

Despite its prosperous appearance after the fire, the rebuilt town of Victor had almost lived out its heyday. The ore bodies in Victor's mines, which produced $100 million by the turn of the century, began to pinch out. Recurring labor confrontations, which began in the district's early days, caused reduced output. As a workers' town, Victor was a hotbed of labor agitation. In 1900, store clerks demanded that merchants change their closing time to 6 P.M. from 8 P.M. And after the 1899 fire, railroad laborers working near the burned depot struck, demanding their wages be increased to $2 per day from $1.75. But it was the strikes at the mines, first in 1894 and later in 1903 that paralyzed Victor. The bloody 1903 confrontation, backed by the Western Federation of Miners, threw thousands of men out of work. The state put Victor under martial law and shipped hundreds of strikers out of Colorado. Finally, the massacre of miners at the Independence, Colorado, depot, which was destroyed by a bomb, led to the end of the strike. Victor never fully recovered.

The final blow came during World War I,

Most of Victor's fine brick buildings are boarded up. *Kendal Atchison*

Villa Grove, 1981. *Kendal Atchison*

when miners left in droves to join the military, and mines were shut down for lack of workers. There was a slight revival during the depression when leasees made $5,000 milling ore scraped off Victor's streets. The Gold Coin Mine in its prosperous days had run short of space to dump low-grade ore and used it to pave the streets.

The mines shut down for good following the outbreak of World War II. The young men boarded up their houses and left; the old ones, living on pensions, crowded around the stoves in the cafes on winter days or sat on benches along the streets in summer, talking of the fortunes to be made when the price of gold, frozen during the depression, was set free. In the mid-1970s the price of gold did indeed begin to rise, causing a run on gold pans in the district's hardware stores. Victor's revival began in the early 1980s when major mining companies once again showed interest in the mines on Battle Mountain. By then it was too late for the old men who had held on. Most of them were dead.

Villa Grove

COUNTY: *Saguache*
LOCATION: *22 mi. south of Poncha Springs*
MAP 13
P.O. est. Jan. 19, 1872

Villa Grove was established in the 1870s as a farming and ranching community and a stopping point for traffic on Otto Mears's Poncha Pass toll road. It became a supply center for the mines on Kerber Creek when gold was discovered at Bonanza and Exchequer. Later, turquoise was found near the town. Originally called Garibaldi, Villa Grove was described by peripatetic George A. Crofutt as merely a "small town in Homan's park."

Villa Grove had a modest boom in 1881 when the Denver & Rio Grande announced it would lay its tracks through the San Luis valley. The town sported a newspaper, one good hotel, the Jack Rabbit Saloon, and a mercantile store that specialized in liquor and tobacco. A reporter touting a local merchant noted: "The consump-

Deserted house at the base of the Sangre de Cristo Mountains near Villa Grove. *Kendal Atchison*

tion of spirituous liquors, both in mechanical arts and for medical purposes, is widespread and of mercantile importance."

Wagon Wheel Gap

COUNTY: *Mineral*
LOCATION: *10 mi. southeast of Creede*
MAP 11
P.O. est. Aug. 27, 1875; discont. Feb. 2, 1895

At the turn of the century, Wagon Wheel Gap was "the garden spot of Colorado," according to one newspaper account, with "the finest medicinal waters in the world." Such publicity was not unfounded. General William Jackson Palmer, who had started the Denver & Rio Grande, was investing thousands in hotels, fishing ponds, and hot springs to attract important trend setters such as Mr. and Mrs. John Campion, who had made a fortune in Leadville mining and owned a resort home at Twin Lakes.

One newspaper article touted:

The depot at Wagon Wheel Gap is an art gallery. *Kendal Atchison*

"Away with your Newport! Away with your Manitou! Away with your ocean breezes and delicious salt air!

"Give us some Wagon Wheel Gap!

"On toast."

As early as the 1870s, Wagon Wheel Gap was attracting tourists to take the waters. The resort, named for the remains of a wagon found in a narrow defile, was being compared to the best spas in the country. "The springs will make Wagon Wheel Gap a rival of Long Branch in a few years," predicted the *Rocky Mountain News* in 1876.

When taking the waters became a less fashionable pursuit, Wagon Wheel Gap declined as a stylish resort to become just a fishing camp.

Wallstreet

COUNTY: *Boulder*
LOCATION: *10 mi. west of Boulder*
MAP 3
P.O. est. Oct. 31, 1895 as Delphi; discont. Sept. 15, 1921

When Charles W. Caryl, an eastern mining promoter, took over the Four Mile Canyon town of Delphi in 1897, he intended to turn it into a workers' utopia. Financed by Wall Street capital, Caryl promptly renamed the town Wall Street (now Wallstreet) and set out to acquire claims from local miners, who would then be hired to work their claims at $3 a day and stock in Caryl's Gold Extraction Mining & Supply Company. There were to be seven classes of workers, ranging from $2-a-day laborers to $25 generals. It is unlikely Caryl's plans extended to the Chinese laborers who worked on the creek, however. The worker plan never came off, and Caryl eventually was arrested for sending obscene matter through the mail.

The Gold Extraction firm was successful for a few years, however. In 1901 the company began construction of a giant stone mill worth $175,000 that processed ore from the Nancy, the Gold Eagle, the Silver Eaglet, and other mines. Beneath the mill was an attractive stone building that served as a company office.

Both mill production and the town peaked in 1903 when the population was three hundred. The quality of ore declined and the mill's effi-

Wallstreet mill. *Courtesy Colorado Historical Society.*

ciency was poor. The company and its assets were sold in a bankruptcy sale, and the machinery was hauled off for work elsewhere, leaving the stone mill to loom over the town like some gloomy medieval ruin.

Ward

COUNTY: *Boulder*
LOCATION: *13 mi. north of Nederland*
MAP 3
P.O. est. Jan. 13, 1863 as Ward District

The history of Ward is one of recurring disasters. In 1899 the town was snowed in for three months before two hundred men, working for three weeks at shoveling snow, managed to clear the tracks of the Whiplash Route of the Colorado & Northwestern, which allowed a train loaded with provisions to reach the town. The mines had been closed for lack of fuel, and the entire town was waiting at the depot for the train.

More disastrous were the fires that regularly hit Ward. In 1866 fire destroyed the newly completed Niwot Mill. A later fire claimed the Big Five Mill, which was rebuilt but burned again in 1949. Ward's most disastrous fire was in 1900 when a fire from an overheated stove in the Mc-Clancy Hotel burned the hotel and forty-five other buildings, wiping out Ward's business district. Fifty-two mine whistles screeched a warning, but telephone lines were destroyed early in the blaze, preventing calls for fire-fighting help to neighboring towns. There was little water available to douse the flames; a disagreement among the city's aldermen had delayed installation of a city water works. The next day the Colorado & Northwestern ran a special relief train to Ward stocked with provisions donated by Boulder merchants, but there was little anyone could do about the $100,000 loss.

It was little wonder that in the 1960s when the Ward school was closed and the Boulder County school district commandeered the school bell, which acted as the town's fire alarm, three indignant Ward women demanded its return. The bell was reinstalled within twenty-four hours.

Ward was rebuilt after each fire. Today's town bears little resemblance to the village that miner Calvin Ward, who discovered the Miser's Dream, founded about 1860. It is a charming

The Wallstreet mill's rock walls look like a fuedal tower. *Kendal Atchison*

community built on a mountainside, with a rambling school, a pretty white church (another church building is a garage), and a number of houses.

The town's politics were as fiery as its history. In 1891 the town sport, Dennis Sullivan, held an elaborate funeral for a local cat, complete with a fancy satin-lined casket, a band, a funeral cortége decorated with crepe, and a stirring oration that was heard solemnly by half the town. The lady who owned the cat was furious. She plotted revenge, and several years later when her husband was elected to the city council, he forced passage of a bill making it illegal to operate a saloon located on a street corner. The only street-corner saloon in Ward was owned by Dennis Sullivan.

Only a few months later, the mayor and several council members were tried for kidnapping a fellow alderman. The council had been divided over an issue, with neither faction mustering a

A replica of this Ward building has been constructed in Jamestown. *Kendal Atchison*

Deserted Ward buildings, 1968. *Sandra Dallas*

deciding vote. Four of the council members arranged to have an opponent arrested on a trumped-up charge, and after he was hauled off to jail, the vote went in their favor.

Not all Ward's residents were rounders. H. A. W. Tabor attempted unsuccessfully to recoup the fortune he lost in the 1893 silver crash by investing in Ward mines.

In 1888, when 15-year-old Otto W. Carrow, who had leased the Star Mine, was paid $1,700 for his first carload of ore, he took the train to Denver and checked into one of the best rooms of the Windsor Hotel. He summoned a tailor and ordered a custom-made suit and a derby hat; he took a cab to the Manhattan Restaurant for a steak dinner, and then he bought a high-wheel bicycle. Owners of the property had the lease declared invalid because of Carrow's age, and he made only $8,000 out of the mine. But he never regretted his Denver spree.

A slow day in Westcliffe. *Courtesy Colorado Historical Society.*

Webster

COUNTY: *Park*
LOCATION: *3 mi. west of Grant*
MAP 4
P.O. est. May 7, 1877; discont. Sept. 30, 1909

As the terminus of the Denver, South Park & Pacific's rail line in the late 1870s, Webster was the departure point for thousands of prospectors, suppliers, con men, prostitutes, and assorted desperados headed into the rich mineral country to the west. Many of them stayed in Webster for a time and plied their trades, turning the town at the foot of Kenosha Pass into a blazing hellhole. Everybody made a buck. One hotel proprietor charged $1 for a worn blanket and enough floor space to throw it on. When he ran out of blankets, he snatched one from an unwary sleeper and sold it again. It was a poor night when he couldn't sell the same blanket three or four times.

Webster's evil ways ended when the rail line was extended into South Park, though the town continued as a way station. A cluster of buildings—one with sky-blue wainscoting—remain, along with several rusting vehicles, the remnants of hippie occupation.

Westcliffe

COUNTY: *Custer*
LOCATION: *46 mi. southwest of Canon City*
MAP 13
P.O. est. July 14, 1881

Settled originally by German colonizers, most of whom went broke trying to farm the Wet Mountain valley, the Westcliffe area boomed when gold and silver were discovered. First called Clifton, Westcliffe was renamed for Westcliffe-on-the-Sea in England, the birthplace of Dr. J. W. Bell, an executive with the Denver & Rio Grande. Bell had planned to run the railroad's southern route through the valley, but the Sangre de Cristo Mountains to the west proved impenetrable, so the route was moved farther south.

Never as glittering as Silver Cliff, only a mile away, Westcliffe proved more enduring, and today it is a far more substantial town. In 1928, Westcliffe wrested the Custer County seat away from Silver Cliff, which had earlier taken the county seat from Rosita.

Many of Silver Cliff's citizens and some of its buildings moved to Westcliffe. They included the Powell House, Silver Cliff's swank hotel,

Westcliffe store, 1981. *Kendal Atchison*

Most West Creek residents fished for gold. *Courtesy Denver Public Library Western History Department.*

and Saint Luke's Church, which was built in Rosita, moved to Silver Cliff, then carted off once more to Westcliffe.

West Creek

COUNTY: *Douglas*
LOCATION: *15 mi. north of Woodland Park*
MAP 14
P.O. est. April 14, 1902; discont. Dec. 6, 1968

When traces of gold were discovered along a tributary of Horse Creek north of Colorado Springs, hundreds of miners flocked to the site in hopes of getting in on another Cripple Creek. The ore failed to live up to expectations, however.

Only two weeks after the town was platted in 1895, half of the 140 lots had been sold, and thirty-five cabins, houses, and tents, along with the chronic boomtown accompaniments of dance halls, saloons, and mining brokerages were in place. Two women, legend says, made a fortune baking bread and selling it for fifteen cents a loaf.

White Pine

COUNTY: *Gunnison*
LOCATION: *43 mi. east of Gunnison*
MAP 8
P.O. est. Aug. 12, 1880; discont. July, 1954

Two groups of prospectors working separately discovered the Iron Duke, the Parole, and the Alwilda mines, all on the same day. Silver stampedes were started on flimsier news, and before the summer of 1879 was over, hundreds of miners had flocked to the Tomichi mining district and its principal city, White Pine. In short order they located the Rights of Man, the Romance, the Excelsior, the Nest Egg, and other mines.

Winters were hard, and the first winter or two most of the miners left for Gunnison as soon as the snow fell. A few stayed on, however, packing in their supplies, drinking, and even composing poems. Two 1880 prospectors, Scott Judy and Doc Hammond, described their winter in verse:

We lived on sow belly, baked beans and strong coffee;

West Creek, 1981. *Kendal Atchison*

Despite rough accommodations, this White Pine hotel was not at a loss for guests. *Courtesy Denver Public Library Western History Department.*

Early White Pine residents deserted the town in winter. Today's residents still do. *Kendal Atchison*

*We done our own cooking and washed our own
 clothes;
We polished the drill like any old-timer,
And put on the rocks our good honest blows.
We drank at Ed Dyart's, the solid old duffer,
We'd wink and say, "Ed, mark her down on the
 slate,
When we strike it we'll ante and then you can
 rub it."
He'd smile and say, "Boys, you are rather too
 late."*

White Pine was laid out in 1881, but by then the community already had a good supply of lodges, dry goods establishments, a blacksmith shop, a stationery store, and, of course, many saloons.

When George A. Root, a 16-year-old boy, arrived in White Pine in 1883 to work as an assistant on the *White Pine Cone,* he wandered into a local saloon his first night in town and described it:

The Horseshoe was approximately 25 x 50 feet in size, contained a pool and billiard table, and about four or five round tables for the accommodation of card players. There must have been close to fifty or sixty in the room at the time we arrived. In the vicinity of the card tables I discovered one could hear more gossip than at any other place in the room even tho the conversation was intermittently interspersed with the clacking of billiard and pool balls, the clinking of glassware on the bar, and such disjointed bits of conversation as "I beg," "Raise you a stack of blues," . . . . The atmosphere was like a fog, everyone apparently puffing away vigorously at a pipe or cigar.

But the scene was not new to him, he said, so he went to bed.

Saloons figured prominently in the life of the camp, Root noted. Once when the town liquor supply ran out, a riot was prevented only by the timely discovery of a few bottles of beer and peach brandy.

The White Pine boom peaked in the mid-1880s. Poor transportation and a squabble between major mine owners that led to the shutdown of several producers contributed to the decline, but the death knell came with the 1893 demonetization of silver. The telegram announcing the crash was followed by others from absentee owners ordering shutdowns of mines, and even the railroads refused to carry silver ore. There was renewed interest several years later when

Winfield's schoolhouse (Chaffee County) is a museum with worn desks and slates. *Kendal Atchison*

the newspapers announced Mark Hanna, national political boss, was looking into White Pine mines, but by then the big mining days in the Tomichi district were over.

A few families stayed on, living in the cabins along White Pine's meandering main street, and as late as 1941 a visitor noted: "The remaining residents still pick away at the rocks."

Winfield

COUNTY: *Chaffee*
LOCATION: *17 mi. west of Granite*
MAP 7
P.O. est. July 5, 1881; discont. Sept. 15, 1912

"We are on the threshold of a prosperity such as the most sanguine has never dreamed of," a correspondent who called himself "An Old Timer" wrote to the *Rocky Mountain News* in 1883. He admitted with modesty uncharacteristic of the mountain camp boomers: "We have never had what is called in the general acceptation [*sic*] of the term a boom."

All that was to change with the development of several mines, including the Tasmania. By 1890, Winfield had fifteen hundred residents, a church in which no service ever was held, and a school. By 1893, with the silver crash, it was nearly deserted.

The town, which had been settled in the 1860s, had a revival in the early 1900s when a dozen companies were formed to explore Winfield's old mines. The town died after World War I when the last ore was shipped out.

Winfield

COUNTY: *Teller*
LOCATION: *5 mi. north of Victor*
MAP 14
No P.O.

Winfield Scott Stratton, a morose Colorado Springs carpenter who was addicted to prospecting, was the Cripple Creek district's first millionaire. His Independence mine brought him millions in profits and another $10 million in 1899

Winfield's brick buildings were torn down recently by a mining company. Only a couple of shacks remain (Teller County). *Kendal Atchison*

when he sold it to an English syndicate. Cripple Creek waited for Stratton to cut loose with his fortune, but the peevish carpenter spent his money buying bicycles for Colorado Springs washerwomen and making bad loans to down-and-out friends.

Stratton was not interested in enjoying his money; he wanted to make more, and in 1901, he announced his "bowl-of-gold" theory. All the veins in Cripple Creek converged on a common point, he believed, and he intended to discover that bowl of gold.

The base of Stratton's operations was Winfield (sometimes called Stratton), a company town founded in 1900 and built of substantial brick buildings with no saloons or dance halls. Stratton's minions moved into Winfield and began work, but the project did not uncover gold and was discontinued when Stratton died a year later.

Winfield itself was more enduring. The town lasted until 1980 when it fell prey to revived mining. A gold-leaching operator who had leased the townsite tore down the buildings, and today only a handful of weathered structures are left.

Yankee

COUNTY: *Clear Creek*
LOCATION: *11 mi. northwest of Idaho Springs*
MAP 1
P.O. est. Nov. 2, 1893; discont. Feb. 28, 1910

Yankee was not named for northern sympa-

thizers as might be expected, but for an enterprising mining man, William H. Yankee, who was, incidentally, a Civil War veteran and a Yankee. The town of Yankee, or Yankee Hill, located on a stage line six miles from Central City, boomed at the turn of the century, when the Yankee Consolidated Mining, Milling & Tunneling Company acquired the rights to nearly a hundred properties. Money flowed in from Ohio, Pennsylvania, and other states, and "miners from all sections of the state are flocking to Yankee and every cabin is filled," reported the *Denver Times.*

The miners also flocked out at regular intervals, according to one old-timer, who said the mining men traveled to Denver once a month to do their brawling. He claimed beer was cheaper in Denver.

In 1902 the *Times* predicted Yankee would get a 100-room hotel, warehouses, and a telephone line. "Clear Creek has many camps which are very valuable," it boomed. "There is very little doubt but that Yankee will eclipse them all."

Today Yankee itself has been eclipsed—by the elements. The foundations of a few cabins and some relics of habitation are all that remain.

Yankee Mine. *Kendal Atchison*

Maps

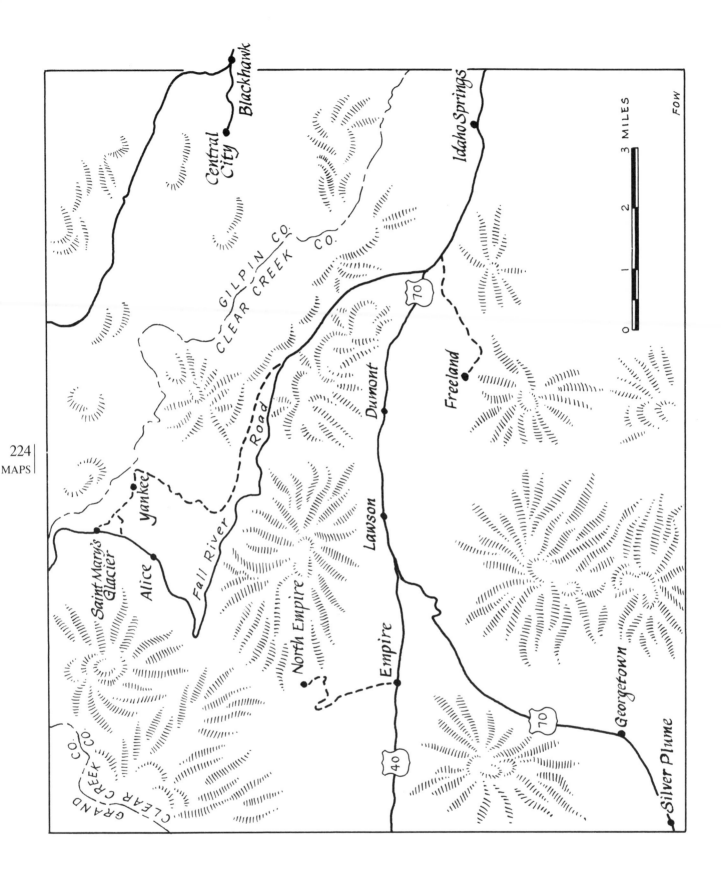

Map 1.

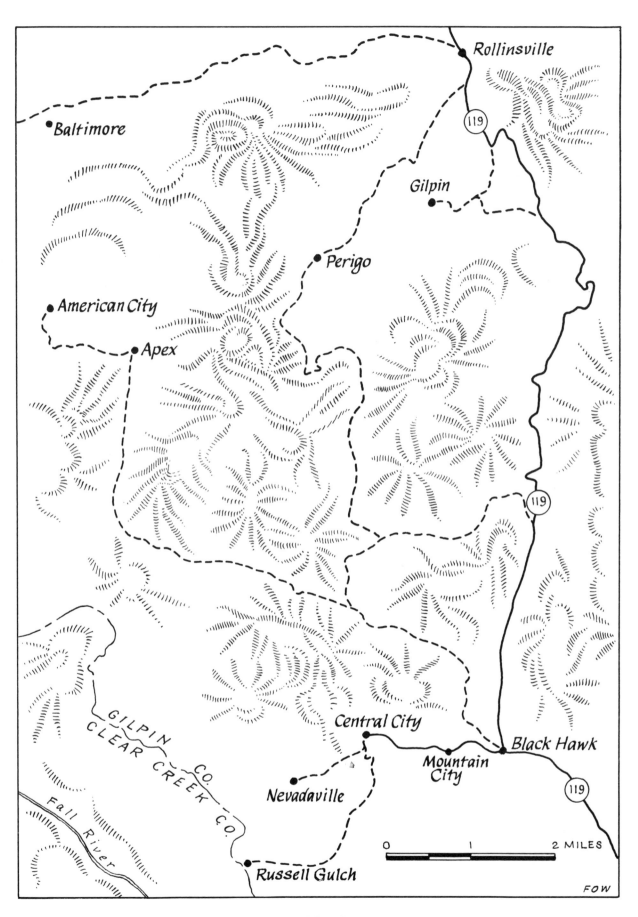

Rollinsville

119

•Baltimore

Gilpin

Perigo

•American City

•Apex

119

GILPIN CO.
CLEAR CREEK CO.

Central City

Black Hawk

Mountain
City

Nevadaville

Fall River

Russell Gulch

0   1   2 MILES

FOW

Map 2.

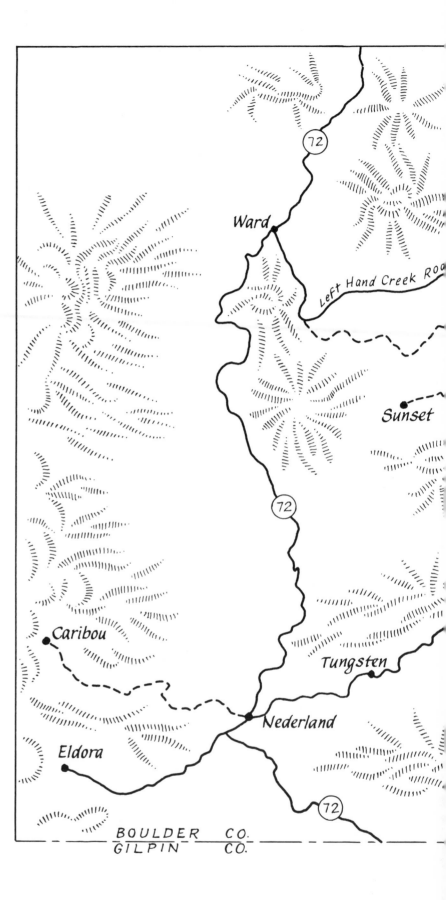

Map 3.

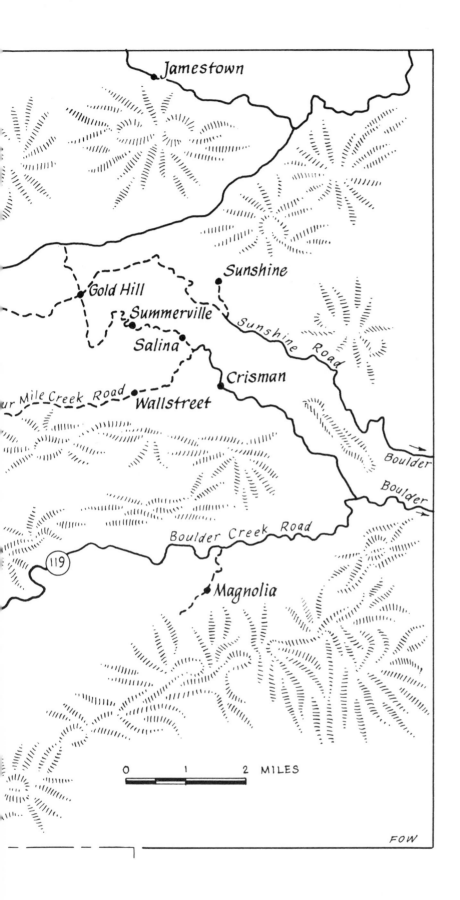

Jamestown

Gold Hill

Sunshine

Summerville

Salina

Sunshine Road

Crisman

ur Mile Creek Road

Wallstreet

Boulder

Boulder

Boulder Creek Road

119

Magnolia

0   1   2   MILES

FOW

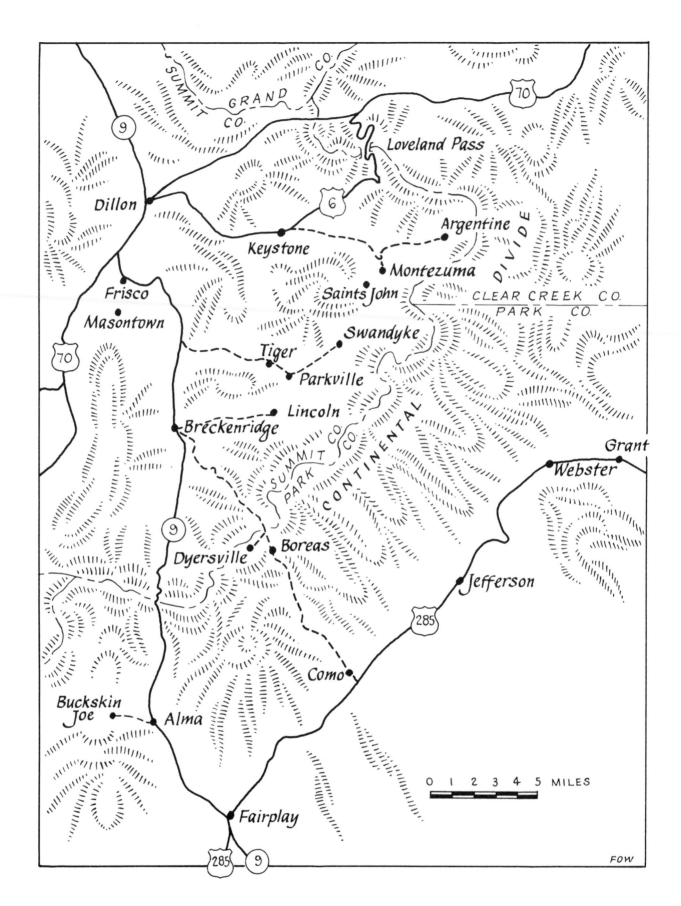

Map 4.

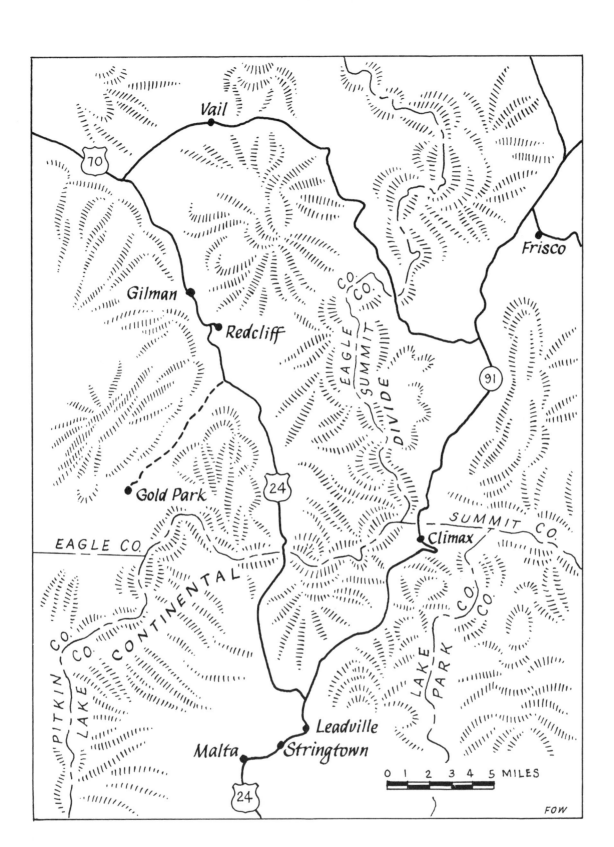

Map 5.

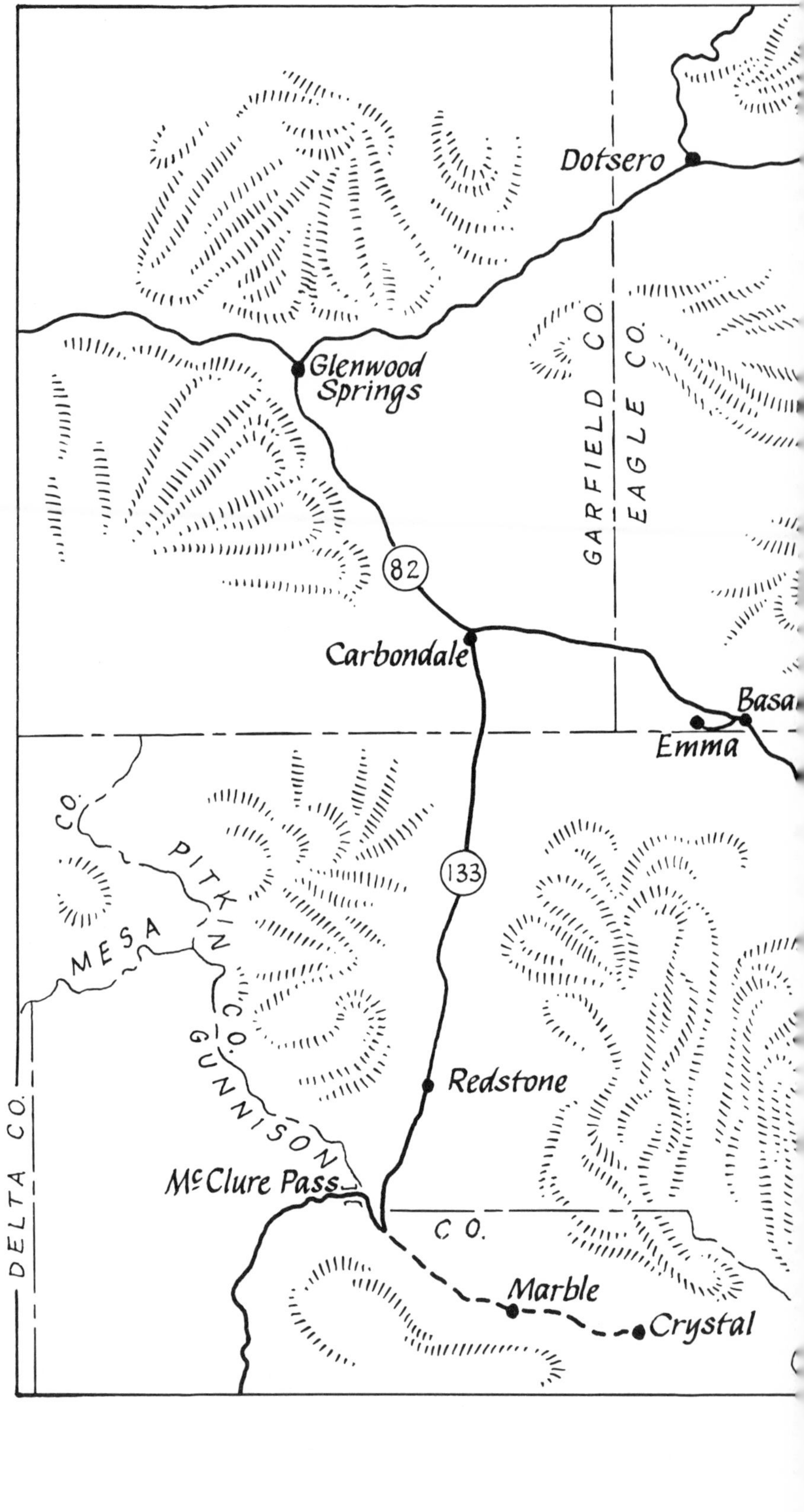
Dotsero
Glenwood Springs
GARFIELD CO.
EAGLE CO.
82
Carbondale
Basa
Emma
CO.
PITKIN CO.
MESA
133
GUNNISON
DELTA CO.
Redstone
McClure Pass
CO.
Marble
Crystal

Map 6.

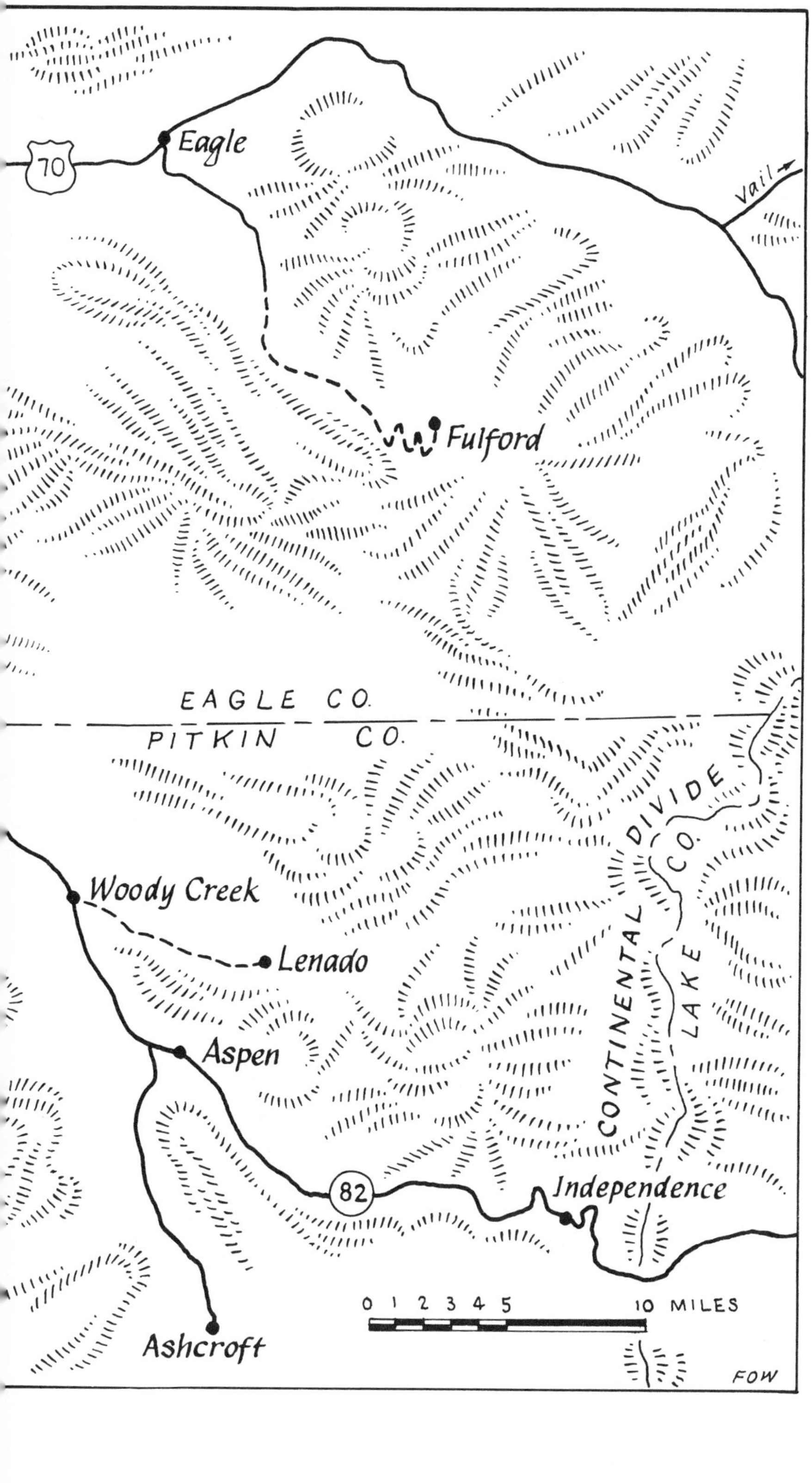

70

Eagle

Vail

Fulford

EAGLE CO.
PITKIN CO.

Woody Creek

Lenado

Aspen

82

Independence

CONTINENTAL DIVIDE

LAKE CO.

Ashcroft

0 1 2 3 4 5   10 MILES

FOW

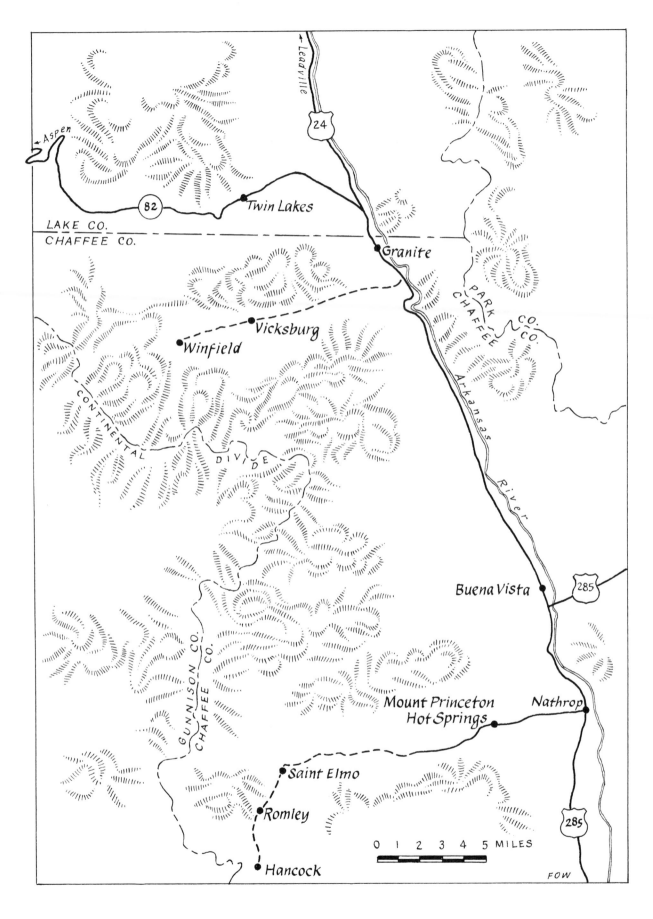

Map 7.

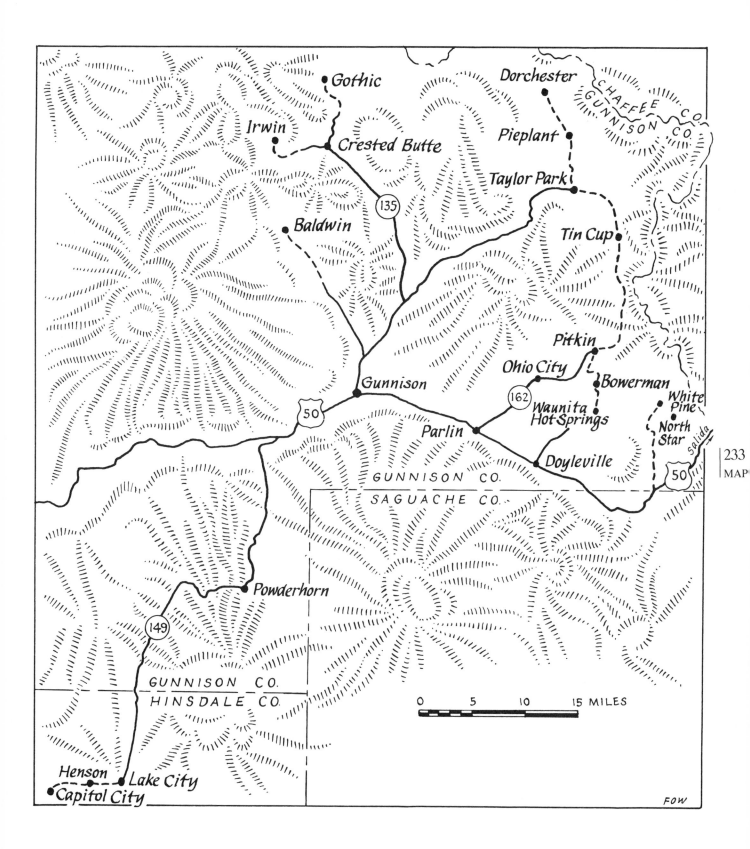

Gothic

Dorchester

Irwin

CHAFFEE CO.

GUNNISON CO.

Pieplant

Crested Butte

Taylor Park

135

Baldwin

Tin Cup

Pitkin

Gunnison

Ohio City

Bowerman

50

162

White Pine

Waunita Hot Springs

North Star

Parlin

Salida

Doyleville

233 MAP

50

GUNNISON CO.

SAGUACHE CO.

Powderhorn

149

GUNNISON CO.

HINSDALE CO.

0   5   10   15 MILES

Henson   Lake City

Capitol City

FOW

Map 8.

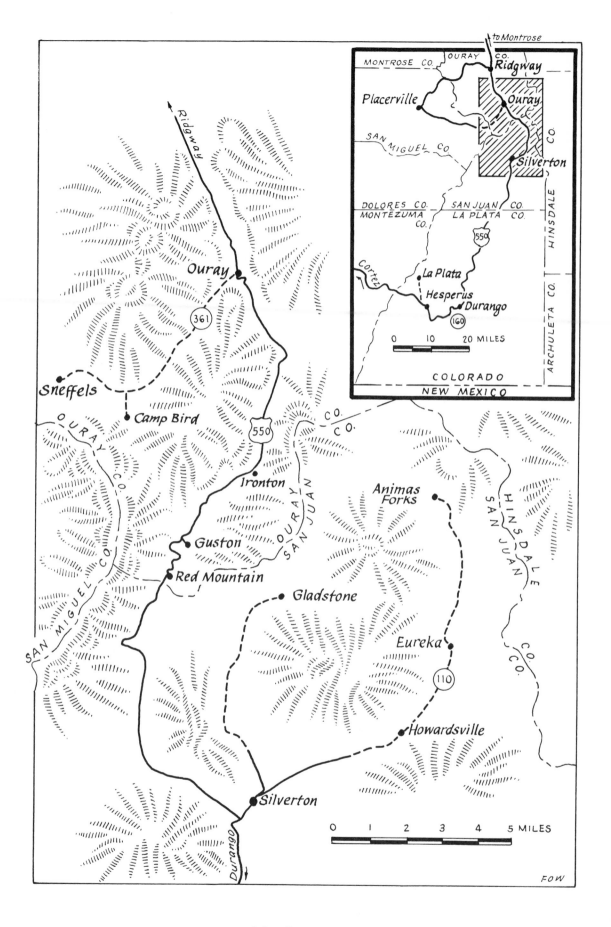

Map 9.

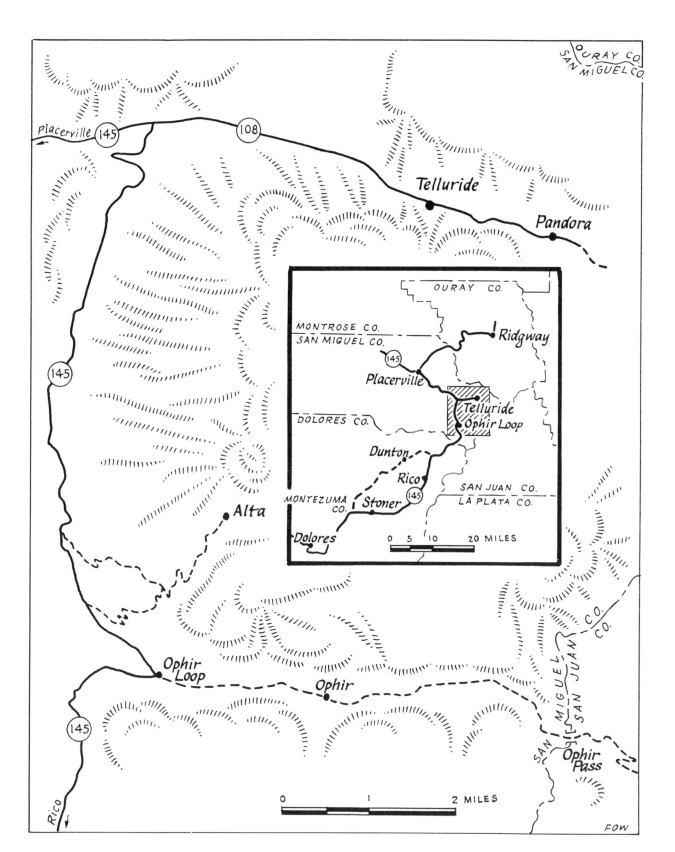

Map 10.

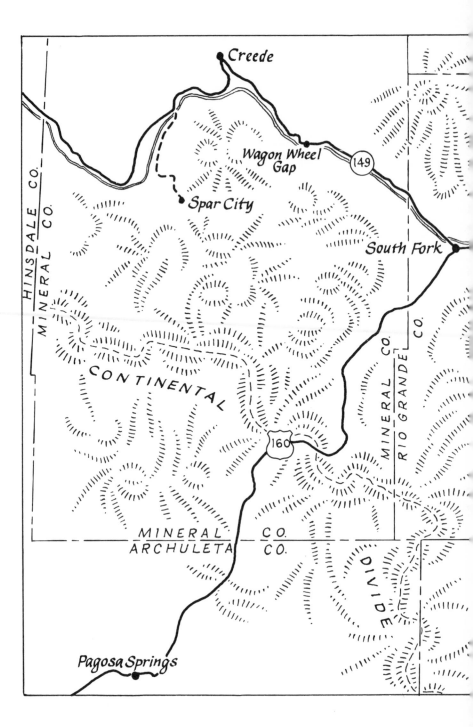

Map 11.

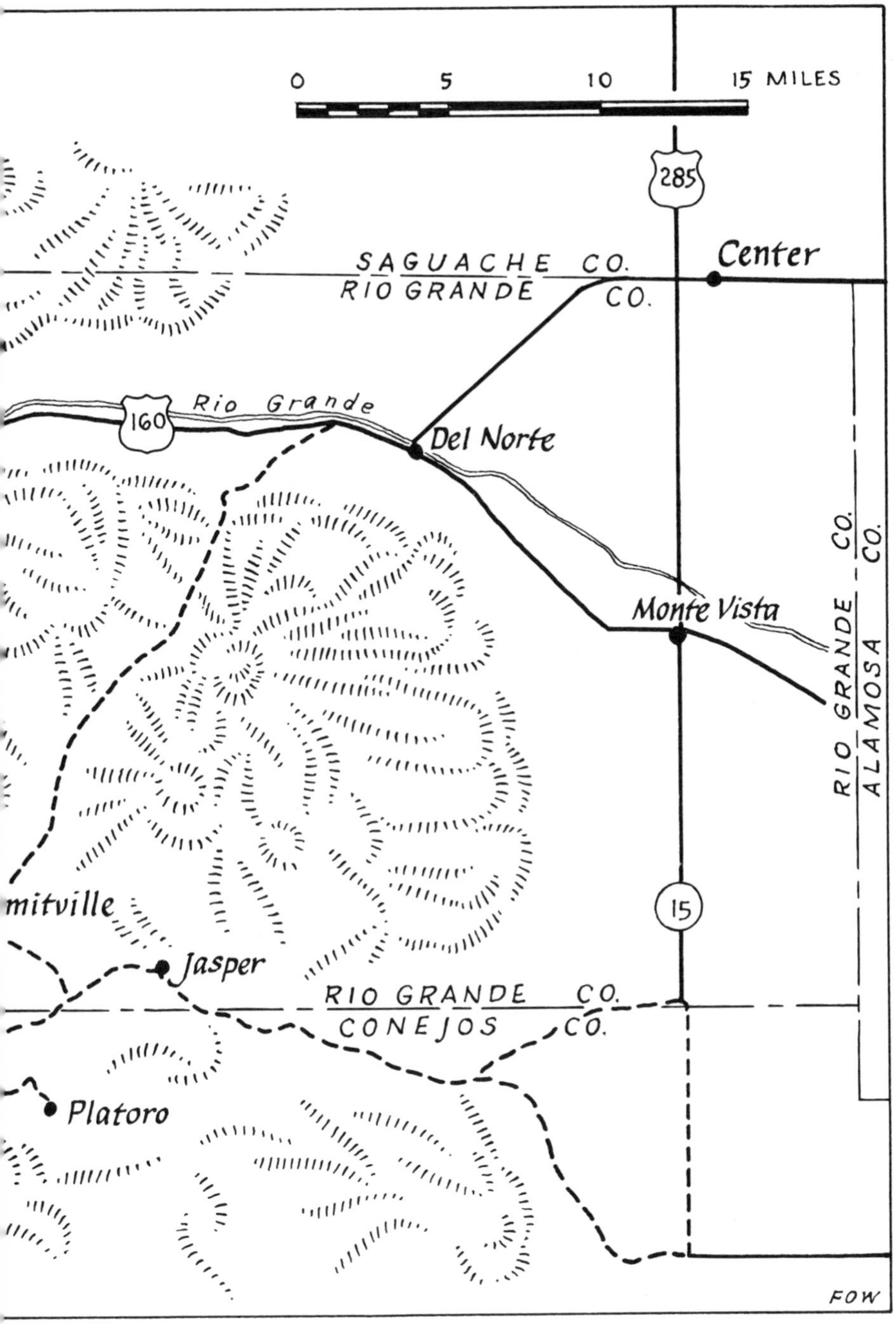
0
5
10
15 MILES
285
SAGUACHE CO.
RIO GRANDE CO.
Center
160
Rio Grande
Del Norte
Monte Vista
RIO GRANDE CO.
ALAMOSA CO.
mitville
15
Jasper
RIO GRANDE CO.
CONEJOS CO.
Platoro
FOW

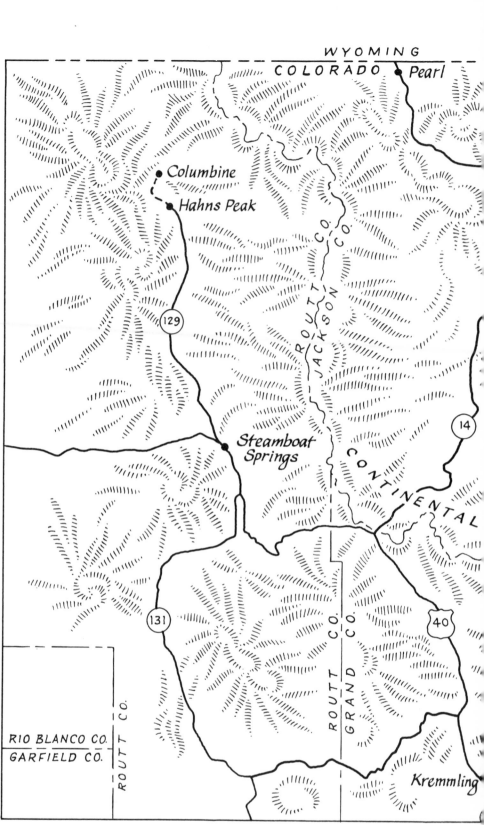

Map 12.

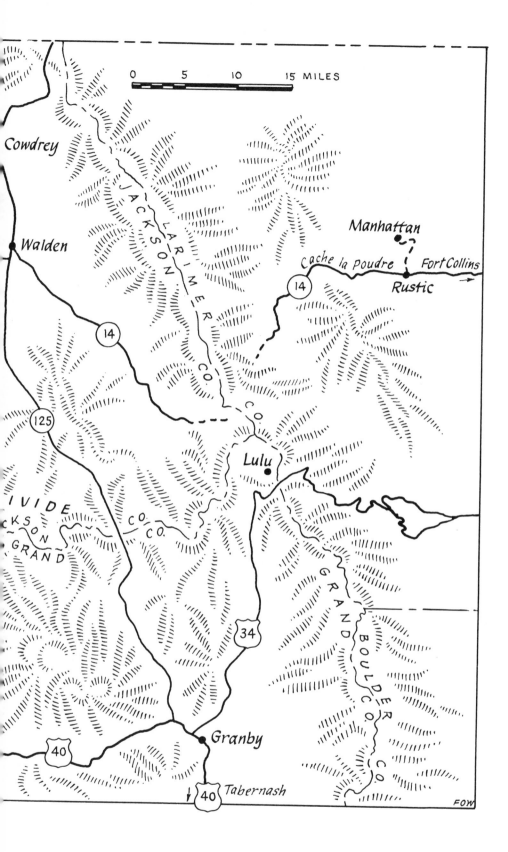

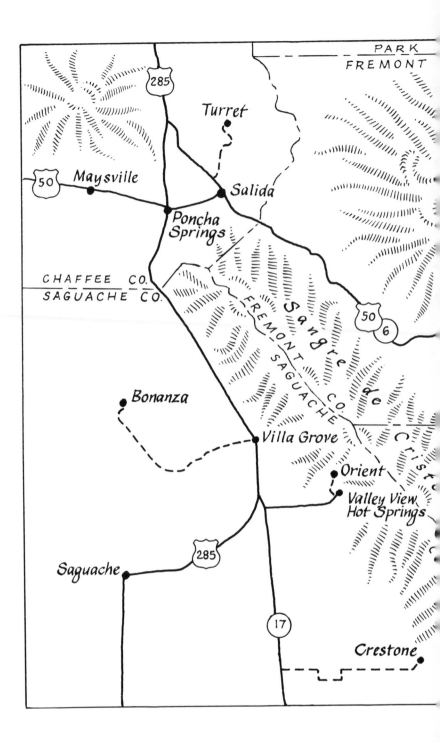

Map 13.

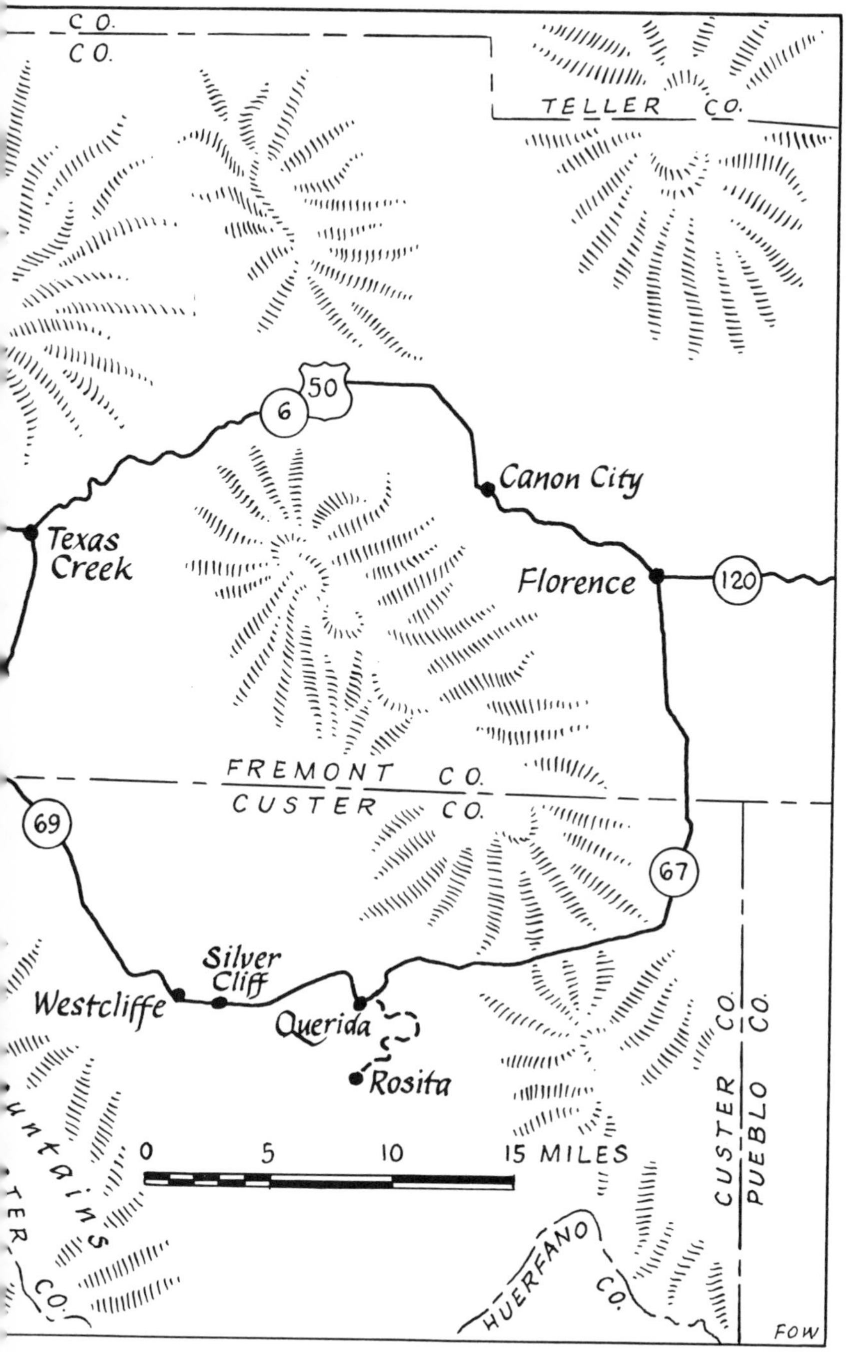
CO.
CO.
TELLER CO.
50
6
Canon City
Texas Creek
Florence
120
FREMONT CO.
CUSTER CO.
69
67
Silver Cliff
Westcliffe
Querida
Rosita
CUSTER CO.
PUEBLO CO.
0 5 10 15 MILES
HUERFANO CO.
FOW

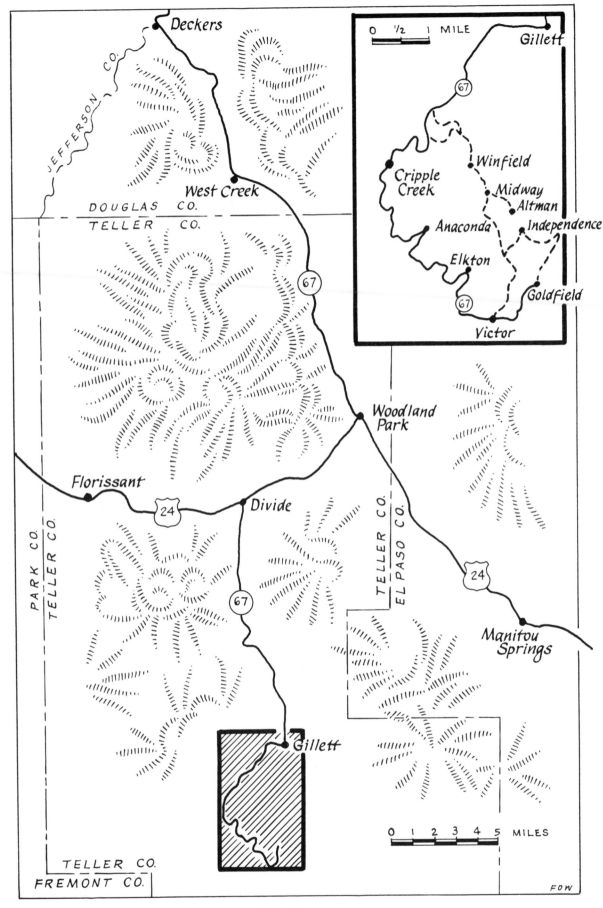

Deckers

JEFFERSON CO.

West Creek

DOUGLAS CO.
TELLER CO.

67

Woodland Park

Florissant

24 Divide

PARK CO.
TELLER CO.

67

TELLER CO.
EL PASO CO.

24

Manitou Springs

Gillett

TELLER CO.
FREMONT CO.

0 ½ 1 MILE

Gillett

67

Winfield

Cripple Creek

Midway
Altman

Anaconda

Independence

Elkton

Goldfield

67

Victor

0 1 2 3 4 5 MILES

FDW

Map 14.

Bibliography

BOOKS

Anonymous. *A Historical, Descriptive, Pictorial and Biographical Work of the Greatest Gold Camp on Earth.* Denver: J. F. Manning (n.d.)

Arps, Louisa Ward. *Chalk Creek, Colorado.* Denver: John Van Male, 1940.

Axford, H. William. *Gilpin County Gold.* Chicago: Swallow Press, 1976.

Backus, Harriet Fish. *Tomboy Bride.* Boulder: Pruett Publishing Co., 1969.

Bancroft, Caroline. *Famous Aspen.* Denver: Bancroft Booklets, 1964.

———. *Guide to Central City.* Denver: World Press, Inc., 1946.

———. *Gulch of Gold.* Boulder: Johnson Publishing Co., 1958.

———. *Tabor's Matchless Mine and Lusty Leadville.* Boulder: Johnson Publishing Co., 1960.

———. *Unique Ghost Towns and Mountain Spots.* Boulder: Johnson Publishing Co., 1961.

Baskin, O. L. *History of the Arkansas Valley, Colorado.* Chicago: O. L. Baskin & Co., 1881. Reprinted Evansville: Unigraphics Inc., 1976.

Bates, Margaret. *A Quick History of Lake City, Colorado.* Colorado Springs: Little London Press, 1973.

Benham, Jack L. *Camp Bird and the Revenue.* Ouray: Bear Creek Publishing Co., 1980.

———. *Ouray.* Ouray: Bear Creek Publishing Co., 1976.

———. *Silverton.* Ouray: Bear Creek Publishing Co., 1977.

Blair, Edward. *Leadville: Colorado's Magic City.* Boulder: Pruett Publishing Co., 1980.

Blair, Kay Reynolds. *Ladies of the Lamplight.* Gunnison: B & B Printers, 1971.

Bowles, Samuel. *The Switzerland of America.* Springfield: Samuel Bowles & Co., 1869.

Brewer, William H. *Rocky Mountain Letters 1869.* Denver: Colorado Mountain Club, 1930.

Brown, Robert L. *Colorado Ghost Towns—Past and Present.* Caldwell: Caxton Printers, 1977.

———. *Ghost Towns of the Colorado Rockies.* Caldwell: Caxton Printers, 1977.

———. *Jeep Trails to Colorado Ghost Towns.* Caldwell: Caxton Printers, 1978.

Buchanan, John W., and Buchanan, Doris G. *The Story of Ghost Town Caribou.* Boulder: Boulder Publishing Co., 1957.

Cornwell, Robert. *Ashcroft: Its Natural and Human History.* Aspen: Aspen Historical Society (n.d.).

Coquoz, Rene L. *The Early Years of Colorado.* New York: Carlton Press, 1965.

———. *King Pleasure Reigned in 1896.* Leadville, 1969.

Crofutt, George A. *Crofutt's Grip-Sack Guide of Colorado.* Omaha: Overland Publishing Co., 1885. Reprinted Boulder: Johnson Books, 1981.

Crum, Josie Moore. *Ouray County, Colorado.* Durango: San Juan History, Inc., 1962.

Davidson, Levette J., ed. *Poems of the Old West.* Denver: University of Denver, 1951.

Davis, Richard Harding. *At a New Mining Camp: Creede of Colorado, 1892.* Olympic Valley: Outbooks, 1977.

Dyer, J. L. *Snow-shoe Itinerant.* Cincinnati: Cranston & Stowe, 1890. Reprinted Breckenridge: Father Dyer United Methodist Church, 1975.

Eberhart, Perry. *Guide to the Colorado Ghost Towns and Mining Camps.* Denver: Sage Books, 1968.

Eichler, George R. *Colorado Place Names.* Boulder: Johnson Publishing Co., 1977.

Ellis, Anne. *The Life of an Ordinary Woman.* New York: Houghton Mifflin Co., 1929. Reprinted Lincoln: University of Nebraska, 1980.

Feitz, Leland. *Cripple Creek.* Colorado Springs: Little London Press, 1967.

———. *Ghost Towns of the Cripple Creek District.* Colorado Springs: Little London Press, 1974.

———. *Myers Avenue.* Colorado Springs: Little London Press, 1967.

———. *A Quick History of Creede.* Colorado Springs: Little London Press, 1969.

———. *A Quick History of Victor.* Colorado Springs: Little London Press, 1969.

Fetter, Richard L., and Fetter, Suzanne. *Telluride: From Pick to Powder.* Caldwell: Caxton Printers, 1979.

Field, Eugene. *A Little Book of Western Verse.* New York: Charles Scribner's Sons, 1894.

Fiester, Mark. *Blasted Beloved Breckenridge.* Boulder: Pruett Publishing Co., 1973.

———. *Look for Me in Heaven.* Boulder: Pruett Publishing Co., 1980.

Fossett, Frank. *Colorado, Its Gold and Silver Mines, Farms and Stock Ranges, and Health and Pleasure Resorts.* New York: C. G. Crawford, 1880. Reprinted Glorieta: Rio Grande Press, Inc., 1976.

Gillette, Ethel Morrow. *Idaho Springs: Saratoga of the Rockies.* New York: Vantage, 1978.

Gilliland, Mary Ellen. *Summit.* Silverthorne: Alpenrose Press, 1980.

Griswold, Don L., and Griswold, Jean H. *The Carbonate Camp Called Leadville.* Denver: University of Denver, 1951.

———. *Colorado's Century of "Cities."* Denver: Smith-Brooks Printing Co., 1958.

Gurnsey, Jann, Heaton, Barbara, and King, Jean.

Mountain Memories: A History of Jimtown, Colorado. (n.p.) 1976.

Hall, Frank. *History of the State of Colorado.* 4 vols. Chicago: Blakely Printing Co., 1889, 1890, 1891, 1895.

Harlan, George. *Postmarks and Places.* Crestone: (n.p.) 1976.

Harrison, Louise C. *Empire and the Berthoud Pass.* Denver: Big Mountain Press, 1964.

Helmers, Dow. *Historic Alpine Tunnel.* Colorado Springs: Century One Press, 1971.

Hill, Alice Polk. *Tales of the Colorado Pioneers.* Denver: Pierson & Gardner, 1884. Reprinted Santa Fe: Rio Grande Press, 1976.

Hollenback, Frank R. *Central City and Black Hawk.* Denver: Sage Books, 1961.

Houston, Grant. *Lake City Reflections.* Gunnison: B & B Printers, 1976.

Howe, M. Hazel. *The Story of Silver Plume.* Idaho Springs: Butler Graphics, 1960.

Johnson, Charlie H., Jr. *The Central City Opera House.* Colorado Springs: Little London Press, 1980.

Kempner, Helen Ashley Anderson. *Bonanza!* Colorado Springs: Little London Press, 1978.

Knight, MacDonald, and Hammock, Leonard. *Early Days on the Eagle.* Eagle (n.p.) 1965.

Lavender, David. *A Rocky Mountain Fantasy: Telluride, Colorado.* Telluride: San Miguel Historical Society (n.d.).

Lee, Mabel Barbee. *Back in Cripple Creek.* Garden City: Doubleday & Co., 1968.

———. *Cripple Creek Days.* Garden City: Doubleday & Co., 1958.

Levine, Brian. *Cities of Gold.* Denver: Stonehenge Books, 1981.

Leyendecker, Liston E. *Georgetown, Colorado's Silver Queen 1859-1876.* Fort Collins: Centennial Publications, 1977.

Livermore, Robert. *Bostonians and Bullion.* Edited by Gene M. Gressley. Lincoln: University of Nebraska, 1968.

Livingston, Harry. *Gold, Men and Central City* (n.p.) (n.d.).

Lotito, Robert F., ed. *Enchanted Central City.* Denver: A. B. Hirschfeld Press (n.d.).

McLean, Evalyn Walsh. *Father Struck It Rich.* Boston: Little, Brown & Co., 1936.

Mazzulla, Fred, and Mazzulla, Jo. *Brass Checks and Red Lights.* Denver (n.p.), 1966.

Mead, Jay, ed. *Silver Plume Walking Tour.* Silver Plume: Tumbleweed Press (n.d.).

Morgan, Gary. *Rails Around the Loop.* Fort Collins: Centennial Publications, 1976.

Morse, Russell A., and Wallis, Mather C. *A Short and Informal Early Days History of the Town of Fairplay.* Fairplay: Centennial Times Publishing Co., 1975.

Pettem, Silvia. *Red Rocks to Riches.* Denver: Stonehenge Books, 1980.

Poor, M. C. *Denver South Park & Pacific.* Denver: Rocky Mountain Railroad Club, 1976.

Rademan, Myles C., ed. *A Useful Guide to Architecture, History and Building in Crested Butte.* Crested Butte: Town of Crested Butte, 1976.

Richardson, Albert D. *Beyond the Mississippi.* Hartford: American Publishing Co., 1867.

Rockwell, Wilson. *Uncompahgre Country.* Denver: Sage Books, 1965.

Rowe, Jim, and Rowe, Louise. *Portal into the Past.* Gunnison: B & B Printers. 1976.

Ruland, Sylvia. *The Lion of Redstone.* Boulder: Johnson Publishing Co., 1981.

Schader, Conrad F. *Tin Cup, Colorado: Silver Link in State History.* Denver: Lynn Publications, 1953.

Schoberlin, Melvin. *From Candles to Footlights.* Denver: Old West Publishing Co., 1941.

Sharp, Verna. *A History of Montezuma, Sts. John, and Argentine.* Dillon: D & L Printing, Inc., 1971.

Shoemaker, Len. *Roaring Fork Valley.* Denver: Sundance, 1958.

Sibley, George. *A Crested Butte Primer.* Gunnison: B & B Printers, 1972.

Simmons, Virginia McConnell. *The San Luis Valley.* Boulder: Pruett Publishing Co., 1979.

Smith, Marion P., and McMechen, Edgar C. *Healy House and Dexter Cabin.* Denver: State Historical Society of Colorado, 1956.

Sommers, Herbert M. *My Story of Early Summitville 1880-1885.* Colorado Springs (n.p.), 1973.

Sprague, Marshall. *Money Mountain.* Boston: Little, Brown & Co., 1953.

Stevenson, Thelma V. *Historic Hahns Peak.* Fort Collins: Robinson Press, 1979.

Stone, Wilbur Fisk. *History of Colorado.* 4 vols. Chicago: S. J. Clarke Publishing Co., 1918.

Street, Julian. *Abroad At Home.* Garden City: Garden City Publishing Co., 1926.

Taylor, Bayard. *Colorado: A Summer Trip.* New York: G. P. Putnam & Son, 1867.

Thompson, Thomas Gray. *Lake City, Colorado.* Oklahoma City: Metro Press, Inc., 1974.

Turk, Gayle. *Wet Mountain Valley.* Colorado Springs: Little London Press, 1977.

Vandenbusche, Duane. *The Gunnison Country.* Gunnison: B & B Printers, 1980.

———, and Myers, Rex. *Marble, Colorado: City of Stone.* Denver: Golden Bell Press, 1970.

Waters, Frank. *Midas of the Rockies.* Chicago: Swallow Press, 1972.

Weber, Rose. *A Quick History of Telluride.* Colorado Springs: Little London Press, 1974.

Wheeler, Col. Homer W. *Buffalo Days.* Indianapolis: Bobbs-Merrill Co., 1925.

Williams, Roger Neville. *The Great Telluride Strike.* Telluride (n.p.), 1977.

Williamson, Ruby G. *Down With Your Dust.* Gunnison: B & B Printers, 1979.

———. *Otto Mears: Pathfinder of the San Juan.* Gunnison: B & B Printers, 1981.

Willison, George F. *Here They Dug the Gold.* New York: Reynal & Hitchcock, 1946.

Wolle, Muriel Sibell. *Ghost Cities of Colorado.* Denver: Smith-Brooks Printing Co., 1933.

———. *Stampede to Timberline.* Denver: Sage Books, 1962.

———. *Timberline Tailings.* Chicago: Sage Books, 1977.

GOVERNMENT DOCUMENT

Civil Works Administration. "Thousand Town File." Unpublished manuscript. Colorado Historical Society.

ARTICLES

Anonymous. "The City of Aspen, Colorado." *Harper's Weekly* (January 19, 1889):59-60.

Anonymous. "The Latest Great Mining Camp." *Mining Industry and Tradesman* 11 (No. 23):229-37.

Anonymous. "Summitville: Colorado's Sensational Gold Camp." *Mining Year Book* (1936), pp. 24, 71.

Ayers, Mary C. "Howardsville in the San Juan." *Colorado Magazine* 28 (October, 1951):241-57.

Bair, Everett. "A Journey to Old St. Elmo, A Glimpse into Her Boom Days." *1958 Brand Book,* 14:199-207. Boulder: Johnson Publishing Co., 1959.

Bartlett, Robert F. "Aspen: The Mining Community 1879-1893." *1950 Brand Book,* 6:133-60. Denver: Univ. of Denver Press, 1951.

Chandler, Allison. "The Story of King Park and Como." *1963 Brand Book,* 19:314-24. Morrison: Buffalo Bull Press, 1964.

Colwell, Raymond. "Lake City." *1950 Brand Book,* 6:111-29. Denver: Univ. of Denver Press, 1951.

Ellithorpe, Ralph C. "Poker, Politics and Gold." *1971 Brand Book,* 27:45-114. Boulder: Johnson Publishing Co., 1972.

Fitz-Mac. "The City of the Clouds." *Great Divide* 4 (December, 1890).

Flynn, Norma L. "Early Mining Camps of South Park." *1951 Brand Book,* 7:135-45. Denver: Artcraft Press, 1952.

Forhan, T. J. "Reminiscences of Irwin or Ruby Camp." *Camp and Plant* 4 (January 9, 1904):605-11.

Griswold, Don L., and Griswold, Jean H. "Mountain Hostelries." *1955 Brand Book,* 11:327-71. Boulder: Johnson Publishing Co., 1956.

Haase, Carl L. "Gothic, Colorado: City of Silver Wires." *Colorado Magazine* 51 (Fall, 1974):294-316.

Hastings, James K. "A Winter in the High Mountains, 1871-72." *Colorado Magazine* 27 (July, 1950):225-33.

Ingersoll, E. "Ups and Downs in Leadville." *Scribner's Monthly* 18 (October, 1879):801-23.

Livingston, Ralph E. "Crestone." *Roundup* 34 (November-December, 1978):3-15.

Mathews, Carl F. "Colorado 'Ghost Towns.'" *1949 Brand Book,* 5:175-94. Denver: Golden Press, 1950.

———. "Rico, Colorado—Once a Roaring Camp." *Colorado Magazine* 28 (January, 1951):37-49.

Melrose, Frances. "Colorado's First and Last Bullfight—1895." *1958 Brand Book,* 14:299-310. Boulder: Johnson Publishing Co., 1959.

Rathbun, Will, and Bathke, Ed. "Bassick and His Wonderful Mine." *1964 Brand Book,* 20:319-49. Boulder: Johnson Publishing Co., 1965.

Rizzari, Francis B. "The Ghost Town of Bowerman." *1949 Brand Book,* 5:1-17. Denver: Golden Press, 1950.

———. "The Personal Life of a Mining Camp." *Roundup* 14 (February, 1958):5-13.

Roller, Elizabeth. "Life in Montezuma, Chihuahua and Sts. Johns." *1964 Brand Book,* 20:61-86. Boulder: Johnson Publishing Co., 1965.

Ryan, Starley. "Pearl, a Forgotten Mountain." *Denver Post Empire Magazine* (September 26, 1976): 12-15.

Smith, Mrs. Loban E. "Altman: A Golden Eyrie." *Leslie's Weekly Illustrated.*

Spring, Agnes Wright. "Old Caribou and Central City." *1958 Brand Book,* 14:3-45. Boulder: Johnson Publishing Co., 1959.

Swanson, Evadene Burris. "Where's Manhattan?" *Colorado Magazine* 48 (February, 1971):147-58.

Wolle, Muriel Sibell. "Irwin, a Ghost Town of the Elk Mountains." *Colorado Magazine* 24 (January, 1947):4-15.

———. "The Midas Touch." *1968 Brand Book* 24:18-48. Boulder: Johnson Publishing Co., 1969.

———. "Tin Cup, One of the Old Boom Towns." *Mining Journal* (January 30, 1946):5.

NEWSPAPERS

Antonio Ledger-News
Ashcroft Journal
Aspen Times
Boulder Daily Camera
Breckenridge Bulletin
Brush Tribune
Canon City Record
Carbonate Chronicle (Leadville)
Clear Creek Echo (Idaho Springs)
Colorado Evening Sun (Denver)
Colorado Miner (Georgetown)
Colorado Springs Gazette
Colorado Springs Sun Gazette & Telegraph
Colorado Transcript
Creede Candle
Cripple Creek Gold Rush
Daily Mining Journal (Black Hawk)
Daily News (Colorado Springs)
Daily Register-Call (Central City)
Denver Daily Tribune

Denver Post
Denver Republican
Denver Times
Denver Tribune
Durango Herald
Elk Mountain Pilot (Crested Butte)
Empire City Echo
Gladstone Times
Glenwood Post
Great Divide (Denver)
Gunnison Review
Gunnison News
Gunnison News-Champion
Gunnison Republican
Herald Democrat (Leadville)
Historic Denver News
Holy Cross Trail (Red Cliff)
Inter-Ocean (Denver)
Kansas City Star
La Plata Miner (Silverton)
Las Animas Leader

Manhattan Prospector
Mining Investor (Colorado Springs)
Mining World (Denver)
Montrose Daily Press
Ouray Herald
Ouray Times
Pine Cone (Apex)
Pueblo Chieftain
Rocky Mountain News (Denver)
Rocky Mountain Sun (Aspen)
San Francisco Chronicle
Silver State Record (Denver)
Silver World (Lake City)
Solid Muldoon (Ouray)
Steamboat Pilot (Steamboat Springs)
Summit County Journal (Breckenridge)
Summit County Leader (Breckenridge)
Sunshine Courier
Telluride Journal
Weekly Register-Call (Central City)

Index

248

Dorchester, Colo.: 66-67
Dougan, Harry: 176
Dougherty, Mike: 46, 152
Douglas County: 217
Doyle, James: 60
Doyle, William: 96
Dry Diggings (see Placerville)
Dumont, Colo.: 67
Dumont, John M.: 67, 79
Dunraven Mine: 129
Dunton, Colo.: 67-69
Dupuy, Louis: 86
Durango, Colo.: 22, 98, 117, 181, 185, 206
Durant Ave. (Aspen): 24
Durant Mine: 18
Dyer, Elias: 95
Dyer, "Father" (see John L. Dyer)
Dyer, John L.: 69-70, 76, 95, 125, 128
Dyersville, Colo.: 69-70

Eagle City (see Ohio City)
Eagle, Colo.: 80
Eagle County: 80, 89, 93, 159-60
Eagle Mine: 7
Eagle River: 89
Eagle River Shaft: 160
East Tin Cup, Colo.: 202
Elbert Guards: 46
El Dorado, Calif.: 71
El Dorado, Colo.: (see Eldora)
Eldora, Colo.: 70-71
Elizabethtown, Colo.: 80
Elk Ave. (Crested Butte): 54-55
Elks Club: 63, 171, 197
Elkton, Colo.: 71-72
Elkton Mine: 71
Ellis, Anne: 30
Emma, Colo.: 71-72
Emma Mine (Dunton): 69
Emma Mine (Spar City): 187
Empire City, Colo. (see Empire)
Empire, Colo.: 73-74, 96, 142
Engle Brothers Exchange Bank: 38
Engle, George: 38
Engle, Peter: 38
Enterprise Mine (Dorchester): 66
Enterprise Mine (Rico): 163, 165
Esmund, John: 188
Esmund Mine: 188
Espinoza brothers (Fairplay killers): 76
Ethel Mine: 51
Eureka Bath Rooms (Silver Cliff): 174
Eureka, Colo.: 74-75, 146
Eureka St. (Central City): 48
Evans, George H.: 40
Excelsior Mine: 217
Exchequer, Colo.: 211
Exchequer Mine: 30

"Face on the Barroom Floor, The": 45
"Face Upon the Floor, The": 45, 48
Fairbanks, Douglas Sr.: 109
Fair Play, Colo. (see Fairplay)
Fairplay, Colo.: 7, 49, 75-78, 111
Fairview Mine: 155
Fancy Creek: 93
Farncomb, Harry: 127
Farncomb Hill: 35, 127
Feathers (Maysville salesman): 133
Feathers Ranch (see Maysville)
Field, Eugene: 91, 93
Fiester, Mark: 127
First National Bank (Central City): 44
First National Bank of Leadville: 124

Fisher (Irwin prospector): 108
Fisher City (see Spar City)
Fisherman Mine: 149
Florence Hayden Dramatic Co.: 160
Foote, Robert: 35, 38
Ford, Bob: 52-53
Forest, Mrs. H. E.: 139
Forest City, Colo.: (see St. Elmo)
Foresters: 141
Forest Queen Mine: 108
Fort Collins, Colo.: 129-30
Fort Peabody: 198
Fossett, Frank: 30, 42, 153
Four Mile Canyon: 213
Four Mile Creek: 174
Fourth of July Mine: 103
Fowler, Eugene: 22
Frank Thaler's saloon: 12
Free America Mine: 117
Freeland, Colo.: 78-79
Freeland Mine: 67, 78-79
Freemont, Colo. (see Cripple Creek)
French Gulch: 127-28
French Mountain: 93
French St. (Breckenridge): 39
Frenchy (man killed in Rico): 163
Frenchy's (Tin Cup saloon): 201
Friends of Alfred E. Packer, The: 116
Frisco, Colo.: 79-80, 133
Frizzel, Ethel (see Ethel Frizzel Carlton)
Front Range: 34
Fryer, George: 121
Fryer Hill: 121
Frying Pan, Colo. (see Basalt)
Fryingpan River: 27
Fulford, Arthur H.: 80
Fulford, Colo.: 80
Fullen, Hiram: 129

Galena City, Colo. (see Capitol City)
Gallagher brothers (Leadville prospectors): 121
Galloping Goose: 75, 167
Gambell, A. D.: 153
Gambell Gulch (see Gamble Gulch)
Gamble Gulch: 89, 153
Gano Downs (Denver store): 40
Garfield, James A.: 71
Garibaldi, Colo. (see Villa Grove)
Gatley Motor Co. (Alma garage): 7
Gee's Addition, Colo. (see Fulford)
Georgetown, Colo.: 79, 80-86, 179, 181
Georgetown Loop: 181
Georgetown Courier: 82
Georgetown Society Inc.: 86
Georgia Gulch: 35, 111-12, 152
Geogiana Mine: 129
Gertrude Mine: 7
Giacomelli family (Silverton confectionary operators): 182
Gibbs, Elijah: 95
Gillett, Colo.: 86-88
Gillette, Ethel Morrow: 103
Gilliland, Mary Ellen: 127
Gilman, Colo.: 88-89
Gilpin, Colo.: 14, 89
Gilpin County: 11, 26, 28, 43, 89, 136, 139, 153, 167, 170
Gilpin, William: 89
Gintown, Colo. (see Creede)
Gish, Lillian: 48
Givens, Mrs. (Eldora hotel operator): 71
Gladstone, Colo.: 89-91
Gladstone Kibosh: 91

Glenwood Springs, Colo.: 18, 27, 71, 161, 206
Goldboat: 39
Gold Brick mining district: 143
Gold Bug Mine: 202
Gold Coin Club: 209
Gold Coin Mine: 206, 211
Gold Creek: 143
Gold Cup Mine: 201
Gold Dirt Mine: 153
Gold Eagle Mine: 213
Golden Age Mine: 109
Golden, Colo.: 44, 47, 101
Golden Fleece Mine (see Hotchkiss Mine)
Golden Transcript: 168, 174
Golden Wonder Mine: 202
Gold Extraction Mining Supply Co.: 213
Goldfield, Colo.: 90-91, 105
Gold King Mine (Alta): 9
Gold King Mine (Silverton): 89, 91, 183
Gold Hill, Colo.: 91-93, 187
Gold Hill Inn: 93
Gold Miner Hotel (Eldora): 71
Gold Pan Co.: 40
Gold Park, Colo.: 93-94
Gold Park Hotel: 93
Gold Park Mining and Milling Co.: 93
Gold Prince Mine: 75
Gold Run Gulch: 174, 187
"Good-bye, Little Girl, Good-bye": 63
Goose Pasture: 39
Gore, Robert: 40
Gothic, Colo.: 94
Gould, Jay's daughter: 104
Graball, Colo.: (see Tarryall)
Graham, Royal R.: 104
Granby, Colo.: 129
Grand County: 129
Grand Hotel (see Grand Imperial Hotel)
Grand Imperial Hotel: 183-84
Grand Junction, Colo.: 27
Grand Lake: 129
Grand Mogul Mine: 91
Grand View Mine: 163
Grand View Saloon: 134-35
Granite, Colo.: 95, 206, 220
Grant, Colo.: 216
Grant, Nellie: 103
Grant, Ulysses S.: 30, 43, 47, 86, 94, 103, 105
Great Divide: 150
Great Logan Mine: 64
Great Western Sugar Co.: 123
Greeley, Horace: 44, 137
Greeley, Salt Lake & Pacific Railroad: 191
Green Mountain: 99
Gregory Diggins: 136-37, 171
Gregory Gulch: 28, 44, 46
Gregory, John: 28, 44, 136, 139, 170
Griffin, Clifford: 181
Griffith, David: 80-81
Griffith, George: 80-81
Grocers and Butchers Protective Assn.: 124
Ground Hog Mine: 192
Groves, Tom: 127
Guggenheim family (founders of Asarco, Inc.): 123, 184
Guinan, Mary Louise Cecelia "Texas": 11
Gunnison Ave. (Lake City): 115
Gunnison, Colo.: 16, 24, 33, 54, 56, 113,

250

252